ARISTOPHANES
Four Comedies

DUDLEY FITTS

ARISTOPHANES
Four Comedies

LYSISTRATA

THE FROGS

THE BIRDS

LADIES' DAY

A Harvest/HBJ Book

HARCOURT
BRACE
JOVANOVICH
NEW YORK AND LONDON

Library of Congress Catalog Card Number: 62-19595

Printed in the United States of America

ISBN 0-15-607900-3

N O P Q R S

CONTENTS

LYSISTRATA

for FREDERICK *and* LEE PETERSON

ποῖ λευκὸν ἵππον

INTRODUCTORY NOTE

i

Lysistrata was written in 412 B.C., and the evidence points to its production at the Athenian festival of the Lenaia in January 411. It is the last of the three plays that Aristophanes devoted to the subject of the war with Sparta—the others being *The Acharnians* and *Peace*—and it is the bravest of them. Never had the situation of Athens been more nearly desperate. The great military and naval expedition to Sicily, that almost maniacal gesture of *hybris,* had been utterly destroyed at Syracuse in 413; and though there were to be seven more years of confusion and despair before the final collapse at the battle of Aigospotomoi, it was clear to Aristophanes, as it must have been to any thinking man, that the cause was lost. *Lysistrata* was an attempt to stem the rush towards annihilation, to save something from the wreckage before it should be too late to save anything. The attempt failed. Nothing was saved. Yet the comedy remains, a generous and shining affirmation of confidence in the ultimate sanity of mankind; and the topical references and symbolic horseplay that attach it to its time neither lessen its enduring urgency nor reduce the importance of what it has to say to us in our similar predicament.

The play is ribald, by any standards. Partly this was an attempt to make laughter succeed where rage and tears, not to speak of common sense, had failed. Partly, too, it was ritualistic, or semi-ritualistic: the origin of Old Comedy in ancient fertility rites is reflected in the theme of *Lysistrata*; and the pseudo-epithalamion in the *éxodos,* like the true ones that conclude *Birds* and *Peace,* seems to have been enforced to a certain extent by tradition. The outrageous and daring plot, however, owes nothing to tradition. It is shock that counts, the elemental shock of good sense insisted upon to the point of absurdity. For what could be more sensible, more wildly absurd, than that the women on both sides should call a sexual strike to halt a war that no

3

longer had meaning or promised hope? 'On both sides'; for Aristophanes addresses himself to Sparta as well as to Athens, and there is no time-wasting talk of international inspections to guard against secret tests, copulations underground or (as in *Birds*) in the air. No one could possibly take Lysistrata's proposition seriously; it is a joke, brutally pure; but the absurd has its own tragic depths, and it may be that our simplicities offer more hope at the end than all our complexities and distinctions.

ii

This translation is based upon a version published in 1954, the first of my attempts to put Aristophanes into English. It was an unequal but generally unsatisfactory attempt, largely because of the many freedoms I permitted myself in handling the text, especially the lyric passages. I have welcomed the opportunity afforded by this collection to rewrite certain passages and to revise others; but since my primary intention was, and is, to write an actable and sayable play, I must warn those who do not know *Lysistrata* in Greek that this is still a free version, not translation *ad litteram expressa*. The low-comedy burlesque of Deep South talk is retained, in spite of the many perfectly lucid objections by scholars, in the passages involving the delegates from Sparta; the Athenian Drunkard who turned up, without textual authority, in the earlier version, has also been kept; and throughout, but especially in the *éxodos,* there has been a conjectural, though I hope discreet, redistribution of speeches.

CONTENTS

PERSONS REPRESENTED:

LYSISTRATA
KALONIKE
MYRRHINE
LAMPITO
CHORUS
COMMISSIONER
KINESIAS
SPARTAN HERALD
SPARTAN AMBASSADOR
A SENTRY

SCENE: *Athens. First, a public square; later, beneath the walls of the Akropolis; later, a courtyard within the Akropolis.*

Until the *éxodos,* the CHORUS is divided into two hemichori: the first, of Old Men; the second, of Old Women. Each of these has its KORYPHAIOS. In the *éxodos,* the hemichori return as Athenians and Spartans.

The supernumeraries include the BABY SON of Kinêsias; STRATYLLIS, a member of the hemichorus of Old Women; various individual speakers, both Spartan and Athenian.

🎬 PROLOGUE

> [*Athens; a public square; early morning;* LYSIS-TRATA *sola*

LYSISTRATA:
　　If someone had invited them to a festival—
　　of Bacchos, say; or to Pan's shrine, or to Aphroditê's
　　over at Kôlias—, you couldn't get through the streets,
　　what with the drums and the dancing. But now,
　　not a woman in sight!
　　　　　　　　Except—oh, yes!
　　　　　　　　　　　　[*Enter* KALONIKE
　　Here's one of my neighbors, at last. Good
　　morning, Kalonikê.

7

KALONIKE:

Good morning, Lysistrata.

Darling,
don't frown so! You'll ruin your face!

LYSISTRATA:

Never mind my face.

Kalonikê,
the way we women behave! Really, I don't blame the men
for what they say about us.

KALONIKE:

No; I imagine they're right.

LYSISTRATA:
For example: I call a meeting
to think out a most important matter—and what hap-
     pens?
The women all stay in bed!

KALONIKE:

Oh, they'll be along.
It's hard to get away, you know: a husband, a cook,
a child . . . Home life can be *so* demanding!

LYSISTRATA:
What I have in mind is even more demanding.

KALONIKE:
Tell me: what is it?

LYSISTRATA:

It's big.

KALONIKE:

Goodness! *How* big?

LYSISTRATA:
Big enough for all of us.

KALONIKE:

But we're not all here!

LYSISTRATA:
We would be, if *that*'s what was up!

No, Kalonikê,
this is something I've been turning over for nights,
long sleepless nights.

KALONIKE:

It must be getting worn down, then,
if you've spent so much time on it.

LYSISTRATA:

Worn down or not,
it comes to this: Only we women can save Greece!

KALONIKE:

Only we women? Poor Greece!

LYSISTRATA:

Just the same,
it's up to us. First, we must liquidate
the Peloponnesians—

KALONIKE:

Fun, fun!

LYSISTRATA:

—and then the Boiotians.

KALONIKE:

Oh! But not those heavenly eels!

LYSISTRATA:

You needn't worry.
I'm not talking about eels. —But here's the point:
If we can get the women from those places—
all those Boiotians and Peloponnesians—
to join us women here, why, we can save
all Greece!

KALONIKE:

But dearest Lysistrata!
How can women do a thing so austere, so
political? We belong at home. Our only armor's
our perfumes, our saffron dresses and
our pretty little shoes!

LYSISTRATA:

Exactly. Those
transparent dresses, the saffron, the
perfume, those pretty shoes—

KALONIKE:

Oh?

LYSISTRATA:

Not a single man would lift
his spear—

KALONIKE:

I'll send my dress to the dyer's tomorrow!

LYSISTRATA:

—or grab a shield—

KALONIKE:
>   The sweetest little negligée—

LYSISTRATA:
—or haul out his sword.

KALONIKE:
>   I know where I can buy
the dreamiest sandals!

LYSISTRATA:
>   Well, so you see. Now, shouldn't
the women have come?

KALONIKE:
>   Come? They should have *flown!*

LYSISTRATA:
Athenians are always late.
>   But imagine!
There's no one here from the South Shore, or from
>   Sálamis.

KALONIKE:
Things are hard over in Sálamis, I swear.
They have to get going at dawn.

LYSISTRATA:
>   And nobody from Acharnai.
I thought they'd be here hours ago.

KALONIKE:
>   Well, you'll get
that awful Theagenês woman: she'll be
a sheet or so in the wind.
>   But look!
Someone at last! Can you see who they are?
>   [*Enter* MYRRHINE *and other women*

LYSISTRATA:
They're from Anagyros.

KALONIKE:
>   They certainly are.
You'd know them anywhere, by the scent.

MYRRHINE:
Sorry to be late, Lysistrata.
>   Oh come,
don't scowl so. Say something!

LYSISTRATA:
>   My dear Myrrhinê,

what is there to say? After all,
you've been pretty casual about the whole thing.

MYRRHINE:

Couldn't find
my girdle in the dark, that's all.

But what *is*
'the whole thing'?

KALONIKE:

No, we've got to wait
for those Boiotians and Peloponnesians.

LYSISTRATA:

That's more like it. —But, look!
Here's Lampitô!

[*Enter* LAMPITO *with women from Sparta*

LYSISTRATA:

Darling Lampitô,
how pretty you are today! What a nice color!
Goodness, you look as though you could strangle a bull!

LAMPITO:

Ah think Ah could! It's the work-out
in the gym every day; and, of co'se that dance of ahs
where y' kick yo' own tail.

KALONIKE:

What an adorable figure!

LAMPITO:

Lawdy, when y' touch me lahk that,
Ah feel lahk a heifer at the altar!

LYSISTRATA:

And this young lady?
Where is she from?

LAMPITO:

Boiotia. Social-Register type.

LYSISTRATA:

Ah. 'Boiotia of the fertile plain.'

KALONIKE:

And if you look,
you'll find the fertile plain has just been mowed.

LYSISTRATA:

And this lady?

LAMPITO:

           Hagh, wahd, handsome. She comes from
    Korinth.

KALONIKE:

High and wide's the word for it.

LAMPITO:

                  Which one of you
called this heah meeting, and why?

LYSISTRATA:

             I did.

LAMPITO:

                 Well, then, tell us:
What's up?

MYRRHINE:

       Yes, darling, what *is* on your mind, after all?

LYSISTRATA:

I'll tell you. —But first, one little question.

MYRRHINE:

                Well?

LYSISTRATA:

It's your husbands. Fathers of your children. Doesn't it
    bother you
that they're always off with the Army? I'll stake my life,
not one of you has a man in the house this minute!

KALONIKE:

Mine's been in Thrace the last five months, keeping an eye
on that General.

MYRRHINE:

       Mine's been in Pylos for seven.

LAMPITO:

               And mahn,
whenever he gets a *dis*charge, he goes raht back
with that li'l ole shield of his, and enlists again!

LYSISTRATA:

And not the ghost of a lover to be found!
From the very day the war began—
             those Milesians!
I could skin them alive!
      —I've not seen so much, even,
as one of those leather consolation prizes.—

But there! What's important is: If I've found a way
to end the war, are you with me?

MYRRHINE:

                              I should *say* so!
Even if I have to pawn my best dress and
drink up the proceeds.

KALONIKE:

                        Me, too! Even if they split me
right up the middle, like a flounder.

LAMPITO:

                            Ah'm shorely with you.
Ah'd crawl up Taÿgetos on mah knees
if that'd bring peace.

LYSISTRATA:

                 All right, then; here it is:
Women! Sisters!
If we really want our men to make peace,
we must be ready to give up—

MYRRHINE:

                       Give up what?
Quick, tell us!

LYSISTRATA:

        But *will* you?

MYRRHINE:

                  We will, even if it kills us.

LYSISTRATA:

Then we must give up going to bed with our men.

                      [*Long silence*
Oh? So now you're sorry? Won't look at me?
Doubtful? Pale? All teary-eyed?

               But come: be frank with me.
Will you do it, or not? Well? Will you do it?

MYRRHINE:

                    I couldn't. No.
Let the war go on.

KALONIKE:

             Nor I. Let the war go on.

LYSISTRATA:

You, you little flounder,
ready to be split up the middle?

KALONIKE:

Lysistrata, no!
I'd walk through fire for you—you *know* 1 would!—, but don't
ask us to give up *that!* Why, there's nothing like it!

LYSISTRATA:
And you?

BOIOTIAN:

No. I must say *I'd* rather walk through fire.

LYSISTRATA:
What an utterly perverted sex we women are!
No wonder poets write tragedies about us.
There's only one thing we can think of.

But you from Sparta:
if you stand by me, we may win yet! Will you?
It means so much!

LAMPITO:

Ah sweah, it means *too* much!
By the Two Goddesses, it does! Asking a girl
to sleep—Heaven knows how long!—in a great big bed
with nobody there but herself! But Ah'll stay with you!
Peace comes first!

LYSISTRATA:

Spoken like a true Spartan!

KALONIKE:
But if—

oh dear!

—if we give up what you tell us to,
will there *be* any peace?

LYSISTRATA:

Why, mercy, of course there will!
We'll just sit snug in our very thinnest gowns,
perfumed and powdered from top to bottom, and those men
simply won't stand still! And when we say No,
they'll go out of their minds! And there's your peace.
You can take my word for it.

LAMPITO:

Ah seem to remember
that Colonel Menelaos threw his sword away
when he saw Helen's breast all bare.

KALONIKE:

But, goodness me!
What if they just get up and leave us?

LYSISTRATA:

In that case
we'll have to fall back on ourselves, I suppose.
But they won't.

KALONIKE:

I must say that's not much help. But
what if they drag us into the bedroom?

LYSISTRATA:

Hang on to the door.

KALONIKE:

What if they slap us?

LYSISTRATA:

If they do, you'd better give in.
But be sulky about it. Do I have to teach you how?
You know there's no fun for men when they have to force
you.
There are millions of ways of getting them to see reason.
Don't you worry: a man
doesn't like it unless the girl co-operates.

KALONIKE:

I suppose so. Oh, all right. We'll go along.

LAMPITO:

Ah imagine us Spahtans can arrange a peace. But you
Athenians! Why, you're just war-mongers!

LYSISTRATA:

Leave that to me.
I know how to make them listen.

LAMPITO:

Ah don't see how.
After all, they've got their boats; and there's lots of money
piled up in the Akropolis.

LYSISTRATA:

The Akropolis? Darling,
we're taking over the Akropolis today!
That's the older women's job. All the rest of us
are going to the Citadel to sacrifice—you understand me?
And once there, we're in for good!

LAMPITO:

Whee! Up the rebels!
Ah can see you're a good strat*ee*gist.

LYSISTRATA:

Well, then, Lampitô,
what we have to do now is take a solemn oath.

LAMPITO:
Say it. We'll sweah.

LYSISTRATA:

This is it.
—But where's our Inner Guard?

—Look, Guard: you see this shield?
Put it down here. Now bring me the victim's entrails.

KALONIKE:
But the oath?

LYSISTRATA:

You remember how in Aischylos' *Seven*
they killed a sheep and swore on a shield? Well, then?

KALONIKE:
But I don't see how you can swear for peace on a shield.

LYSISTRATA:
What else do you suggest?

KALONIKE:

Why not a white horse?
We could swear by that.

LYSISTRATA:

And where will you get a white horse?

KALONIKE:
I never thought of that. *What* can we do?

LYSISTRATA:

I have it!
Let's set this big black wine-bowl on the ground
and pour in a gallon or so of Thasian, and swear
not to add one drop of water.

LAMPITO:

Ah lahk *that* oath!

LYSISTRATA:
Bring the bowl and the wine-jug.

KALONIKE:

Oh, what a simply *huge* one!

LYSISTRATA:

Set it down. Girls, place your hands on the gift-offering.

O Goddess of Persuasion! And thou, O Loving-cup
Look upon this our sacrifice, and
be gracious!

KALONIKE:

See the blood spill out. How red and pretty it is!

LAMPITO:

And Ah must say it smells good.

MYRRHINE:

Let me swear first!

KALONIKE:

No, by Aphroditê, we'll match for it!

LYSISTRATA:

Lampitô: all of you women: come, touch the bowl,
and repeat after me—remember, this is an oath—:
I WILL HAVE NOTHING TO DO WITH MY HUS-
   BAND OR MY LOVER

KALONIKE:

I will have nothing to do with my husband or my lover

LYSISTRATA:

THOUGH HE COME TO ME IN PITIABLE CONDI-
   TION

KALONIKE:

Though he come to me in pitiable condition
(Oh Lysistrata! This is killing me!)

LYSISTRATA:

IN MY HOUSE I WILL BE UNTOUCHABLE

KALONIKE:

In my house I will be untouchable

LYSISTRATA:

IN MY THINNEST SAFFRON SILK

KALONIKE:

In my thinnest saffron silk

LYSISTRATA:

AND MAKE HIM LONG FOR ME.

KALONIKE:

And make him long for me.

LYSISTRATA:

I WILL NOT GIVE MYSELF

KALONIKE:
  I will not give myself

LYSISTRATA:
  AND IF HE CONSTRAINS ME

KALONIKE:
  And if he constrains me

LYSISTRATA:
  I WILL BE COLD AS ICE AND NEVER MOVE

KALONIKE.
  I will be cold as ice and never move

LYSISTRATA:
  I WILL NOT LIFT MY SLIPPERS TOWARD THE
    CEILING

KALONIKE:
  I will not lift my slippers toward the ceiling

LYSISTRATA:
  OR CROUCH ON ALL FOURS LIKE THE LIONESS
    IN THE CARVING

KALONIKE:
  Or crouch on all fours like the lioness in the carving

LYSISTRATA:
  AND IF I KEEP THIS OATH LET ME DRINK FROM
    THIS BOWL

KALONIKE:
  And if I keep this oath let me drink from this bowl

LYSISTRATA:
  IF NOT, LET MY OWN BOWL BE FILLED WITH
    WATER.

KALONIKE:
  If not, let my own bowl be filled with water.

LYSISTRATA:
  You have all sworn?

MYRRHINE:
                    We have.

LYSISTRATA:
                    Then thus
  I sacrifice the victim.

                              [*Drinks largely*

KALONIKE:
                    Save some for us!
  Here's to you, darling, and to you, and to you!

[*Loud cries off-stage*

LAMPITO:
What's all *that* whoozy-goozy?

LYSISTRATA:
Just what I told you.
The older women have taken the Akropolis.
Now you, Lampitô,
rush back to Sparta. We'll take care of things here. Leave
these girls here for hostages.
The rest of you,
up to the Citadel: and mind you push in the bolts.

KALONIKE:
But the men? Won't they be after us?

LYSISTRATA:
Just you leave
the men to me. There's not fire enough in the world,
or threats either, to make me open these doors
except on my own terms.

KALONIKE:
I hope not, by Aphroditê!
After all,
we've got a reputation for bitchiness to live up to.

[*Exeunt*

🎗 PÁRODOS: CHORAL EPISODE

[*The hillside just under the Akropolis. Enter*
CHORUS OF OLD MEN *with burning torches and
braziers; much puffing and coughing*

KORYPHAIOS^m:
Forward march, Drakês, old friend: never you mind
that damn big log banging hell down on your back.

CHORUS^m:
There's this to be said for longevity: [STROPHE 1
You see things you thought that you'd never see.
   Look, Strymodôros, who would have thought it?
   We've caught it—
the New Femininity!
The wives of our bosom, our board, our bed—

Now, by the gods, they've gone ahead
And taken the Citadel (Heaven knows why!),
Profanèd the sacred statuar-y,
>   And barred the doors,
>   The subversive whores!

KORYPHAIOS^m:

Shake a leg there, Philûrgos, man: the Akropolis or
     bust!
Put the kindling around here. We'll build one almighty
     big
bonfire for the whole bunch of bitches, every last one;
and the first we fry will be old Lykôn's woman.

CHORUS^m:

>   [ANTISTROPHE 1
They're not going to give me the old horse-laugh!
No, by Deméter, they won't pull this off!
     Think of Kleómenês: even he
     Didn't go free
>   till he brought me his stuff.
A good man he was, all stinking and shaggy,
Bare as an eel except for the bag he
Covered his rear with. God, what a mess!
Never a bath in six years, I'd guess.
>   Pure Sparta, man!
>   He also ran.

KORYPHAIOS^m:

That was a siege, friends! Seventeen ranks strong
we slept at the Gate. And shall we not do as much
against these women, whom God and Euripides hate?
If we don't, I'll turn in my medals from Marathon.

CHORUS^m:

>   [STROPHE 2

>   Onward and upward! A little push,
>   And we're there.
>   Ouch, my shoulders! I could wish
>   For a pair

Of good strong oxen. Keep your eye
   On the fire there, it mustn't die.
      Akh! Akh!
   The smoke would make a cadaver cough!

Holy Heraklês, a hot spark   [ANTISTROPHE 2
   Bit my eye!
Damn this hellfire, damn this work!
   So say I.
Onward and upward just the same.
(Lachês, remember the Goddess: for shame!)
      Akh! Akh!
   The smoke would make a cadaver cough!

KORYPHAIOS^m:

At last (and let us give suitable thanks to God
for his infinite mercies) I have managed to bring
my personal flame to the common goal. It breathes, it
   lives.
Now, gentlemen, let us consider. Shall we insert
the torch, say, into the brazier, and thus extract
a kindling brand? And shall we then, do you think,
push on to the gate like valiant sheep? On the whole, yes.
But I would have you consider this, too: if they—
I refer to the women—should refuse to open,
what then? Do we set the doors afire
and smoke them out? At ease, men. Meditate.
Akh, the smoke! Woof! What we really need
is the loan of a general or two from the Samos Command.
At least we've got this lumber off our backs.
That's something. And now let's look to our fire.

O Pot, brave Brazier, touch my torch with flame!
Victory, Goddess, I invoke thy name!
Strike down these paradigms of female pride,
And we shall hang our trophies up inside.
               [*Enter* CHORUS OF OLD WOMEN *on the walls of the*
               Akropolis, carrying jars *of water*
KORYPHAIOS^w:

Smoke, girls, smoke! There's smoke all over the place!
Probably fire, too. Hurry, girls! Fire! Fire!

CHORUS^W:

Nikodikê, run!   [STROPHE 1
Or Kalykê's done
To a turn, and poor Kritylla's
Smoked like a ham.
               Damn
These old men! Are we too late?
I nearly died down at the place
Where we fill our jars:
   Slaves pushing and jostling—
   Such a hustling
I never saw in all my days.

But here's water at last.   [ANTISTROPHE 1
Haste, sisters, haste!
Slosh it on them, slosh it down,
The silly old wrecks!
             Sex
Almighty! What they want's
A hot bath? Good. Send one down.
Athêna of Athens town,
   Trito-born! Helm of Gold!
   Cripple the old
Firemen! Help us help them drown!

      [*The* OLD MEN *capture a woman,* STRATYLLIS

STRATYLLIS:
  Let me go! Let me go!
KORYPHAIOS^W:
             You walking corpses,
  have you no shame?
KORYPHAIOS^m:
             I wouldn't have believed it!
  An army of women in the Akropolis!
KORYPHAIOS^W:
  So we scare you, do we? Grandpa, you've seen
  only our pickets yet!
KORYPHAIOS^m:
           Hey, Phaidrias!
  Help me with the necks of these jabbering hens!

KORYPHAIOS^w:

Down with your pots, girls! We'll need both hands
if these antiques attack us.

KORYPHAIOS^m:

Want your face kicked in?

KORYPHAIOS^w:

Want your balls chewed off?

KORYPHAIOS^m:

Look out! I've got a stick!

KORYPHAIOS^w:

You lay a half-inch of your stick on Stratyllis,
and you'll never stick again!

KORYPHAIOS^m:

Fall apart!

KORYPHAIOS^w:

I'll spit up your guts!

KORYPHAIOS^m:

Euripides! Master!
How well you knew women!

KORYPHAIOS^w:

Listen to him! Rhodippê,
up with the pots!

KORYPHAIOS^m:

Demolition of God,
what good are your pots?

KORYPHAIOS^w:

You refugee from the tomb,
what good is your fire?

KORYPHAIOS^m:

Good enough to make a pyre
to barbecue you!

KORYPHAIOS^w:

We'll squizzle your kindling!

KORYPHAIOS^m:

You think so?

KORYPHAIOS^w:

Yah! Just hang around a while!

KORYPHAIOS^m:

Want a touch of my torch?

KORYPHAIOS^w:

It needs a good soaping.

KORYPHAIOS^m:
How about you?
KORYPHAIOS^w:
Soap for a senile bridegroom!
KORYPHAIOS^m:
Senile? Hold your trap!
KORYPHAIOS^w:
Just *you* try to hold it!
KORYPHAIOS^m:
The yammer of women!
KORYPHAIOS^w:
Oh is that so?
You're not in the jury room now, you know.
KORYPHAIOS^m:
Gentlemen, I beg you, burn off that woman's hair!
KORYPHAIOS^w:
Let it come down!
                    [*They empty their pots on the men*
KORYPHAIOS^m:
What a way to drown!
KORYPHAIOS^w:
Hot, hey?
KORYPHAIOS^m:
Say,
enough!
KORYPHAIOS^w:
Dandruff
needs watering. I'll make you
nice and fresh.
KORYPHAIOS^m:
For God's sake, you,
hold off!

🏵 SCENE I

[*Enter a* COMMISSIONER *accompanied by four constables*

COMMISSIONER:
These degenerate women! What a racket of little drums,
what a yapping for Adonis on every house-top!

It's like the time in the Assembly when I was listening
to a speech—out of order, as usual—by that fool
Demostratos, all about troops for Sicily,
that kind of nonsense—
      and there was his wife
trotting around in circles howling
Alas for Adonis!—
     and Demostratos insisting
we must draft every last Zakynthian that can walk—
and his wife up there on the roof,
drunk as an owl, yowling
Oh weep for Adonis!—
     and that damned ox Demostratos
mooing away through the rumpus. That's what we get
for putting up with this wretched woman-business!

KORYPHAIOS^m:
 Sir, you haven't heard the half of it. They laughed at us!
 Insulted us! They took pitchers of water
 and nearly drowned us! We're still wringing out our
  clothes,
 for all the world like unhousebroken brats.

COMMISSIONER:
 Serves you right, by Poseidon!
 Whose fault is it if these women-folk of ours
 get out of hand? We coddle them,
 we teach them to be wasteful and loose. You'll see a husband
 go into a jeweler's. 'Look,' he'll say,
 'jeweler,' he'll say, 'you remember that gold choker
 'you made for my wife? Well, she went to a dance last
  night
 'and broke the clasp. Now, I've got to go to Sálamis,
 'and can't be bothered. Run over to my house tonight,
 'will you, and see if you can put it together for her.'
 Or another one
 goes to a cobbler—a good strong workman, too,
 with an awl that was never meant for child's play. 'Here,'
 he'll tell him, 'one of my wife's shoes is pinching
 'her little toe. Could you come up about noon
 'and stretch it out for her?'
      Well, what do you expect?

Look at me, for example. I'm a Public Officer,
and it's one of my duties to pay off the sailors.
And where's the money? Up there in the Akropolis!
And those blasted women slam the door in my face!
But what are we waiting for?
                              —Look here, constable,
stop sniffing around for a tavern, and get us
some crowbars. We'll force their gates! As a matter of
    fact,
I'll do a little forcing myself.
                    [*Enter* LYSISTRATA, *above, with* MYRRHINE, KALO-
                    NIKE, *and the* BOIOTIAN

LYSISTRATA:
                              No need of forcing.
Here I am, of my own accord. And all this talk
about locked doors—! We don't need locked doors,
but just the least bit of common sense.

COMMISSIONER:
    Is that so, ma'am!
                    —Where's my constable?
                                        —Constable,
arrest that woman, and tie her hands behind her.

LYSISTRATA:
    If he touches me, I swear by Artemis
    there'll be one scamp dropped from the public pay-roll
        tomorrow!

COMMISSIONER:
    Well, constable? You're not afraid, I suppose? Grab her,
    two of you, around the middle!

KALONIKE:
                              No, by Pándrosos!
    Lay a hand on her, and I'll jump on you so hard
    your guts will come out the back door!

COMMISSIONER:
                                   That's what *you* think!
    Where's the sergeant?—Here, you: tie up that trollop
        first,
    the one with the pretty talk!

MYRRHINE:
                              By the Moon-Goddess,
    just try! They'll have to scoop you up with a spoon!

COMMISSIONER:
Another one!

Officer, seize that woman!

I swear
I'll put an end to this riot!

BOIOTIAN:

By the Taurian,
one inch closer, you'll be one screaming bald-head!

COMMISSIONER:
Lord, what a mess! And my constables seem ineffective.
But—women get the best of us? By God, no!

—Skythians!
Close ranks and forward march!

LYSISTRATA:

'Forward,' indeed!
By the Two Goddesses, what's the sense in *that*?
They're up against four companies of women
armed from top to bottom.

COMMISSIONER:

Forward, my Skythians!

LYSISTRATA:
Forward, yourselves, dear comrades!
You grainlettucebeanseedmarket girls!
You garlicandonionbreadbakery girls!
Give it to 'em! Knock 'em down! Scratch 'em!
Tell 'em what you think of 'em!

[*General mêlée; the Skythians yield*
—Ah, that's enough!
Sound a retreat: good soldiers don't rob the dead.

COMMISSIONER:
A nice day *this* has been for the police!

LYSISTRATA:
Well, there you are.—Did you really think we women
would be driven like slaves? Maybe now you'll admit
that a woman knows something about spirit.

COMMISSIONER:

Spirit enough,
especially spirits in bottles! Dear Lord Apollo!

KORYPHAIOS^m:
Your Honor, there's no use talking to them. Words
mean nothing whatever to wild animals like these.

Think of the sousing they gave us! and the water
was not, I believe, of the purest.

KORYPHAIOS^w:

You shouldn't have come after us. And if you try it again,
you'll be one eye short!—Although, as a matter of fact,
what I like best is just to stay at home and read,
like a sweet little bride: never hurting a soul, no,
never going out. But if you *must* shake hornets' nests,
look out for the hornets.

CHORUS^m:

Of all the beasts that God hath wrought   [STROPHE 1
   What monster's worse than woman?
Who shall encompass with his thought
   Their guile unending? No man.

They've seized the Heights, the Rock, the Shrine—
   But to what end? I wot not.
Sure there's some clue to their design!
   Have you the key? I thought not.

KORYPHAIOS^m:

We might question them, I suppose. But I warn you, sir,
don't believe anything you hear! It would be un-Athenian
not to get to the bottom of this plot.

COMMISSIONER:

                                        Very well.
My first question is this: Why, so help you God,
did you bar the gates of the Akropolis?

LYSISTRATA:

                                        Why?
To keep the money, of course. No money, no war.

COMMISSIONER:

You think that money's the cause of war?

LYSISTRATA:

                                        I do.
Money brought about that Peisandros business
and all the other attacks on the State. Well and good!
They'll not get another cent here!

COMMISSIONER:

                                        And what will you do?

LYSISTRATA:
What a question! From now on, we intend
to control the Treasury.
COMMISSIONER:
Control the Treasury!
LYSISTRATA:
Why not? Does that seem strange? After all,
we control our household budgets.
COMMISSIONER:
But that's different!

LYSISTRATA:
'Different'? What do you mean?
COMMISSIONER:
I mean simply this:
it's the Treasury that pays for National Defense.
LYSISTRATA:
Unnecessary. We propose to abolish war.
COMMISSIONER:
Good God.—And National Security?
LYSISTRATA:
Leave that to us.

COMMISSIONER:
You?
LYSISTRATA:
Us.
COMMISSIONER:
We're done for, then!
LYSISTRATA:
Never mind.
We women will save you in spite of yourselves.
COMMISSIONER:
What nonsense!

LYSISTRATA:
If you like. But you must accept it, like it or not.
COMMISSIONER:
Why, this is downright subversion!
LYSISTRATA:
Maybe it is.
But we're going to save you, Judge.
COMMISSIONER:
I don't *want* to be saved.

LYSISTRATA:

Tut. The death-wish. All the more reason.

COMMISSIONER:

                                                           But the idea

of women bothering themselves about peace and war!

LYSISTRATA:

Will you listen to me?

COMMISSIONER:

                              Yes. But be brief, or I'll—

LYSISTRATA:

This is no time for stupid threats.

COMMISSIONER:

                                 By the gods,

I can't stand any more!

AN OLD WOMAN:

                            Can't stand? Well, well.

COMMISSIONER:

That's enough out of you, you old buzzard!

Now, Lysistrata: tell me what you're thinking.

LYSISTRATA:

Glad to.

               Ever since this war began

We women have been watching you men, agreeing with
    you,

keeping our thoughts to ourselves. That doesn't mean

we were happy: we weren't, for we saw how things were
    going;

but we'd listen to you at dinner

arguing this way and that.

                  —Oh you, and your big

Top Secrets!—

              And then we'd grin like little patriots

(though goodness knows we didn't feel like grinning) and
    ask you:

'Dear, did the Armistice come up in Assembly today?'

And you'd say, 'None of your business! Pipe down!',
    you'd say.

And so we would.

AN OLD WOMAN:

                   I wouldn't have, by God!

COMMISSIONER:
　　You'd have taken a beating, then!
　　　　　　　　　　　　　—Go on.
LYSISTRATA:
　　Well, we'd be quiet. But then, you know, all at once
　　you men would think up something worse than ever.
　　Even *I* could see it was fatal. And, 'Darling,' I'd say,
　　'have you gone completely mad?' And my husband would
　　　　　look at me
　　and say, 'Wife, you've got your weaving to attend to.
　　'Mind your tongue, if you don't want a slap. "War's
　　' "a man's affair"'!'
COMMISSIONER:
　　　　　　　　　　Good words, and well pronounced.
LYSISTRATA:
　　You're a fool if you think so.
　　　　　　　　　　　　　　　It was hard enough
　　to put up with all this banquet-hall strategy.
　　But then we'd hear you out in the public square:
　　'Nobody left for the draft-quota here in Athens?'
　　you'd say; and, 'No,' someone else would say, 'not a man!'
　　And so we women decided to rescue Greece.
　　You might as well listen to us now: you'll have to, later.
COMMISSIONER:
　　You rescue Greece? Absurd.
LYSISTRATA:
　　　　　　　　　　You're the absurd one.
COMMISSIONER:
　　You expect me to take orders from a woman?
　　　　　　　　　　　　　　　　I'd die first!
LYSISTRATA:
　　Heavens, if that's what's bothering you, take my veil,
　　here, and wrap it around your poor head.
KALONIKE:
　　　　　　　　　　　　　　Yes,
　　and you can have my market-basket, too.
　　Go home, tighten your girdle, do the washing, mind
　　your beans! 'War's
　　a woman's affair'!
KORYPHAIOS^w:
　　　　　　　Ground pitchers! Close ranks!

CHORUS^w:

[ANTISTROPHE

> This is a dance that I know well,
> My knees shall never yield.
> Wobble and creak I may, but still
> I'll keep the well-fought field.
>
> Valor and grace march on before,
> Love prods us from behind.
> Our slogan is EXCELSIOR,
> Our watchword SAVE MANKIND.

KORYPHAIOS^w:

Women, remember your grandmothers! Remember
that little old mother of yours, what a stinger she was!
On, on, never slacken. There's a strong wind astern!

LYSISTRATA:

O Erôs of delight! O Aphroditê! Kyprian!
If ever desire has drenched our breasts or dreamed
in our thighs, let it work so now on the men of Hellas
that they shall tail us through the land, slaves, slaves
to Woman, Breaker of Armies!

COMMISSIONER:

And if we do?

LYSISTRATA:

Well, for one thing, we shan't have to watch you
going to market, a spear in one hand, and heaven knows
what in the other.

KALONIKE:

Nicely said, by Aphroditê!

LYSISTRATA:

As things stand now, you're neither men nor women.
Armor clanking with kitchen pans and pots—
you sound like a pack of Korybantês!

COMMISSIONER:

A man must do what a man must do.

LYSISTRATA:

So I'm told.
But to see a General, complete with Gorgon-shield,
jingling along the dock to buy a couple of herrings!

KALONIKE:

I saw a Captain the other day—lovely fellow he was,

nice curly hair—sitting on his horse; and—can you believe it?—
he'd just bought some soup, and was pouring it into his
helmet!
And there was a soldier from Thrace
swishing his lance like something out of Euripides,
and the poor fruit-store woman got so scared
that she ran away and let him have his figs free!

COMMISSIONER:
All this is beside the point.
                                    Will you be so kind
as to tell me how you mean to save Greece?

LYSISTRATA:
                                                Of course.
Nothing could be simpler.

COMMISSIONER:
                            I assure you, I'm all ears.

LYSISTRATA:
Do you know anything about weaving?
Say the yarn gets tangled: we thread it
this way and that through the skein, up and down,
until it's free. And it's like that with war.
We'll send our envoys
up and down, this way and that, all over Greece,
until it's finished.

COMMISSIONER:
                    Yarn? Thread? Skein?
Are you out of your mind? I tell you,
war is a serious business.

LYSISTRATA:
                        So serious
that I'd like to go on talking about weaving.

COMMISSIONER:
All right. Go ahead.

LYSISTRATA:
                        The first thing we have to do
is to wash our yarn, get the dirt out of it.
You see? Isn't there too much dirt here in Athens?
You must wash those men away.
                                Then our spoiled wool—
that's like your job-hunters, out for a life

of no work and big pay. Back to the basket,
citizens or not, allies or not,
or friendly immigrants.

And your colonies?
Hanks of wool lost in various places. Pull them
together, weave them into one great whole,
and our voters are clothed for ever.

COMMISSIONER:

It would take a woman
to reduce state questions to a matter of carding and
weaving.

LYSISTRATA:

You fool! Who were the mothers whose sons sailed off
to fight for Athens in Sicily?

COMMISSIONER:

Enough!
I beg you, do not call back those memories.

LYSISTRATA:

And then,
instead of the love that every woman needs,
we have only our single beds, where we can dream
of our husbands off with the Army.

Bad enough for wives!
But what about our girls, getting older every day,
and older, and no kisses?

COMMISSIONER:

Men get older, too.

LYSISTRATA:

Not in the same sense.
A soldier's discharged,
and he may be bald and toothless, yet he'll find
a pretty young thing to go to bed with.

But a woman!
Her beauty is gone with the first grey hair.
She can spend her time
consulting the oracles and the fortune-tellers,
but they'll never send her a husband.

COMMISSIONER:

Still, if a man can rise to the occasion—

LYSISTRATA:
Rise? Rise, yourself!

[*Furiously*
Go invest in a coffin!
You've money enough.
I'll bake you
a cake for the Underworld.
And here's your funeral
wreath!

[*She pours water upon him*

MYRRHINE:
And here's another!

[*More water*

KALONIKE:
And here's
my contribution!

[*More water*

LYSISTRATA:
What are you waiting for?
All aboard Styx Ferry!
Charôn's calling for you!
It's sailing-time: don't disrupt the schedule!

COMMISSIONER:
The insolence of women! And to me!
No, by God, I'll go back to town and show
the rest of the Commission what might happen to them.

[*Exit* COMMISSIONER

LYSISTRATA:
Really, I suppose we should have laid out his corpse
on the doorstep, in the usual way.
But never mind.
We'll give him the rites of the dead tomorrow morning.

[*Exit* LYSISTRATA *with* MYRRHINE *and* KALONIKE

🎭 PARÁBASIS: CHORAL EPISODE

KORYPHAIOS^m:

[ODE 1
Sons of Liberty, awake! The day of glory is at hand.

CHORUS^m:

> I smell tyranny afoot, I smell it rising from the land.
> I scent a trace of Hippias, I sniff upon the breeze
> A dismal Spartan hogo that suggests King Kleisthenês.
>> Strip, strip for action, brothers!
>> Our wives, aunts, sisters, mothers
> Have sold us out: the streets are full of godless female
>> rages.
> Shall we stand by and let our women confiscate our wages?

KORYPHAIOS^m:

[EPIRRHEMA 1

> Gentlemen, it's a disgrace to Athens, a disgrace
> to all that Athens stands for, if we allow these grandmas
> to jabber about spears and shields and making friends
> with the Spartans. What's a Spartan? Give me a wild wolf
> any day. No. They want the Tyranny back, I suppose.
> Are we going to take that? No. Let us look like
> the innocent serpent, but be the flower under it,
> as the poet sings. And just to begin with,
> I propose to poke a number of teeth
> down the gullet of that harridan over there.

KORYPHAIOS^w:

[ANTODE 1

> Oh, is that so? When you get home, your own mammá
>> won't know you!

CHORUS^w:

> Who do you think we are, you senile bravos? Well, I'll
>> show you.
> I bore the sacred vessels in my eighth year, and at ten
> I was pounding out the barley for Athêna Goddess; then
>> They made me Little Bear
>> At the Braunonian Fair;
> I'd held the Holy Basket by the time I was of age,
> The Blessed Dry Figs had adorned my plump décolletage.

KORYPHAIOS^w:

[ANTEPIRRHEMA 1

> A 'disgrace to Athens', am I, just at the moment
> I'm giving Athens the best advice she ever had?

Don't I pay taxes to the State? Yes, I pay them
in baby boys. And what do you contribute,
you impotent horrors? Nothing but waste: all
our Treasury, dating back to the Persian Wars,
gone! rifled! And not a penny out of your pockets!
Well, then? Can you cough up an answer to that?
Look out for your own gullet, or you'll get a crack
from this old brogan that'll make your teeth see stars!

CHORUS^m:

> Oh insolence!   [ODE 2
> Am I unmanned?
> Incontinence!
> Shall my scarred hand
> Strike never a blow
> To curb this flow-
> ing female curse?
>
> Leipsydrion!
> Shall I betray
> The laurels won
> On that great day?
> Come, shake a leg,
> Shed old age, beg
> The years reverse!

KORYPHAIOS^m:

[EPIRRHEMA 2
Give them an inch, and we're done for! We'll have them
launching boats next and planning naval strategy,
sailing down on us like so many Artemisias.
Or maybe they have ideas about the cavalry.
That's fair enough, women are certainly good
in the saddle. Just look at Mikôn's paintings,
all those Amazons wrestling with all those men!
On the whole, a straitjacket's their best uniform.

CHORUS^w:

> Tangle with me,   [ANTODE 2
> And you'll get cramps.
> Ferocity

's no use now, Gramps!
By the Two,
I'll get through
To you wrecks yet!

I'll scramble your eggs,
I'll burn your beans,
With my two legs.
You'll see such scenes
As never yet
Your two eyes met.
A curse? You bet!

KORYPHAIOS^w:

[ANTEPIRRHEMA 2
If Lampitô stands by me, and that delicious Theban girl,
Ismênia—what good are *you*? You and your seven
Resolutions! Resolutions? Rationing Boiotian eels
and making our girls go without them at Hekatê's Feast!
That was statesmanship! And we'll have to put up with it
and all the rest of your decrepit legislation
until some patriot—God give him strength!—
grabs you by the neck and kicks you off the Rock.

✿ SCENE II

[*Re-enter* LYSISTRATA *and her lieutenants*

KORYPHAIOS^w [*Tragic tone*]:
    Great Queen, fair Architect of our emprise,
    Why lookst thou on us with foreboding eyes?

LYSISTRATA:
    The behavior of these idiotic women!
    There's something about the female temperament
    that I can't bear!
KORYPHAIOS^w:
                    What in the world do you mean?
LYSISTRATA:
    Exactly what I say.

KORYPHAIOS^w:

What dreadful thing has happened?
Come, tell us: we're all your friends.

LYSISTRATA:

It isn't easy
to say it; yet, God knows, we can't hush it up.

KORYPHAIOS^w:
Well, then? Out with it!

LYSISTRATA:

To put it bluntly,
we're dying to get laid.

KORYPHAIOS^w:

Almighty God!

LYSISTRATA:
Why bring God into it?—No, it's just as I say.
I can't manage them any longer: they've gone man-crazy,
they're all trying to get out.

Why, look:
one of them was sneaking out the back door
over there by Pan's cave; another
was sliding down the walls with rope and tackle;
another was climbing aboard a sparrow, ready to take off
for the nearest brothel—I dragged *her* back by the hair!
They're all finding some reason to leave.

Look there!
There goes another one.

—Just a minute, you!
Where are you off to so fast?

FIRST WOMAN:

I've got to get home.
I've a lot of Milesian wool, and the worms are spoiling it.

LYSISTRATA:
Oh bother you and your worms! Get back inside!

FIRST WOMAN:
I'll be back right away, I swear I will.
I just want to get it stretched out on my bed.

LYSISTRATA:
You'll do no such thing. You'll stay right here.

FIRST WOMAN:

And my wool?
You want it ruined?

LYSISTRATA:

Yes, for all I care.

SECOND WOMAN:

Oh dear! My lovely new flax from Amorgos—
I left it at home, all uncarded!

LYSISTRATA:

Another one!

And all she wants is someone to card her flax.
Get back in there!

SECOND WOMAN:

But I swear by the Moon-Goddess,
the minute I get it done, I'll be back!

LYSISTRATA:

I say No.

If you, why not all the other women as well?

THIRD WOMAN:

O Lady Eileithyia! Radiant goddess! Thou
intercessor for women in childbirth! Stay, I pray thee,
oh stay this parturition. Shall I pollute
a sacred spot?

LYSISTRATA:

And what's the matter with *you*?

THIRD WOMAN:

I'm having a baby—any minute now.

LYSISTRATA:

But you weren't pregnant yesterday.

THIRD WOMAN:

Well, I am today.

Let me go home for a midwife, Lysistrata:
there's not much time.

LYSISTRATA:

I never heard such nonsense.

What's that bulging under your cloak?

THIRD WOMAN:

A little baby boy.

LYSISTRATA:

It certainly isn't. But it's something hollow,
like a basin or— Why, it's the helmet of Athêna!
And you said you were having a baby.

THIRD WOMAN:

Well, I am! So there!

LYSISTRATA:

Then why the helmet?

THIRD WOMAN:

I was afraid that my pains
might begin here in the Akropolis; and I wanted
to drop my chick into it, just as the dear doves do.

LYSISTRATA:

Lies! Evasions!—But at least one thing's clear:
you can't leave the place before your purification.

THIRD WOMAN:

But I can't stay here in the Akropolis! Last night I
    dreamed
of the Snake.

FIRST WOMAN:

And those horrible owls, the noise they make!
I can't get a bit of sleep; I'm just about dead.

LYSISTRATA:

You useless girls, that's enough: Let's have no more lying.
Of course you want your men. But don't you imagine
that they want you just as much? I'll give you my word,
their nights must be pretty hard.

Just stick it out!
A little patience, that's all, and our battle's won.
I have heard an Oracle. Should you like to hear it?

FIRST WOMAN:

An Oracle? Yes, tell us!

LYSISTRATA:

Here is what it says:
WHEN SWALLOWS SHALL THE HOOPOE SHUN
    AND SPURN HIS HOT DESIRE,
ZEUS WILL PERFECT WHAT THEY'VE BEGUN
    AND SET THE LOWER HIGHER.

FIRST WOMAN:

Does that mean we'll be on top?

LYSISTRATA:

BUT IF THE SWALLOWS SHALL FALL OUT
    AND TAKE THE HOOPOE'S BAIT,
A CURSE MUST MARK THEIR HOUR OF DOUBT,
    INFAMY SEAL THEIR FATE.

THIRD WOMAN:

I swear, *that* Oracle's all too clear.

FIRST WOMAN:

                                        Oh the dear gods!

LYSISTRATA:

Let's not be downhearted, girls. Back to our places!
The god has spoken. How can we possibly fail him?
                    [*Exit* LYSISTRATA *with the dissident women*

🎜 CHORAL EPISODE

CHORUS^m:

                                             [STROPHE

I know a little story that I learned way back in school
Goes like this:
Once upon a time there was a young man—and no fool—
Named Melanion; and his
One aversi-on was marriage. He loathed the very thought.
So he ran off to the hills, and in a special grot
Raised a dog, and spent his days
Hunting rabbits. And it says
That he never never never did come home.
It might be called a refuge *from* the womb.
All right,
            all right,
                    all right!
We're as bright as young Melanion, and we hate the very
        sight
Of you women!

A MAN:

How about a kiss, old lady?

A WOMAN:

Here's an onion for your eye!

A MAN:

A kick in the guts, then?

A WOMAN:

Try, old bristle-tail, just try!

A MAN:

Yet they say Myronidês
On hands and knees
Looked just as shaggy fore and aft as I!

CHORUS^w:

[ANTISTROPHE

Well, *I* know a little story, and it's just as good as yours.
Goes like this:
Once there was a man named Timon—a rough diamond,
    of course,
And that whiskery face of his
Looked like murder in the shrubbery. By God, he was a
    son
Of the Furies, let me tell you! And what did he do but run
From the world and all its ways,
Cursing mankind! And it says
That his choicest execrations as of then
Were leveled almost wholly at *old* men.
All right,
       all right,
           all right!
But there's one thing about Timon: he could always stand
    the sight
Of us women.

A WOMAN:
How about a crack in the jaw, Pop?
A MAN:
I can take it, Ma—no fear!
A WOMAN:
How about a kick in the face?
A MAN:
You'd reveal your old caboose?
A WOMAN:
What I'd show,
I'll have you know,
Is an instrument you're too far gone to use.

SCENE III

[*Re-enter* LYSISTRATA

LYSISTRATA:
Oh, quick, girls, quick! Come here!

A WOMAN:

What is it?

LYSISTRATA:

A man.

A man simply bulging with love.

O Kyprian Queen,
O Paphian, O Kythereian! Hear us and aid us!

A WOMAN:
Where is this enemy?

LYSISTRATA:

Over there, by Demêter's shrine.

A WOMAN:
Damned if he isn't. But who *is* he?

MYRRHINE:

My husband.

Kinêsias.

LYSISTRATA:

Oh then, get busy! Tease him! Undermine him!
Wreck him! Give him everything—kissing, tickling,
    nudging,
whatever you generally torture him with—: give him
    everything
except what we swore on the wine we would not give.

MYRRHINE:
Trust me.

LYSISTRATA:

I do. But I'll help you get him started.
The rest of you women, stay back.

[*Enter* KINESIAS

KINESIAS:

Oh God! Oh my God!
I'm stiff from lack of exercise. All I can do to stand up.

LYSISTRATA:
Halt! Who are you, approaching our lines?

KINESIAS:

Me? I.

LYSISTRATA:
A man?

KINESIAS:

You have eyes, haven't you?

LYSISTRATA:

Go away.

KINESIAS:

Who says so?

LYSISTRATA:

Officer of the Day.

KINESIAS:

Officer, I beg you,
by all the gods at once, bring Myrrhinê out.

LYSISTRATA:

Myrrhinê? And who, my good sir, are you?

KINESIAS:

Kinêsias. Last name's Pennison. Her husband.

LYSISTRATA:

Oh, of course. I beg your pardon. We're glad to see you.
We've heard so much about you. Dearest Myrrhinê
is always talking about 'Kinêsias'—never nibbles an egg
or an apple without saying
'Here's to Kinêsias!'

KINESIAS:

Do you really mean it?

LYSISTRATA:

I do.
When we're discussing men, she always says
'Well, after all, there's nobody like Kinêsias!'

KINESIAS:

Good God.—Well, then, please send her down here.

LYSISTRATA:

And what do *I* get out of it?

KINESIAS:

A standing promise.

LYSISTRATA:

I'll take it up with her.

[*Exit* LYSISTRATA

KINESIAS:

But be quick about it!
Lord, what's life without a wife? Can't eat. Can't sleep.
Every time I go home, the place is so empty, so
insufferably sad. Love's killing me. Oh,
hurry!

[*Enter* MANES, *a slave, with* KINESIAS' *baby; the voice of* MYRRHINE *is heard off-stage.*

MYRRHINE:

But of course I love him! Adore him!—But no, he hates love. No. I won't go down.

[*Enter* MYRRHINE, *above*

KINESIAS:

Myrrhinê!
Darlingest Myrrhinette! Come down quick!

MYRRHINE:

Certainly not.

KINESIAS:

Not? But why, Myrrhinê?

MYRRHINE:

Why? You don't need me.

KINESIAS:

Need you? My God, *look* at me!

MYRRHINE:

So long!

[*Turns to go*

KINESIAS:

Myrrhinê, Myrrhinê, Myrrhinê!
If not for my sake, for our child!

[*Pinches* BABY
—All right, you: pipe up!

BABY:

Mummie! Mummie! Mummie!

KINESIAS:

You hear that?
Pitiful, I call it. Six days now
with never a bath; no food; enough to break your heart!

MYRRHINE:

My darlingest child! What a father *you* acquired!

KINESIAS:

At least come down for his sake.

MYRRHINE:

I suppose I must.
Oh, this mother business!

[*Exit*

KINESIAS:

How pretty she is! And yourger!

The harder she treats me, the more bothered I get.
                                        [MYRRHINE *enters, below*
MYRRHINE:

                                        Dearest child,
you're as sweet as your father's horrid. Give me a kiss.
KINESIAS:

Now don't you see how wrong it was to get involved
in this scheming League of women? It's bad
for us both.
MYRRHINE:

                Keep your hands to yourself!
KINESIAS:

                                        But our house
going to rack and ruin?
MYRRHINE:

                        I don't care.
KINESIAS:

                                And your knitting
all torn to pieces by the chickens? Don't you care?
MYRRHINE:

Not at all.
KINESIAS:

                And our debt to Aphroditê?
Oh, *won't* you come back?
MYRRHINE:

                        No.—At least, not until you men
make a treaty and stop this war.
KINESIAS:

                        Why, I suppose
that might be arranged.
MYRRHINE:

                        Oh? Well, I suppose
I might come down then. But meanwhile,
I've sworn not to.
KINESIAS:

                Don't worry.—Now, let's have fun.
MYRRHINE:

No! Stop it! I said no!
                        —Although, of course,
I *do* love you.

KINESIAS:

                    I know you do. Darling Myrrhinê:
come, shall we?

MYRRHINE:

            Are you out of your mind? In front of the child?

KINESIAS:

Take him home, Manês.

                                [*Exit* MANES *with* BABY
                        There. He's gone.
                                            Come on!

There's nothing to stop us now.

MYRRHINE:

                            You devil! But where?

KINESIAS:

In Pan's cave. What could be snugger than that?

MYRRHINE:

But my purification before I go back to the Citadel?

KINESIAS:

Wash in the Klepsydra.

MYRRHINE:

                    And my oath?

KINESIAS:

                        Leave the oath to me.
After all, I'm the man.

MYRRHINE:

                    Well . . . if you say so.
                            I'll go find a bed.

KINESIAS:

Oh, bother a bed! The ground's good enough for me.

MYRRHINE:

No. You're a bad man, but you deserve something better
    than dirt.

                                    [*Exit* MYRRHINE

KINESIAS:

What a love she is! And how thoughtful!

                                [*Re-enter* MYRRHINE

MYRRHINE:

                            Here's your bed.
Now let me get my clothes off.

                            But, good horrors!

We haven't a mattress.

KINESIAS:

Oh, forget the mattress!

MYRRHINE:

No.

Just lying on blankets? Too sordid.

KINESIAS:

Give me a kiss.

MYRRHINE:

Just a second.

[*Exit* MYRRHINE

KINESIAS:

I swear, I'll explode!

[*Re-enter* MYRRHINE

MYRRHINE:

Here's your mattress.

I'll just take my dress off.   But look—

where's our pillow?

KINESIAS:

I don't *need* a pillow!

MYRRHINE:

Well, *I* do.

[*Exit* MYRRHINE

KINESIAS:

I don't suppose even Heraklês

would stand for this!

[*Re-enter* MYRRHINE

MYRRHINE:

There we are. Ups-a-daisy!

KINESIAS:

So we are. Well, come to bed.

MYRRHINE:

But I wonder:

is everything ready now?

KINESIAS:

I can swear to that. Come, darling!

MYRRHINE:

Just getting out of my girdle.

But remember, now,

what you promised about the treaty.

KINESIAS:

                                  Yes, yes, yes!

MYRRHINE:
But no coverlet!

KINESIAS:

                      Damn it, I'll be
your coverlet!

MYRRHINE:

                Be right back.

                        [*Exit* MYRRHINE

KINESIAS:

                   This girl and her coverlets
will be the death of me.

                    [*Re-enter* MYRRHINE

MYRRHINE:

               Here we are. Up you go!

KINESIAS:
Up? I've been up for ages.

MYRRHINE:

                  Some perfume?

KINESIAS:
No, by Apollo!

MYRRHINE:

               Yes, by Aphroditê!
I don't care whether you want it or not.

                      [*Exit* MYRRHINE

KINESIAS:
For love's sake, hurry!

                    [*Re-enter* MYRRHINE

MYRRHINE:
Here, in your hand. Rub it right in.

KINESIAS:

                  Never cared for perfume.
And this is particularly strong. Still, here goes.

MYRRHINE:
What a nitwit I am! I brought you the Rhodian bottle.

KINESIAS:
Forget it.

MYRRHINE:

              No trouble at all. You just wait here.

                    [*Exit* MYRRHINE

KINESIAS:

God damn the man who invented perfume!

[*Re-enter* MYRRHINE

MYRRHINE:

At last! The right bottle!

KINESIAS:

I've got the rightest
bottle of all, and it's right here waiting for you.
Darling, forget everything else. Do come to bed.

MYRRHINE:

Just let me get my shoes off.

—And, by the way,
you'll vote for the treaty?

KINESIAS:

I'll think about it.

[MYRRHINE *runs away*

There! That's done it! The damned woman,
she gets me all bothered, she half kills me,
and off she runs! What'll I do? Where
can I get laid?

—And you, little prodding pal,
who's going to take care of *you*? No, you and I
had better get down to old Foxdog's Nursing Clinic.

CHORUS[m]:

Alas for the woes of man, alas
Specifically for you.
She's brought you to a pretty pass:
What are you going to do?
Split, heart! Sag, flesh! Proud spirit, crack!
Myrrhinê's got you on your back.

KINESIAS:

The agony, the protraction!

KORYPHAIOS[m]:

Friend,
What woman's worth a damn?
They bitch us all, world without end.

KINESIAS:

Yet they're so damned sweet, man!

KORYPHAIOS^m:

> Calamitous, that's what I say.
> You should have learned that much today.

CHORUS^m:

> O blessed Zeus, roll womankind
>   Up into one great ball;
> Blast them aloft on a high wind,
>   And once there, let them fall.
> Down, down they'll come, the pretty dears,
> And split themselves on our thick spears.

> > > > [*Exit* KINESIAS

᪥ SCENE IV

> > > > [*Enter a* SPARTAN HERALD

HERALD:

> Gentlemen, Ah beg you will be so kind
> as to direct me to the Central Committee.
> Ah have a communication.

> > > [*Re-enter* COMMISSIONER

COMMISSIONER:

> > > Are you a man,
> or a fertility symbol?

HERALD:

> > > Ah refuse to answer that question!
> Ah'm a certified herald from Spahta, and Ah've come
> to talk about an ahmistice.

COMMISSIONER:

> > > Then why
> that spear under your cloak?

HERALD:

> > > Ah have no speah!

COMMISSIONER:

> You don't walk naturally, with your tunic
> poked out so. You have a tumor, maybe,
> or a hernia?

HERALD:

> > You lost yo' mahnd, man?

COMMISSIONER.

Well,
something's up, I can see that. And I don't like it.

HERALD:
Colonel, Ah resent this.

COMMISSIONER:

So I see. But what *is* it?

HERALD:

A staff
with a message from Spahta.

COMMISSIONER:

Oh. I know about those staffs
Well, then, man, speak out: How are things in Sparta?

HERALD:
Hahd, Colonel, hahd! We're at a standstill.
Cain't seem to think of anything but women.

COMMISSIONER:
How curious! Tell me, do you Spartans think
that maybe Pan's to blame?

HERALD:
Pan? No. Lampitô and her little naked friends.
They won't let a man come nigh them.

COMMISSIONER:
How are you handling it?

HERALD:

Losing our mahnds,
if y' want to know, and walking around hunched over
lahk men carrying candles in a gale.
The women have swohn they'll have nothing to do with
us
until we get a treaty.

COMMISSIONER:

Yes. I know.
It's a general uprising, sir, in all parts of Greece.
But as for the answer—
Sir: go back to Sparta
and have them send us your Armistice Commission.
I'll arrange things in Athens.
And I may say
that my standing is good enough to make them listen.

HERALD:
   A man after mah own haht! Seh, Ah thank you.

   [*Exit* HERALD

🏵 CHORAL EPISODE

CHORUS^m:

Oh these women! Where will you find   [STROPHE
A slavering beast that's more unkind?
   Where a hotter fire?
Give me a panther, any day.
He's not so merciless as they,
   And panthers don't conspire.

CHORUS^w:

We may be hard, you silly old ass,   [ANTISTROPHE
But who brought you to this stupid pass?
   You're the ones to blame.
Fighting with us, your oldest friends,
Simply to serve your selfish ends—
   Really, you have no shame!

KORYPHAIOS^m:
   No, I'm through with women for ever.
KORYPHAIOS^w:

                              If you say so.
   Still, you might put some clothes on. You look too absurd
   standing around naked. Come, get into this cloak.
KORYPHAIOS^m:
   Thank you; you're right. I merely took it off
   because I was in such a temper.
KORYPHAIOS^w:

                              That's much better.
   Now you resemble a man again.
                              Why have you been so horrid?
   And look: there's some sort of insect in your eye.
   Shall I take it out?
KORYPHAIOS^m:

                  An insect, is it? So that's
   what's been bothering me. Lord, yes: take it out!

KORYPHAIOS^w:
You might be more polite.
                              —But, heavens!
What an enormous mosquito!
KORYPHAIOS^m:
                              You've saved my life.
That mosquito was drilling an artesian well
in my left eye.
KORYPHAIOS^w:
                    Let me wipe
those tears away.—And now: one little kiss?
KORYPHAIOS^m:
No, no kisses.
KORYPHAIOS^w:
                    You're so difficult.
KORYPHAIOS^m:
You impossible women! How you do get around us!
The poet was right: Can't live with you, or without you.
But let's be friends.
And to celebrate, you might join us in an Ode.

CHORUS^{m and w}:
                    Let it never be said   [STROPHE 1
                    That my tongue is malicious:
                    Both by word and by deed
I would set an example that's noble and gracious.
                    We've had sorrow and care
                    Till we're sick of the tune.
                    Is there anyone here
                    Who would like a small loan?
                    My purse is crammed,
                    As you'll soon find;
And you needn't pay me back if the Peace gets signed.

                    I've invited to lunch   [STROPHE 2
                    Some Karystian rips—
                    An esurient bunch,
But I've ordered a menu to water their lips.
                    I can still make soup
                    And slaughter a pig.
                    You're all coming, I hope?

But a bath first, I beg!
       Walk right up
       As though you owned the place,
And you'll get the front door slammed to in your face.

🎗 SCENE V

[*Enter* SPARTAN AMBASSADOR, *with entourage*

KORYPHAIOS[m]:
The Commission has arrived from Sparta.
                              How oddly
they're walking!
                 Gentlemen, welcome to Athens!
How is life in Lakonia?
AMBASSADOR:
                          Need we discuss that?
Simply use your eyes.
CHORUS[m]:
                       The poor man's right:
                       What a sight!
AMBASSADOR:
                              Words fail me.
But come, gentlemen, call in your Commissioners,
and let's get down to a Peace.
CHORAGOS[m]:
                              The state we're in! Can't bear
a stitch below the waist. It's a kind of pelvic
paralysis.
COMMISSIONER:
             Won't somebody call Lysistrata? —Gentlemen,
we're no better off than you.
AMBASSADOR:
                          So I see.
A SPARTAN:
Seh, do y'all feel a certain strain
early in the morning?
AN ATHENIAN:
                       I do, sir. It's worse than a strain.

A few more days, and there's nothing for us but Kleis-
    thenês,
that broken blossom.

CHORAGOS^m:

                    But you'd better get dressed again.
You know these people going around Athens with chisels,
looking for statues of Hermês.

ATHENIAN:

                        Sir, you are right.

SPARTAN:

He certainly is! Ah'll put mah own clothes back on.

                [*Enter* ATHENIAN COMMISSIONERS

COMMISSIONER:

Gentlemen from Sparta, welcome. This
    is a sorry business.

SPARTAN: [*To one of his own group:*
Colonel, we got dressed just in time. Ah sweah.
if they'd seen us the way we were, there'd have been a
    new wah
between the states.

COMMISSIONER:

Shall we call the meeting to order?

                    Now, Lakonians,
    what's your proposal?

AMBASSADOR:

              We propose to consider peace.

COMMISSIONER:

Good. That's on our minds, too.

                  —Summon Lysistrata.
We'll never get anywhere without her.

AMBASSADOR:

                    Lysistrata?
Summon Lysis-*any*body! Only, summon!

KORYPHAIOS^m:

             No need to summon:
here she is, herself.

                [*Enter* LYSISTRATA

COMMISSIONER:

        Lysistrata! Lion of women!
This is your hour to be

hard and yielding, outspoken and shy, austere and
gentle. You see here
the best brains of Hellas (confused, I admit,
by your devious charming) met as one man
to turn the future over to you.

LYSISTRATA:

                        That's fair enough,
unless you men take it into your heads
to turn to each other instead of to us. But I'd know
soon enough if you did.

                     —Where is Reconciliation?
Go, some of you: bring her here.

                       [Exeunt two women
                  And now, women,
lead the Spartan delegates to me: not roughly
or insultingly, as our men handle them, but gently,
politely, as ladies should. Take them by the hand,
or by anything else if they won't give you their hands.

               [The SPARTANS *are escorted over*
There. —The Athenians next, by any convenient handle.

                  [The ATHENIANS *are escorted*
Stand there, please. —Now, all of you, listen to me.

        [During the following speech the two women
        re-enter, carrying an enormous statue of a naked
        girl; this is RECONCILIATION.
I'm only a woman, I know; but I've a mind,
and, I think, not a bad one: I owe it to my father
and to listening to the local politicians.
So much for that.

               Now, gentlemen,
since I have you here, I intend to give you a scolding.
We are all Greeks.
Must I remind you of Thermopylai, of Olympia,
of Delphoi? names deep in all our hearts?
Are they not a common heritage?

                     Yet you men
go raiding through the country from both sides,
Greek killing Greek, storming down Greek cities—
and all the time the Barbarian across the sea
is waiting for his chance!

                —That's my first point.

AN ATHENIAN:
Lord! I can hardly contain myself.

LYSISTRATA:
As for you Spartans:
Was it so long ago that Perikleidês
came here to beg our help? I can see him still,
his grey face, his sombre gown. And what did he want?
An army from Athens. All Messênê
was hot at your heels, and the sea-god splitting your land.
Well, Kimôn and his men,
four thousand strong, marched out and saved all Sparta.
And what thanks do we get? You come back to murder
us.

AN ATHENIAN:
They're aggressors, Lysistrata!

A SPARTAN:
Ah admit it.
When Ah look at those laigs, Ah sweah Ah'll aggress
mahself!

LYSISTRATA:
And you, Athenians: do you think you're blameless?
Remember that bad time when we were helpless,
and an army came from Sparta,
and that was the end of the Thessalian menace,
the end of Hippias and his allies.
And that was Sparta,
and only Sparta; but for Sparta, we'd be
cringing slaves today, not free Athenians.
  [*From this point, the male responses are less to*
  LYSISTRATA *than to the statue*

A SPARTAN:
A well shaped speech.

AN ATHENIAN:
Certainly it has its points.

LYSISTRATA:
Why are we fighting each other? With all this history
of favors given and taken, what stands in the way
of making peace?

AMBASSADOR:
Spahta is ready, ma'am,
so 'long as we get that place back.

LYSISTRATA:

What place, man?

AMBASSADOR:

Ah refer to Pylos.

COMMISSIONER:

Not a chance, by God!

LYSISTRATA:

Give it to them, friend.

COMMISSIONER:

But—what shall we have to bargain with?

LYSISTRATA:

Demand something in exchange.

COMMISSIONER:

Good idea. —Well, then:
Cockeville first, and the Happy Hills, and the country
between the Legs of Mégara.

AMBASSADOR:

Mah government objects.

LYSISTRATA:

Over-ruled. Why fuss about a pair of legs?

[*General assent. The statue is removed.*

AN ATHENIAN:

I want to get out of these clothes and start my plowing.

A SPARTAN:

Ah'll fertilize mahn first, by the Heavenly Twins!

LYSISTRATA:

And so you shall,
once you've made peace. If you are serious,
go, both of you, and talk with your allies.

COMMISSIONER:

Too much talk already. No, we'll stand together.
We've only one end in view. All that we want
is our women; and I speak for our allies.

AMBASSADOR:

Mah government concurs.

AN ATHENIAN:

So does Karystos.

LYSISTRATA:

Good. —But before you come inside
to join your wives at supper, you must perform

the usual lustration. Then we'll open
our baskets for you, and all that we have is yours.
But you must promise upright good behavior
from this day on. Then each man home with his woman!

AN ATHENIAN:
Let's get it over with.

A SPARTAN:
                              Lead on. Ah follow.

AN ATHENIAN:
Quick as a cat can wink!

                              [*Exeunt all but the* CHORUSES

CHORUS^w:
                    Embroideries ánd   [ANTISTROPHE 1
                    Twinkling ornaments ánd
                    Pretty dresses—I hand
Them all over to you, and with never a qualm.
                    They'll be nice for your daughters
                    On festival days
                    When the girls bring the Goddess
                    The ritual prize.
                         Come in, one and all:
                         Take what you will.
I've nothing here so tightly corked that you can't make
    it spill.

                    You may search my house,   [ANTISTROPHE 2
                    But you'll not find
                    The least thing of use,
Unless your two eyes are keener than mine.
                    Your numberless brats
                    Are half starved? and your slaves?
                    Courage, grandpa! I've lots
                    Of grain left, and big loaves.
                         I'll fill your guts,
                         I'll go the whole hog;
But if you come too close to me, remember: 'ware the
    dog!

                              [*Exeunt* CHORUSES

❧ ÉXODOS

[*A* DRUNKEN CITIZEN *enters, approaches the gate, and is halted by a sentry*

CITIZEN:
Open. The. Door.

SENTRY:
Now, friend, just shove along!
—So you want to sit down. If it weren't such an old joke,
I'd tickle your tail with this torch. Just the sort of gag
this audience appreciates.

CITIZEN:
I. Stay. Right. Here.

SENTRY:
Get away from there, or I'll scalp you! The gentlemen
from Sparta
are just coming back from dinner.
[*Exit* CITIZEN; *the general company re-enters;
the two* CHORUSES *now represent* SPARTANS *and*
ATHENIANS.

A SPARTAN:
Ah must say,
Ah never tasted better grub.

AN ATHENIAN:
And those Lakonians!
They're gentlemen, by the Lord! Just goes to show,
a drink to the wise is sufficient.

COMMISSIONER:
And why not?
A sober man's an ass.
Men of Athens, mark my words: the only efficient
Ambassador's a drunk Ambassador. Is that clear?
Look: we go to Sparta,
and when we get there we're dead sober. The result?
Everyone cackling at everyone else. They make speeches;
and even if we understand, we get it all wrong
when we file our reports in Athens. But today—!
Everybody's happy. Couldn't tell the difference
between *Drink to Me Only* and
The Star-Spangled Athens.

What's a few lies,
washed down in good strong drink?

[*Re-enter the* DRUNKEN CITIZEN

SENTRY:

God almighty,

he's back again!

CITIZEN:

I. Resume. My. Place.

A SPARTAN: [*To an* ATHENIAN

Ah beg yo', seh,
take yo' instrument in yo' hand and play for us.
Ah'm told
yo' understand the in*tr*icacies of the floot?
Ah'd lahk to execute a song and dance
in honor of Athens,

and, of cohse, of Spahta.

CITIZEN:

Toot. On. Your. Flute.

[*The following song is a solo—an aria—accompanied by the flute. The* CHORUS OF SPARTANS *begins a slow dance.*

A SPARTAN:

O Memory,
Let the Muse speak once more
In my young voice. Sing glory.
Sing Artemision's shore,
Where Athens fluttered the Persians. *Alalai,*
Sing glory, that great
Victory! Sing also
Our Leonidas and his men,
Those wild boars, sweat and blood
Down in a red drench. Then, then
The barbarians broke, though they had stood
Numberless as the sands before!

O Artemis,
Virgin Goddess, whose darts
Flash in our forests: approve
This pact of peace and join our hearts,

From this day on, in love.
Huntress, descend!

LYSISTRATA:
All that will come in time.
But now, Lakonians,
take home your wives. Athenians, take yours.
Each man be kind to his woman; and you, women,
be equally kind. Never again, pray God,
shall we lose our way in such madness.

KORYPHAIOS^a:

                                And now
let's dance our joy.
            [*From this point the dance becomes general*

CHORUS^a:
Dance, you Graces
                    Artemis, dance
Dance, Phoibos, Lord of dancing
                            Dance,
In a scurry of Maenads, Lord Dionysos
                    Dance, Zeus Thunderer
            Dance, Lady Hêra
Queen of the Sky
                    Dance, dance, all you gods
Dance witness everlasting of our pact
Evohí Evohé
Dance for the dearest
                    the Bringer of Peace
Deathless Aphroditê!

COMMISSIONER:
Now let us have another song from Sparta.

CHORUS^s:

            From Taÿgetos, from Taÿgetos,
            Lakonian Muse, come down.
            Sing to the Lord Apollo
            Who rules Amyklai Town.

            Sing Athêna of the House of Brass!

Sing Lêda's Twins, that chivalry
  Resplendent on the shore
Of our Eurôtas; sing the girls
  That dance along before:

Sparkling in dust their gleaming feet,
  Their hair a Bacchant fire,
And Lêda's daughter, thyrsos raised,
  Leads their triumphant choir.

CHORUSES s and a:

Evohé!
          Evohai!
                    Evohé!
                              We pass
          Dancing
                    dancing
                              to greet
Athêna of the House of Brass.

NOTES

Page

9: *those heavenly eels*: See note on BOIOTIA.

11: *that dance of ahs*: Athenian girls were brought up in seclusion. In Sparta, however, girls were expected to participate in athletic exercises. The 'dance' referred to here is the strenuous *bibasis*, in which the executant must strike her buttocks with her heels.

11: *Lawdy*: She swears 'by the Two,' which, in Sparta, meant the Heavenly Twins, Kastor and Polydeukês. The Athenian 'by the Two' was reserved to women only, and referred to Demêter and Persephonê.

12: *that General*: His name was Eukratês, and Σ describes him as 'an Athenian general, for sale, a traitor, and a mercenary'.

13: *drink up the proceeds*: The Athenian women were frequently satirized as being heavy drinkers.—The joke here, such as it is, depends upon a rhetorical trope by which the expected conclusion of a sentence is twisted into an unexpected incongruity. Thus, one would have expected Myrrhinê to say that she would pawn her best dress and contribute the proceeds to the Cause.

14: *when he saw Helen's breast*: An allusion to Euripides' *Andromachê*, 627, *sqq;* where Menelaos, about to stab his faithless wife, is overcome by her beauty and drops his sword.

16: *Where's our Inner Guard?*: See note on SKYTHIANS.

16: *Why not a white horse?*: Obscure; Σ observes that 'the horse' is a schema of coitus, but he also remarks that the Amazons (see note on MIKON) were accustomed to sacrifice white horses. According to Herodotos, the Amazons, furious horsewomen, were noted for their white (we should say 'ash-blonde') hair.

20: *the sacred statuar-y*: The august statue of Athêna Polias, which fell from Heaven upon the Akropolis.

22: *Trito-born!*: Name for Athêna, who, according to some accounts, was born near Lake Tritonis, in Libya.

25: *troops for Sicily*: A reference to the elaborate Sicilian Expedition (415 B.C.), in which Athens suffered a calamitous defeat from which she never recovered. (See note on DEMOSTRATOS.)

31: *"War's / a man's affair"*: Quoted from *Iliad* VI:492; Hektor to Andromachê.

36: *I bore the vessels*: Annually, four girls of high birth, between the ages of seven and eleven, were appointed acolytes to Athêna in the Akropolis.

36: *I was pounding out the barley*: At the age of ten, an aristocratic girl was eligible to be chosen as Mill-maid; her duty was to grind the sacred grain for Athêna.

36: *Little Bear*: See note on BRAURON.

36: *the Holy Basket*: The highest distinction of all. According to Σ, the baskets containing objects sacred to Athêna were of gold.

37: *our Treasury*: A sum of money, originally contributed by Athens and her allies, intended to finance an extension of the sea-war against Persia. Since the failure of the Sicilian Expedition, the contributions of the allies had fallen off; and the fund itself was now being raided by Athenian politicians.

39: *Pan's cave*: A grotto on the north side of the Akropolis, beneath the walls.

41: *the Snake*: This divine Snake was the Guardian of the Temple, the peculiar Safeguard of the Akropolis. He never appeared; but each month a succulent cake was set out for him, and it always vanished overnight.

41: *those horrible owls*: The Owl was sacred to Athêna.

46: *Oh, this mother business!*: A parody of Euripides, *Iph. Aul.* 917.

57: *looking for statues*: The statues were the Hermai, stone posts set up in various parts of Athens. Just before the sailing of the Sicilian Expedition, a group of anonymous vandals mutilated these statues with chisels. This and the women's Adonis-dirge (see note on ADONIS) were considered unhappy auguries.

57: *Summon Lysis-anybody!*: He actually says 'Lysistratos,' grasping at random for a name. Lysistrata's name means Dissolver of Armies.

64: *Athêna of the House of Brass*: This famous temple stood on the Akropolis of Sparta.

THE FROGS

for JOHN CIARDI

Ed egli a me: 'Ritorna a tua scienza,
  Che vuol, quanto la cosa è più perfetta,
  Più senta il bene, e così la doglienza,
Tuttochè questa gente maledetta
  In vera perfezion giammai non vada,
  Di là, più che di qua, essere aspetta.'
Noi aggirammo a tondo quella strada,
  Parlando più assai ch'io non ridico:
  Venimmo al punto dove si digrada:
Quivi trovammo Pluto il gran nimico.

INTRODUCTORY NOTE

I

Frogs was produced at the Lenaian Festival of 405 B.C., in the twenty-sixth year of the Peloponnesian War, only a few months before the final surrender of Athens to Sparta at the battle of Aigospotamoi. The competing comedies were the *Muses* of Phrynichos and the *Kleophôn* of Plato *Comicus*. Aristophanes took first prize, and his play was so well received that there was an augmented repeat performance. It has been a favourite ever since, though largely (like *Gulliver's Travels,* which it resembles) for the wrong reasons.

The plot of the comedy is simple, though somewhat inconsistent. Euripides had died in 406, to be followed almost immediately by Sophoklês. The future of drama seemed unpromising, at best; so Dionysos, the god presiding over the theatre, resolved to go down into Hadês, release Euripides, and bring him back to Athens. *Frogs* is the account of his experiences on this infernal errand. Disguised as Heraklês, who had made his own descent into Hell, and accompanied by Xanthias, a kind of Sancho Panza, Dionysos gets his directions from Heraklês, obligingly works his passage across the Styx in Charon's ferry, and arrives at his destination on the great Feast of Demêter and Persephonê, just in time to encounter the Initiates on their way to the celebration of the annual Mysteries at Eleusis. After a series of ribald mishaps he finds himself appointed judge—who could be a better choice?—of a poetry contest. It seems that Euripides, in his usual pushing way, has managed to seize the Chair of Poetry from Aischylos, who has been Laureate ever since his death in 456. The populace is happy enough with the usurpal, but a few strong-minded ghosts insist that Euripides should at least be tested by fair competition; and since Sophoklês ('he's happy anywhere') refuses to intervene unless Aischylos is defeated, the two poets contend publicly before Pluto's palace. Aischylos wins, and as a

71

reward he is permitted to return with Dionysos *in luminis oras*.

Such a plot has obvious, not to say vulgar, attractions, and they are played for all they are worth. There is a dismaying encounter with the archetype of all insolent doorkeepers; there is a slapstick scene in which the god and his companion are belaboured by loutish underlings; there are indelicate physical and mental situations in which no man, let alone a god, should be expected to involve himself; and there is, of course, the unseen boisterous chorus of Frogs which Yale-cheers Dionysos across the Styx. The material for the *agôn*, however, is at first sight less attractive. Euripides and Aischylos attack each other's work by anatomizing or parodying the poetry itself. If appreciation of this method made considerable demands upon the literary background of the ordinary Athenian playgoer—and some commentators have thought the demands so excessive that Aristophanes must have provided his subsequent audience with a libretto—it throws an even heavier burden upon us, especially since most of the plays cited are lost. It must be confessed, too, that Aristophanes knows a good joke when he gets hold of one, and has no intention of letting it go until he has extracted the last possible laugh. In spite of such disadvantages, what might have been the duller part of the play is actually its passionate core: the philosophical criticism implicit in the poetry contest itself. And it is here that the inconsistency is evident. At the beginning of the play Dionysos goes in quest of Euripides because he is a fashionable, decadent, effeminate god who has been captivated by a fashionable, decadent, 'modernist' dramatist. There is no question of serious purpose. But in the end he decides that Aischylos, not Euripides, must be returned to Athens, because the salvation of the state depends upon restoring the manly conservative principles for which the elder poet stands. What has happened is not unusual in comic satire: the initial raillery has become serious.

When we compare *Frogs* with the earlier war plays—*Peace,* for example, or *Lysistrata*—we are struck by an apparent difference of emphasis. The War itself is handled less overtly. Of course there are the usual attacks upon reckless demagogues and bone-headed commanders, the usual jokes about slaves liberated because of military service and honest citizens persecuted for dissident opinions; but the War was the whole thing in *Lysistrata,* when there was still some hope of a reasonable peace, whereas in *Frogs* the references are intermittent, almost muted, as though the poet were trying to escape from actuality into a Hadês of dream. It is easy enough to read the play as a yielding, to see its theme in the grim last words of the *parábasis:* 'If we win, there will be praise for us. If we lose, we shall have the consolation of losing handsomely and to the applause of wise men.' But such a reading, I think, is superficial. Aristophanes had never imagined that the War could be won by either side. Wars were as futile in his day as they are in ours. Even the gay *Lysistrata*—though it is not so gay as it looks—showed that the spirit of unconditional surrender could be as harmful to Athens as to Sparta; and in *Frogs,* with conditions incomparably worse, with collapse only a matter of months away, the poet is surer than ever that his point is sound. His play, therefore, is almost an I-told-you-so tract; with the difference that he now regards the War, desperate as it is, as only another symptom of the disease of his time. What we call pragmatism or materialism is the element that he deplores in the new teaching of the Sophists, the modernism of his age.

What an age! we are accustomed to say. But Aristophanes would not agree. It is undeniable that the greatest comic genius of antiquity, surely as mordant a satirist as the world has ever known, was a reactionary of reactionaries. There is nothing of the modernist in Aristophanes. Even what looks like 'advanced' blasphemy to us—his scandalous treatment of Dionysos, for instance—is demonstrably and firmly traditional. Living early in the very period of Athenian development that seems to us so exciting in retrospect—the brilliant innovations in art, in rhetoric, in philosophical speculation, in science—he found it only hateful, a prelude to the abyss. He would have agreed with the dimmest of Sokratês' judges that Sokratês was in truth a demented iconoclast, a perverter of young minds. Consequently he seized upon Euripides as symbolizing in literature all that was dangerous in the new radical theories. If we are really to understand *Frogs,* we must apprehend the deeper animus beneath the comic surface. We must see that the attack upon the Sophists in general, and upon Euripides in particular, is something more than a splenetic crotchet, a slap at a fashionable dramatist. *Frogs* is a moral and political polemic disguised as literary criticism. The laughter is enormous, of course, and we respond with laughter; but the poem transcends topicality and fun, and may even have a meaning for our own day.

II

In translating *Lysistrata* I set myself certain principles that I have not essentially altered. I have kept the dialogue as close to the Greek as I could, making allowances for local references and other details that could not be brought across without an even more formidable apparatus of notes than the one I have provided. In the lyric and choral passages I have taken more freedom. It is idle to speak—at least it is idle to speak to me—of recreating Aristophanes in corresponding English metres. There are no corresponding English metres. There are not even equivalent English metres. If I were an accomplished lyrist, I might compose strophes and antistrophes of significance and weight; but I suspect that they would be as unlike Aristophanes as the choruses I have written here, and, in an artistic sense, worse. My solution is modest; and I can only warn the reader that the Greek lyrics are very complicated indeed and occasionally of great beauty. My other departure is equally modest. Since the original is almost as rich as *Finnegans Wake* in literary allusion and rhetorical parody—indeed, it is a haunted text—I have sprinkled my version with comparable allusions to English literature. When I began my work I had some idea of substituting lines from Shakspere and Dryden, possibly, for the Aischylean and Euripidean verses quoted in the *agôn* and elsewhere; but this quickly turned out to be impractical. My only willed perversity is the substitution of a passage of Aischylean Pistolese for the lyric interlude immediately preceding the poetry contest. Perhaps Dionysos will pardon me for that.

The fact remains that translation from any language means sacrifice and compromise. Especially when one is dealing with the dead: slavish fidelity is stupid, and not even fidelity; and the attempt to 'modernize' generally beats itself insensible. All the translator can hope for, working within his own limitations, is to extract what is viable for him, put it into as credible a shape as he can command, and communicate to someone else an idea, however spectral, of the original. The dream of any poet is *Volito vivos per ora virum*. The translator has a duty to the shades.

III

I have used chiefly the Coulon text, published in Paris in 1928; but I have followed Oxford in some instances, and have been attracted to certain conjectures by that testy but fertile editor, J. Van Leeuwen. I am obviously indebted to the latter's copious Notes, and for the *scholia* have consulted the edition of Dindorf (1838).

CONTENTS

SCENE: *After the Prologue, the scene shifts from before the house of* HERAKLES *(presumably in Athens) to the hither shore of the Infernal Lake; thence to the other shore. From the* Párodos *on, we are in deepest Hell, before* PLUTO's *palace.*

The supernumeraries include four undertaker's assistants, women in the train of the CHORUS OF INITIATES, three Skythian constables, and a decaying prostitute.

🎐 PROLOGUE

[*A street before the house of* HERAKLES. *Enter the god* DIONYSOS, *wearing a saffron gown partly covered by a lion skin, carrying a huge club; and his slave* XANTHIAS, *bent double under an enormous amount of luggage, riding on an ass.*

XANTHIAS:
   Well, Master, we seem to be here. I suppose you want me
   to entertain the audience with one of my jokes?
DIONYSOS:
   By all means. Anything but the one that goes
   'Stop, you're killing me!' I couldn't stand that again.
XANTHIAS:
Something funnier, maybe?
DIONYSOS
                              Yes; but not 'That's what *she* said'.
XANTHIAS:
   You're fussy today
DIONYSOS:
                         Oh, come on! Whatever you like,
   except—
XANTHIAS:
                  Except?
DIONYSOS:
                           Don't shrug that knapsack back and forth
   and say, 'Ouch! Out from under!'
XANTHIAS:
                              But if I *don't* get out from under
   pretty damned soon, there'll be a disaster in the rear.
DIONYSOS:
   I swear, you make me sick.
XANTHIAS:
                                 Then what was the point
   of loading me down with this trash, if I can't behave
   like those low-comedy porters of Phrynichos,
      not to mention Messrs Lykis and Ameípsias?
DIONYSOS:
   Forget them. Any comedy of theirs
   ages a man by a good ten years.
XANTHIAS:
                                   Maybe; but my back
   won't hold up much longer.
DIONYSOS:
                               Who ever heard
   such insolence! Here I am, Dionysos, son of
   Juice, hobbling along, wearing myself out; and you

with a first-class donkey, the gift of my own hands,
to save you the trouble of carrying the load!
XANTHIAS:
You mean I'm not carrying it?
DIONYSOS:

                    No; the donkey is.

XANTHIAS:
If you say so. But it's strange.
DIONYSOS:

               What's strange?

XANTHIAS:

                    This nothing
that seems to weigh so much.
DIONYSOS:

              That's the donkey's business.

XANTHIAS:
No, by God, it's mine!
DIONYSOS:

            You're supported, not supporting.

XANTHIAS:
My shoulder's insupportable!
DIONYSOS:

        Well, if my donkey's no help to you,
pick him up and carry him for a while.
XANTHIAS:

               If only I were
a Navy veteran!
DIONYSOS:

       Why?

XANTHIAS:

       Why, then I could answer you
man to man, not like a damnèd slave.
DIONYSOS:
Get down, you imbecile! We've arrived.

             [XANTHIAS *dismounts.*
Hey, you, doorkeeper!

         Porter!

           Open up!
     [*The voice of* HERAKLES *is heard, within.*

HERAKLES:
In Hell's name, what's out there? Sounds like a centaur
kicking the door in.

[Enter HERAKLES

For God's sake, what have we here?

DIONYSOS: *[Aside, to* XANTHIAS
Boy.

XANTHIAS:
        Yes?

DIONYSOS:
              You've observed?

XANTHIAS:
                        Observed what?

DIONYSOS:
                              Damn it, observed
the way I scared him!

XANTHIAS:
                  Who's crazy now?

HERAKLES:
                              I swear by Demêter,
I can't help laughing, rude as it is.—Forgive me.

DIONYSOS:
Take courage, man, and draw near. We need your help.

HERAKLES:
This lion skin! this saffron gown! bedroom slippers and
a new shillelagh! What in the world are you?
Somehow I don't get the point.

DIONYSOS:
                        Give ear:
I was under Admiral Kleisthenês—

HERAKLES:
                        Must have been fun.

DIONYSOS:
                                    We sent
twelve or thirteen to the bottom.

HERAKLES:
                        Between you?

DIONYSOS:
                                    Yes.

XANTHIAS:
Wake up, the dream's over.

DIONYSOS:

No, let me tell you:
I was reclining in the poop, perusing
a play by Euripides—the *Andrómeda,* I remember—
when suddenly my breast was wrenched with a wild desire.

HERAKLES:

A big one?

DIONYSOS:

Gigantic.

HERAKLES:

For a woman?

DIONYSOS:

Certainly not!

HERAKLES:

Of course not. A boy, then?

DIONYSOS:

Brother, you're insulting.

HERAKLES:

Good God. You mean you wanted a full-grown man?

DIONYSOS:

Come, really, Heraklês!

HERAKLES:

Well, the only thing left
would seem to be Kleisthenês.

DIONYSOS:

Brother, don't make fun of me.
This passion of mine is tearing me to pieces.

HERAKLES:

Divulge, Brother, divulge.

DIONYSOS:

No, I can't; at least, not directly;
but maybe a hint—
Tell me, O Heraklês:
hast ever been seized by a craving for pea soup?

HERAKLES:

Over and over again.

DIONYSOS:

'Spake not my tongue plainly',
or must I elaborate?

HERAKLES:

      I see pea soup

in my mind's eye.

DIONYSOS:

     Just such a longing consumeth me now

for Euripides.

HERAKLES:

    For Euripides? But he's dead!

DIONYSOS:

No merely human force shall hinder me

from seeking him out.

HERAKLES:

      You mean you'd go down to Hell?

DIONYSOS:

Deeper, if need be.

HERAKLES:

     But why?

DIONYSOS:

       My heart is fixed

on that mighty poet. As he himself has written:

  Many men no more are.

  Those that are, no good are.

HERAKLES:

How about Iophôn?

DIONYSOS:

     The only good poet left alive,

and sometimes I have my doubts about *him*.

HERAKLES:

       Well; but Sophoklês?

If you must drag a literary man back from the grave,

why not him? He's worth a dozen Euripideses.

DIONYSOS:

Not until I'm sure that Iophôn can stand

on his own feet, without help from Sophoklês. Besides,

Euripides knows all the tricks. He'll find a way

to get out of Hell. But Sophoklês—

why, he's contented anywhere!

HERAKLES:

     And Agathôn?

DIONYSOS:

Departed. Much regretted by his friends.

HERAKLES:
  I didn't know. Departed whither?
DIONYSOS:
                                          Thither,
  to the Banquet o' th' Blest.
HERAKLES:
                      You don't say. How about Xenoklês?
DIONYSOS:
  To hell with Xenoklês.
HERAKLES:
                              Pythángelos, then?
XANTHIAS: [*Aside*
                                          I wish to God
  someone would mention Xanthias. My aching back!
HERAKLES:
  In fact, there must be thousands of pretty scribblers
  who can outrun your Euripides by miles
  when it comes to tragic jabber.
DIONYSOS:
                                  Scrannel pipes,
  I tell you; chirping birdlets; the death of Art.
  One tragedy, and they're spent
  without giving Melpomenê so much as a *frisson*.
  I don't care where you look,
  you won't find a poet today who is really
  generative.
HERAKLES:
            Generative?
DIONYSOS:
                        Yes, generative. I mean
  a poet who can sing of 'the skyey sky of Zeus',
  or 'fleet-flitting Time', or 'when last
  your eye I eyed', or (best of all, in my judgment)
  'Sworn hath my tongue; my soul stands yet unpledged'.
HERAKLES:
  You really like that sort of thing?
DIONYSOS:
                              Mad about it.
HERAKLES:
  But it's trash, and you know it.

DIONYSOS:
        'O thou rash intruder,
creep not into my mind'; you've one of your own.
HERAKLES:
 Have you no critical sense?
DIONYSOS:
         I'll accept
kitchen criticism from you; no other kind.
XANTHIAS: [*Aside*
 And still not a word about *me*!
DIONYSOS:
        But now, to business.
I'm on my way to Hell in your uniform,
and of course I turn to you for information.
What was it like down there when you stole the Dog?
The natives? The hospitality? The general tone of the
  place?
The sights? The shops?
Whorehouses, taverns, restaurants, the hotels
with the fewest bedbugs?
XANTHIAS: [*Aside*
    Still not a word!
HERAKLES:
          You're raving.
Do you really have the courage to go to Hell?
DIONYSOS:
 Are you deaf? Tell me the best route (not too hot,
yet not too cold) to the Houses of the Dead.
HERAKLES:
 The best route, hey? Take a rope and hang yourself.
DIONYSOS:
 No. Delicate throat.
HERAKLES:
      How about hemlock?
DIONYSOS:
 No. Feet get cold, legs swell up.
HERAKLES:
 I'll tell you the quickest way.
DIONYSOS:
      Good. I hate walking.

HERAKLES:
Go out to Potterville—
DIONYSOS:

Yes?

HERAKLES:

Climb the tallest tower—

DIONYSOS:
Yes?
HERAKLES:
And wait for the start of the torch-race.
When the fans shout 'Throw down the torch!',
then you just throw yourself—
DIONYSOS:

Where?

HERAKLES:

Down.

DIONYSOS:

Oh.

But that might scramble my brains.
No, give me
a better route than that.
HERAKLES:
You're hard to please.
DIONYSOS:
Tell me how *you* got there.
HERAKLES:
That was a long, long trip.
Well, first you come to an enormous dismal lake—
DIONYSOS:
How do you get across?
HERAKLES:
There's an old man
who runs a little ferry. Two pennies round trip.
DIONYSOS:
Dear me. Even Hell's gone commercial.
HERAKLES:
It was Theseus
started the custom.
Well, after you get over,
you'll meet mobs of snakes and all kinds of disgusting
beasts.

DIONYSOS:
   You can't scare *me*! I've been seeing them all my life.
HERAKLES:
   Then a great swamp with an almighty stink.
   Here they throw criminals: pathics who cheat their boys
   of pay for the pleasure they've had; stingy hosts;
   men who maul their mothers or flatten their fathers;
   perjured persons—
DIONYSOS:
                    And don't forget to add
   the publishers of Morismos, and those fools
   who admire the lyric spasms of Kinêsias.
HERAKLES:
   And then a grove with lovely light and the sound
   of soft flutes everywhere, and happy crowds
   of men and women, and laughter, and applause.
DIONYSOS:
   Who are these men and women?
HERAKLES:
                             The Initiates.
XANTHIAS: [*Aside*
   And I am the Initiated Ass! No, I've had enough.
HERAKLES:
   These will tell you whatever you need to know.
   They live quite near the road, at Pluto's gates.
   —Good-bye, Brother, and good luck!
DIONYSOS:
                             The same to you.
                             [*Exit* HERAKLES
   Xanthias, pick up the baggage.
XANTHIAS:
                        Before I've laid it down?
DIONYSOS:
   And make it quick!
XANTHIAS:
                    No! Please! Hire someone who's going there!
DIONYSOS:
   What if I can't find someone?
XANTHAIS:
                        Then I suppose
   I'll have to go.

DIONYSOS:

Fair enough.

—But here comes a dead man.

[*Enter, R, four undertaker's assistants carrying a* CORPSE *on an elaborate litter*

—My dear sir,

you, I mean, the Late Lamented,

Mr Corpse: will you carry my luggage with you to Hell?

CORPSE:

How heavy?

DIONYSOS:

Look at it.

CORPSE:

Hm. Let's say two drachmai.

DIONYSOS:

Too much.

CORPSE:

On your way, men!

DIONYSOS:

Wait a minute!

I'm sure we can strike a bargain.

CORPSE:

I said two drachmai.

DIONYSOS:

Nine obols?

CORPSE:

Not on your death!

—Go on, men.

[*Exeunt bearers, L, with* CORPSE

XANTHIAS:

That cadaver's too clever. To hell with him.

Master,

I'm with you!

DIONYSOS:

My noble Xanthias.

[XANTHIAS *retrieves the baggage and remounts his donkey; exeunt,* L.

✿ SCENE I

[The shore of a great lake separating our world from the world below. CHARON *is discovered standing in a dilapidated skiff. Enter* DIONYSOS *and* XANTHIAS.

DIONYSOS:
What's that?
XANTHIAS:
That? A lake.
DIONYSOS:
By God, the very one
he told us about!
XANTHIAS:
Yes. And there's the boat.
DIONYSOS:
So it is, by Poseidon!
XANTHIAS:
And there's old Charôn himself!
DIONYSOS:
Greetings, Charôn!
XANTHIAS:
Greetings, Charôn!
BOTH:
***GREETINGS,
CHARON!***
*[*CHARON *raises a large megaphone and addresses them.*
CHARON:
Who are you, coming from the world of woe and care?
Who are you, coming to Lethê? to the Mare's Nest?
to the Land of Dogdays? to Perdition Plaza? to
Hell in all its glory?
DIONYSOS:
Me.
CHARON:
All aboard, then.
And hurry up: we're runing behind schedule.
DIONYSOS:
Does this ship really touch at those ports?

CHARON:

                                    With *you* aboard, yes.

  Come, be quick!

DIONYSOS:

                  This way, Xanthias.

CHARON:

                              No slaves on my boat!

  Unless, of course, he's a Navy veteran.

XANTHIAS:

                                No.

  God knows I tried, but they wouldn't take me. Bad eyes.

CHARON:

  Walk around the lake, then.

XANTHIAS:

                      Where do I meet you?

CHARON:

  At old Arid's tavern by the Desiccated Rock.

DIONYSOS:

                                  Got it?

XANTHIAS:

  I've got it, all right.

                  —Must've met a black cat this morning!

            [*Exit* XANTHIAS; DIONYSOS *struggles into the boat.*

CHARON:

  Sit down. There's your oar.

                —All aboard! Anyone else coming?

                [DIONYSOS *sits down on an oar.*

  What in hell do you think you're doing?

DIONYSOS:

                    Just what you told me:

  I'm sitting on my oar.

CHARON:

                You gastric hyperbole!

  Sit there, on the bench!

DIONYSOS:

             All right.

CHARON:

                  Flex your biceps,

  stick out your hands

DIONYSOS:

            All right.

CHARON:
                                    And row, man, row!

DIONYSOS:
    Me? Row? Unshipbroken, unoceanized, unoared?
    How can I row?

CHARON:
                    Easiest thing in the world. Just try,
    and you'll have the most marvelous music to help you on.

DIONYSOS:
    What music?

CHARON:
                    Frogswans. A grade-A troupe.

DIONYSOS:
                                        I'm ready.
    Give me the stroke.

CHARON:
                    O opóp! O opóp!
                    [*The skiff leaves the shore, wobbling.*

🎗 KOMMOS: CHORAL EPISODE

                    [*The* ACCESSORY CHORUS *of* FROGS *is heard, off-
                    stage.*

FROGS:
                    Brekekekéx koáx koáx
                    Brekekekéx koáx koáx!
    We are the swamp-children
                            Greeny and tiny,
    Fluting our voices
                        As all in time we
                    Sing our koáx koáx
                    Koáx koáx koáx
    For Dionysos
                    Nysa-born
    On the Winey Festival
                            When the throng
    Lurches in through his temple gate,
    Every man as drunk as a hake.
                    Brekekekéx koáx koáx
                    Brekekekéx koáx koáx!

DIONYSOS:
My arse is sore, koáx koáx.

FROGS:
Brekekekéx koáx koáx.

DIONYSOS:
And you don't give a damn, koáx.

FROGS:
Brekekekéx koáx koáx.

DIONYSOS:
Go jump in the lake, koáx, koáx!
Let's have a different tune, koáx!

FROGS:
Different? What a
                    Meddlesome fool!
Pan and the Muses
                    Love us, our whole
            Koáx koáx koáx
            Koáx koáx koáx
Draws down Apollo
                    Golden-lyred:
Ours are the marsh-reeds
                    God-inspired
That sing to his heavenly fingering
Their music with our own mingling
            Brekckckéx koáx koáx.

DIONYSOS:
My hands are ablaze, my bottom's a wreck!
In a minute or two you'll hear it speak.

FROGS:
Brekekekéx koáx koáx!

DIONYSOS:
Silence, you lily-pad lyrists, koáx!

FROGS:
No, we must sing. The
    Sunshine will bring the
        Glint to the pools,
            The shimmer of reeds,
And when Zeus descends
    In rain on our heads
        We'll leap with our friends
            And pipe from our souls
                Brekekekéx koáx koáx!

DIONYSOS:
       Brekekekéx koáx koáx!
  Come, that's enough!
FROGS:
         We've hardly begun!
DIONYSOS:
  I suppose you think that rowing is fun?
     *[A furious increase in volume and tempo to the
     end of the chorus*
FROGS:
       Brekekekéx koáx koáx!
DIONYSOS:
       Brekekekéx koáx koáx!
  I wish you'd die!
FROGS:
        We'll swell up and cry
       Brekekekéx koáx koáx!
       Brekekekéx koáx koáx!
DIONYSOS:
       Brekekekéx koáx koáx!
  I can beat you at that koáx koáx!
FROGS:
  The devil you can, koáx, koáx!
DIONYSOS:
  I will, by God, if it takes all day!
       Brekekekéx koáx koáx!
  Go and koáx yourselves away!
     KOAX KOAX *KOAX!*
     [He breaks wind hugely; the FROGS *are silent.*
  There! That settles your damned koáx!
     [The boat has reached the opposite shore.

  🙚 SCENE II

     *[The shore of Hell; in the background, an ex-
     panse of weary grey land; the air is faintly brown*

CHARON:
  Easy all. Oars in. Step right out and pay
  at the gate.

DIONYSOS:

Here's your money.

[*Exit* CHARON

—Xanthias!

Xanthias! Where in hell is Xanthias?

XANTHIAS [*offstage*]:

Coming, coming!

DIONYSOS:

Late, as usual.

[*Enter* XANTHIAS, R

XANTHIAS:

Welcome to the underworld, Chief!

DIONYSOS:

What's in that direction?

XANTHIAS:

Murk and mud.

DIONYSOS:

Did you see those damned souls he told us about?

XANTHIAS:

Didn't you?

DIONYSOS:

Yes, by Poseidon! And I still do.

[*Points to the audience*

—Well, what's next?

XANTHIAS:

I think we ought to get out of here. This is the place
where that awful menagerie is, the one
Heraklês mentioned.

DIONYSOS:

Oh, *him.* He was just blustering,
trying to scare me off, because he knows
I'm unbeatable in battle. 'Breathes there the man
with soul so drunk' as Heraklês? Unlikely.
Oh for a beast, a monstrous beast,
to justify my valiant coming hither!

[XANTHIAS *feigns acute terror.*

XANTHIAS:

Did you hear that noise?

DIONYSOS:

No. Where? Where?

XANTHIAS:
Over there, in back of you.
DIONYSOS:
You get in back of me!
XANTHIAS:
Now it's in front of us.
DIONYSOS:
Come on, stand in front!
XANTHIAS:
Almighty Zeus, what a monster!
DIONYSOS:
What is it like?
XANTHIAS:
Horrible. Keeps changing its shape, too. First it's an ox,
then it's a mule, and now
it's the prettiest girl.
DIONYSOS:
Girl? Where? Lead me to her!
XANTHIAS:
Now she's turned into a mastiff.
DIONYSOS:
It's the Empûsa!
XANTHIAS:
A face like a bonfire!
DIONYSOS:
Legs of brass?
XANTHIAS:
Yes, one of them.
The other one's donkey-manure.
DIONYSOS:
Where can I hide?
XANTHIAS:
Me, too.
DIONYSOS [to the audience]:
Is there a doctor in the house?
XANTHIAS:
Lord Heraklês, we're done for!
DIONYSOS:
Name not that hateful name.
XANTHIAS:
'Lord Dionysos', then.

DIONYSOS:
                         Nor that.

XANTHIAS:
                         It's all right, Master.

DIONYSOS:
  What do you mean?

XANTHIAS:
                    As Hegélochos would say,
  'After the storm I see the clam again.'
  The Empûsa's pushed off.

DIONYSOS:
                         Swear it by Zeus.

XANTHIAS:
  I swear it.

DIONYSOS:
           Swear it again.

XANTHIAS:
                         I
  swear it.

DIONYSOS:
        Again.

XANTHIAS:
           I swear it.

DIONYSOS:
                    I went all white
  when I saw the Empûsa.

XANTHIAS:
                    Yes; and part of your robe
  went all brown.

DIONYSOS:
              Alas, what god is to blame
  for this dreadful visitation?

XANTHIAS:
                       Might it not be
  'the skyey sky of Zeus', or 'fleet-flitting Time'?
                       [A sound of flutes, off R
  Hark!

DIONYSOS:
        What?

XANTHIAS:
           Can't you hear them?

DIONYSOS:

What?

XANTHIAS:

The flutes.

DIONYSOS:

Yes; and the wind blows the scent of crackling torches.
They are celebrating the Mysteries.

XANTHIAS:

Then let's be quiet, and hide over there and watch.
[*The* CHORUS OF INITIATES *is heard offstage,* R.

CHORUS:

Iacchos! O Iacchos!
Iacchos! O Iacchos!

XANTHIAS:

The Initiates, Master, the ones
he told us about. That is their holy ground
where they sing of you, as they do in the Agora.

DIONYSOS:

I think so, too; but until we're sure of it
let's lie low and listen.

CHORUS:

O Iacchos!   [STROPHE
    God of many hymns!
Come to this meadow of delight
                    Come
  Dancing with laurel
                The bright
Flowers circling the holy hair that streams
        Gold in the golden air
                    Whirl our choirs
    In the maze of the Graces
                Iô!
    As the quick feet go.

XANTHIAS:

O Persephoneia! Lady! Demêter's daughter!
What a heavenly smell of pork!

DIONYSOS:
                              Oh, do be quiet!
A sniff of sausage, and you can't control yourself.

CHORUS:
Up the torches   [ANTISTROPHE
        Let them flare again
Radiant god
           Pure star of our night
  The glade's aflame:
                and care, and age—how light-
ly borne in the Bacchants' train!
    Lead us, bright glancer
                Whirl our choirs
   In the maze of the Graces
               Ió!
     As the quick feet go.

✿ PÁRODOS

> [*The scene has changed to the innermost part of Hell, before the palace of* PLUTO. *Enter,* R, *the* CHORUS OF INITIATES: *twenty-four men vested in white, crowned, carrying torches. They are accompanied by a throng of women who dance to the choral passages, although they take no part in the singing. The* KORYPHAIOS *assumes the rôle of the Hierophant, or President of the Mysteries.*

KORYPHAIOS:
Silence, O ye profane! Make way for our mystical Chorus,
    Ye to the Muses unknown * yé unvers'd in their dance!
Leave us, all ye unskill'd in the art of mighty Kratínos,
    Lovers of ancient jokes * friends of the easy laugh!
Let the bad man depart, fomenter of civic subversion,
    Venal commander in war * traitor on land or sea,
Public servant for sale, chéap déaler in contraband oar-
        locks,
    Sails and caulking pitch,* dallier with the foe,
Cyclic chorister dropping his filth at the shrinelets of
        Hékat',

Orator hating the poet, * grudging him his poor pay.
Let them be gone, I say, and I say it again, and a third
time.
Yield to the holy choir! * Brothers, begin the song!

CHORUS:

Oh sacred dance in the sacred fields, [STROPHE 1
Oh mystery of laughter!
We sing the praise of Her who shields
Her City from disaster:

Athêna goddess, swift to save [ANTISTROPHE 1
In times of mortal treason,
Queen of our joy this side the grave,
Our hope in every season.

KORYPHAIOS:

Now let us raise a hymn to Demêter, Queen of the deep
fields,
Goddess of waving wheat * crowned with the harvest-
gold.

CHORUS:

Demêter, Mistress of our mysteries, [STROPHE 2
Be with us today.
Satire and laughter-barbed sobrieties
Make up our play:

[ANTISTROPHE 2
When the last scene is done, the final wry
Verse has been said,
Grant me to wear the victor's wreath on my
Ecstatic head!

KORYPHAIOS:

Sing the adorable god who leads us all in our dancing,
Sing Dionysos the fair, * draw him to us in song.

CHORUS [*three solo voices with choral responsory*]:

A:

    Iacchos, festal Musician, come down to us now:
    The journey is long to the Goddess; we're dying to go.
        Dionysos, lead me.

B:

    Our costumes are tatters and worse, to cut the expense.
    Anything for a laugh; it won't matter a century hence.
        Dionysos, lead me.

C:

    I just glimpsed the prettiest girl in this part of the town
    And a pink little nipple popped through a rip in her
        gown!
        Dionysos, lead me.

DIONYSOS:

    I'd like to play with that pink little nipple.

XANTHIAS:

                                Me, too!

KORYPHAIOS:

    For Archedémos let us drop
      A small but lyric tear.
    No voter yet; but that won't stop
      His antics, never fear!
        Demagogue, prig, fop, and liar:
        Hell scarify him with its fire!

CHORUS:

    They say that Kleisthenês, in tears
      On his Sebinos' tomb,
  Is pulling out his nether hairs
      And prophesying doom.
        Pederast, pig, effeminate:
        From such as him God save the State!

KORYPHAIOS:

    I've heard the ever-valiant son
      Of Hippobine the Mighty
    Routs hosts of women one by one,
      No armour but his nighty—
        But that is made of lion skin:
        The girls look once, and then give in.

DIONYSOS: [*Politely, to the* CHORUS
    Can any of you gentlemen
    Direct me to the place
    That Pluto holds his revels in?
    I long to see his face.
        We're strangers here, my slave and I:
        We just came in on the last ferr-y.

KORYPHAIOS:
    Stranger, rejoice! Your journey's at
    An end. You see that gate?
    Enter to grow in wisdom. That
    Is all I care to state.
        All men who come from earth a-helling
        Are welcome in that aústere dwelling.

DIONYSOS:
    Pick up the bags, then, Xanthias.
XANTHIAS:
        That's all I needed, Master!
    A Korinthian baggomania's
    Consuming you, by Kastor!
        If Korinth really is 'God's City',
        Xanthias is—well, no self-pity!

        [DIONYSOS *and* XANTHIAS *approach* PLUTO's *gate.*

KORYPHAIOS:
    Let us dance.
    Dance to Demêter with flowers, to the goddess of flowers
        undying!
    Jewel her meadow with song! * Meanwhile, I will de-
        part,
    Torch in hand, with these maidens (themselves the kin-
        dlers of torches)
    To a secluded spot. * Béar úp! I'm sure *I* shall!
        [*Exit* KORYPHAIOS *with the company of women*

CHORUS:
            Ah the sweet dance   [STROPHE 3
                        the graced
            Rose-ritual
                    in places

Secret
     fair:
          O blest
Plain of all

Souls' desire!   [ANTISTROPHE 3
               O Fire
Hélios:
          good men
Hail thee
          find in thee
                    kindliest
Goodness to all!

SCENE III

> [DIONYSOS *stands timidly at* PLUTO'S *gate; sud-
> denly he turns back.*

DIONYSOS:
Xanthias, how does one knock at the door of Hell?
We mustn't violate local etiquette.
XANTHIAS:
Go ahead and knock. Remember, you're Heraklês!
> [DIONYSOS *knocks.*
DIONYSOS:
Anyone home?
AIAKOS [*within*]:
               Who wants to know?
DIONYSOS:

                    Heraklês the Remorseless.
> [AIAKOS *bursts from the house.*
AIAKOS:
O wretched, rash, intruding, hateful cheat!
Rogue of rogues, all rogues excelling! Dog-
napper—
          and that behind my back!
                         Never mind:
This time I've got you!
               Ay, and gloomhearted Styx
and the bloodthrobbing jetty of Acheron and

the ranging ghastly dogs of Kokytos await you!
Echidna shall rip you with her hundred mouths!
Tartessan eels shall gnaw your lungs away!
Teithrasian Gorgons shall chew your liver and lights!
Just you wait here: I'll be back with them in a minute.
                    [*He re-enters the house, slams the door.*

DIONYSOS:
Xanthias.

XANTHIAS:
            What's the matter?

DIONYSOS:
                        I seem to have soiled myself.
'Invoke the god.'

XANTHIAS:
            Nonsense. Pull yourself together.
What if someone should see you?

DIONYSOS:
                        I am dying, Xanthias, dying.
Bring me a sponge and apply it to my heart.

XANTHIAS:
Here you are. Apply it yourself.
        [DIONYSOS *takes the sponge and washes himself.*
                        Merciful God,
Is *that* where your heart is?

DIONYSOS:
                        Yes; it seems to have sunk.

XANTHIAS:
You colossal coward, disgrace of gods and men!

DIONYSOS:
Who calls me coward? Did I not ask for a sponge?
A weaker man would never have dared.

XANTHIAS:
                        How so?

DIONYSOS:
He'd have lain there, radiating. But *I* faced the matter,
and now I'm as good as new.

XANTHIAS:
                        Poseidon, what a man!

DIONYSOS:
Exactly.—But you,
weren't you appalled by that dreadful speech of his?

XANTHIAS:
  Me? Not at all.
DIONYSOS:
                    I congratulate you.
                              — Here,
  since you're so heroic, take my lion skin
  and my club. I'll carry the baggage.
XANTHIAS:
                              I hear and I obey.
  Give me your uniform, quick. Here's mine, and the
      luggage.
                              [*After the exchange:*
  You behold a new kind of god, a Xanthioheraklês.
  Do *I* look like a coward?
DIONYSOS:
                    You look like hell to me!
  [*He picks up the baggage and they start to leave,*
  XANTHIAS *leading the way.*

🎨 SCENE IV

              [*The door suddenly opens.* DIONYSOS *cringes in*
              terror behind XANTHIAS. *Enter from the house a*
              pretty MAID-SERVANT *to Persephonê*

MAID:
  Welcome, dearest Heraklês!
  So nice to have you back again! Her Majesty
  no sooner heard you were here than she baked a mountain
      of bread
  with her own hands, put three or four pots of peas
  on the fire, roasted an immense ox, and made
  I don't know how many hundreds of little cookies and
      cakes.
  Come in, do!
XANTHIAS:
                    You're very kind, but I'm not hungry.
MAID:
  Mercy, but you *must* be!
                    I forgot to mention

that there's chicken, too, and wine, and the darlingest
  dessert.

XANTHIAS:

Thank you, but no.

MAID:

You're *always* teasing!

Well, what about
a flute-girl (a real artist) and two or three
ballerinas?

XANTHIAS:

Did you say ballerinas?

MAID:

Lovely girls, too,
all perfumed and plucked, not one of them over fifteen.
Come in:
the fish is broiled to a turn, and they're setting the table.

XANTHIAS:

That's different! Tell the girls I'm on my way.

[*Exit* MAID

Slave, pick up the luggage and follow me.

DIONYSOS:

Stop right there! I let you play Heraklês
for the fun of it. Did you think I was serious?
Xanthias, don't be a fool. Pick up the baggage.

XANTHIAS:

You mean you didn't mean what you meant?

DIONYSOS:

I mean
that I'm the master here. Take off that lion skin.

XANTHIAS:

Witness, O gods from whom no secrets are hid,
how the man treats me!

DIONYSOS:

Idiot, thou art the man!
How can a deathbound slave be Alkmenê's son?

XANTHIAS:

Oh, I suppose so. Here you are.

[*They exchange costumes.*

But the day will come
when you'll need my help. By God, just wait till then!

DIONYSOS:
  Xanthias.

XANTHIAS:
       Yes?

DIONYSOS:
           Xanthias, I swear
that I love you beyond all men living or dead.

XANTHIAS:
  Hey, none of that! I'm through being Heraklês.

DIONYSOS:
  Oh please, please, Xanthy!

XANTHIAS:
               As you said yourself,
how can a deathbound slave be Alkmenê's son?

DIONYSOS:
  I know, I know. You're angry, and I don't blame you.
Hit me, if you want to.
            But this time, Xanthias,
if I try to take back the lion skin, may I be
cast out root and branch with my wife and children—
and you can toss in old blear-eyed Archedémos.

XANTHIAS:
  All right. If you really mean that, I'll play along.
                     [*They exchange rôles.*

CHORUS:
    Nice work! You have the clothes again, [ANTISTROPHE
    And now *you*'re Heraklês.
  Swagger and strut, and strut again:
         For if you fail
         To make men quail,
   He'll beat you to your knees.
      Permit me to recite the adage:
      'The coward always bears the baggage.'

XANTHIAS:
    Friends, you have harped my fear aright:
      He'll cheat me if he can.
  But I'll be fierce, and growl, and bite,
         And goggle so
         That all will know

I'm a catastrophic man.
            Be with me now, propitious Fate!
            I hear a knocking at the gate.

[*The door opens. Enter* AIAKOS *carrying a horse-whip, accompanied by three Skythian constables*

AIAKOS:
    Arrest that dog-thief and be quick about it.
    His time has come!
DIONYSOS: [*Aside*
                Somebody's in for it.
XANTHIAS:
                                Go to hell!
    One step more, and you get a taste of my club!
AIAKOS:
    Tut. Resisting an officer!
                    —Ditylas, Skeblyas,
    and you, Pardokas: come here and get him.
            [*The constables disarm* XANTHIAS *and bind him.*
    There. Now he'll get the kind of treatment
    a dog-rustler deserves.
DIONYSOS: [*Aside*
                A horrid fate!
XANTHIAS:
    I hope to die if I was ever here before,
    or if I stole so much as a hair of your dog!
    But I'll be generous:
    suppose you torture that lousy slave of mine.
    If he proves me guilty, I don't care what you do to me.
AIAKOS:
    Well . . . What kind of torture do you suggest?
XANTHIAS:
    Oh, the rack, or hang him by the thumbs, or stretch him
    on the ladder, or flay him, or pour vinegar up his nose,
    or pile stones upon him—it's all one to me.
AIAKOS:
    Excellent, excellent! But suppose I damage him
    permanently? You won't bring suit, I hope?
XANTHIAS:
    Certainly not. I make no conditions at all.
AIAKOS:
    Better do it here, so that you can watch what he says.

—Here you, put down the baggage. And swear to tell the truth and nothing but the truth.

DIONYSOS:

One moment.

You can not torture me. I am a god.

AIAKOS:

What say?

DIONYSOS:

I said that I

am Dionysos, son of Zeus Almighty.

That person is my slave.

AIAKOS [*to* XANTHIAS]:

Did you hear that?

XANTHIAS:

Yes. Incredible blasphemy.

But whip him!

If he's a god, he'll never feel a thing.

DIONYSOS [*to* XANTHIAS]:

You say *you*'re a god. Why don't you get whipped too?

XANTHIAS:

That's reasonable.

—All right, whip us both; and the one who cries *Uncle!*, or shows the least sign of feeling pain—that one's no god.

AIAKOS:

Good. You understand justice.

—All right: strip, both of you.

XANTHIAS:

The procedure?

AIAKOS:

Simple. First I hit one, then the other.

XANTHIAS:

Brilliant!

[*He lashes* XANTHIAS' *buttocks.*

AIAKOS:

Take that!

XANTHIAS:

Well, why don't you begin?

AIAKOS:

I did!

XANTHIAS:

Ridiculous.

AIAKOS: [*Lashes* DIONYSOS
    Then let's try the other.

DIONYSOS:
  Come on; haven't got all day!

AIAKOS:
           You didn't feel that?

DIONYSOS:
  Never a feel.

AIAKOS:
      Strange. Back to the first one.
                  [*Lashes* XANTHIAS

XANTHIAS:
  Oh my God!

AIAKOS:
     Felt it, hev?

XANTHIAS:
          Not at all. I was thinking
of the Festival of Heraklês Diomeios.

AIAKOS:
             Hm.
  The religious type.
       Well, let's have a go at the other one.
                  [*Lashes* DIONYSOS

DIONYSOS:
  Oooh! Oooh¹

AIAKOS:
     What's the matter?

DIONYSOS:
          Look at the gorgeous cavalry!

AIAKOS:
  Then why the tears?

DIONYSOS:
        Some onions popped into my mind.

AIAKOS:
  And you don't give a damn for the whipping?

DIONYSOS:
            Not a damn.

AIAKOS:
  What's going on here?
               [*Lashes* XANTHIAS

XANTHIAS:

Oh, please! please!

AIAKOS:

'Please' what?

XANTHIAS:

Got a thorn in my heel. Please pull it out for me.

AIAKOS:

Funny, aren't you?

—Well, it's your turn again.

[*Lashes* DIONYSOS

DIONYSOS:

Oh Apollo!

'Regent of Delos and of Delphoi.'

XANTHIAS:

He felt that, all right. Just listen to him!

DIONYSOS:

Not a bit.

I was merely reciting a verse from Hippónax.

XANTHIAS:

You're not getting anywhere. Hit him in the groin.

AIAKOS:

You're right, I'm not getting anywhere. Turn around!

[*Lashes* XANTHIAS' *belly*

XANTHIAS:

Poseidon!

AIAKOS:

Aha! At last!

XANTHIAS:

'Thou holding sway
o'er th' Aigaian cliffs and the winedark wave!'

AIAKOS:

No, by Demêter, it's beyond me! I can't tell
which one of you is the god.

Come in: I'll ask Persephoneia
and the King to decide. After all, they're gods themselves.

XANTHIAS:

A good idea; but I wish you'd thought of it sooner.

[*Exeunt into the house*

🎵 PARÁBASIS

[*The* CHORUS *turns and faces the audience, the*
KORYPHAIOS *standing apart from the group*

CHORUS:

      Descend, O Muse: strike with divine fire   [ODE
            Our mystic choir.
      Grant us the grace of song, that we
            Harmoniously
        May charm this audience,
        Ten thousand men of sense
      Whose hearts are angry when they see
      Kleophôn on his Thracian tree—
            That twittering split-tongued swallow
              Whose hollow
        Trillings tell
        Of Philomel
      'So rudely forced'.
            (As well he may:
        For if the jurymen should vote
        Acquittal, we would cut his throat.)

KORYPHAIOS:

                    [EPIRRHEMA
There is no function more noble than that of the god-
    touched Chorus
    Teaching the City in song. * Hear what we have in our
    hearts!
First, we pray for an end to unequal justice in Athens.
    Phrynichos with his tricks, * desperate wrestling-holds,
May have tripped some of us up. If he has, we beg you
    forget it.
    Must we reject our own? * Do we not need each man?
Shall we, because of one battle, make slaves the peers of
    Plataians
    (No, I approve your decree. * Then, for once, you were
    wise.)
And debase these neighbours of ours whose fathers and
    grandfathers, fighting

Oúr fight in oúr ships, * saved the City from shame?
Should they not have, as the dark comes down, storms
    bursting about us,
    Rights that are common to all? * Is there no Greek
    faith left?
Pride and revenge are human; but pride can be death,
    and revenge is
    Joy in the act, but pain * when the cleared brain
    reflects.

CHORUS:

       'If aught of skill in augury   [ANTODE
            Dwelleth in me',
    I say that tiny Kleigenês,
         That foe of peace,
      That drunken latrine-sweeper,
      That monkey-gaited creeper,
   Smells coming trouble—yes, and worse.
   (I'm always decorous in verse.)
        Else why does he every night,
          When he's tight,
    Insist
    On a club in his fist?
   It's plain enough:
            as he's weaving home,
    He fears some citizen may take it
    Into his head to strip him naked.

KORYPHAIOS:

                   [ANTEPIRRHEMA
Yet there are sensible men and good in Athêna's City,
    True as an ancient coin, * gold against modern brass.
Everyone knows the gold, here in Greece and the out-
    landish nations:
    How often we toss it aside, * stretch out our hands for
    what's new!
So with our dealings with men: When we find one worthy
    of honour,
    Old Athenian stock, * brave for his country, wise.

Skilled in the arts, a scholar, an athlete, a soldier, a
poet—
What do we do with *him*? * Drive him away from our
sight!
No, we prefer the brass: the connivers, the bland politi-
cians,
Faddists from overseas, * parvenus, plausible scamps,
Slippery scum that the City would once have disdained
to consider
Even as scapegoats fit * for the expiatory rites.
Ah, we are mad, we are mad! And we may go down in
our madness,
Or God may restore our sense.* Victory? It may be.
But if we fall, let us fall so that children to come will
remember
Sane men meeting their fate, * not a surd grunt in the
dark!

🎱 SCENE V

[*Enter from the house* XANTHIAS *and a* SERVANT
TO PLUTO. XANTHIAS *has resumed his own cloth-
ing.*

SERVANT:
A great man, your master, by God the Saviour, yes,
a very great man!
XANTHIAS:
Well, yes, I suppose so.
First prize for guzzling and nuzzling, at any rate.
SERVANT:
Do not belittle those accomplishments.
I liked the way
he finally proved you were lying, and then didn't try
the Outraged Employer routine.
XANTHIAS:
He didn't dare to.
SERVANT:
By God! As one servant to another,
that's the way I like to hear a servant talk.

XANTHIAS:
You do?
SERVANT:
Yes. I like to get off by myself
and think up horrible things about my master.
XANTHIAS:
Well, well! And when he beats you?
SERVANT:
Grist to my mill.

XANTHIAS:
My, my! And if he catches you spying on him?
SERVANT:
Man, it's heaven!

XANTHIAS:
O God of Kinship!
You listen to the family secrets?
SERVANT:
I do.
XANTHIAS:
And spread them around?
SERVANT:
Yes. There's nothing like it,
except maybe a good strong emission.
XANTHIAS:
O Phoibos Apollo!
Come, let me kiss that hand.
    [They embrace; loud cries from within
    What's that?
SERVANT:
Aischylos and Euripides, I imagine.
XANTHIAS:
Oh?

SERVANT:
It's a damned nuisance. Hell's foundations quiver.
XANTHIAS:
Since when?
SERVANT:
We've a custom here, you see,
that when a great artist or scientist arrives
and can prove that he's better than any of his rivals,

we invite him to lunch in the Prytaneion
right next to Pluto.

XANTHIAS:

I begin to see.

SERVANT:

Of course, if an even greater man comes along,
the first has to yield his place.

XANTHIAS:

But how does this
touch Aischylos?

SERVANT:

Why, as the greatest of poets,
he was on the Tragedy Foundation.

XANTHIAS:

And now who's on it?

SERVANT:

Euripides, I'm sorry to say. When he died and came down
here,
he began giving public readings from his plays
before our audience of pickpockets, barratrists,
adulterers, parricides—the general run of Hell.
His metrical writhings and convolutions pleased them,
so they gave him the crown; and poor Aischylos
had to resign the Chair.

XANTHIAS:

There was no protest?

SERVANT:

Yes, from a certain faction.
They insisted that we should hold a poetry contest
to determine which artist really deserved the Chair.

XANTHIAS: [Indicating audience
You mean this assembly of jailbirds?

SERVANT:

I do indeed.
Their howling smote the stars.

XANTHIAS:

No one supported Aischylos?

SERVANT:

Respectable men
[Indicating audience
are few in this place.

Just take a look at that crowd!

XANTHIAS:
Well, what has Pluto decided?

SERVANT:
Oh, we'll have the contest.
The two of them will recite—and then, the judgment

XANTHIAS:
Do you mean to tell me
that Sophoklês hasn't announced *his* candidacy?

SERVANT:
No. *That* one's a gentleman! When he arrived here
he kissed Aischylos and took him by the hand.
He could have had part of the Chair, too, for Aischylos
offered
to share it with him. But no; as Kleidemidês puts it,
'He sitteth i' th' reserve'.
That is to say,
if Aischylos gets the verdict, he'll be content;
but if Euripides wins,
by God, we'll have Sophoklês in there on his own.

XANTHIAS:
When do they start?

SERVANT:
Any minute now. Just where you're standing
the frenzy of poetic strife will rage,
and Thespis will be weighed.

XANTHIAS:
What do you mean?
Can tragedies be weighed?

SERVANT:
Of course they can.
More than that: there'll be compasses and rulers
and T-squares—

XANTHIAS:
What for? Are you building a brick wall?

SERVANT:
Also wedges, and instruments to calculate
diameters.
Euripides has sworn
that he'll dissect each drama verse by verse.

XANTHIAS:

Aischylos isn't taking this lightly?

SERVANT:

If you could see him!

He's glaring like a bull.

XANTHIAS:

Who's to be judge?

SERVANT:

Ah, that was the question! Real critics are scarce in this
place.

And besides,

Aischylos never did get along with Athens.

XANTHIAS:

I suppose he disliked the criminal majority.

SERVANT:

Yes; and he always held that art was wasted there.

At any rate,

they finally agreed on your master Dionysos.

He *does* know his poetry, after all.

—But look!

They're coming. Let's go in. This is no place

for us servants when our masters are about.

Come, Xanthias.

[*They enter the house; the* KORYPHAIOS *indulges
in an Aischylean tirade.*

KORYPHAIOS:

The rage! The cardiac tumult! Psychic disasters!

The fury of the thunder-kissing bard when he perceives

his piddling opponent picking his dentures with dactyls!

Regard his orbs, how they roll: one this way, one the
other!

Ah the logotomy! Verb breasting adverb, the cristate
nouns

plunging 'gainst pavid pronouns. Let the bull stylistic

(husband of cows) rise up and whirl his whiskers!

Ah the lambent raiding of verse, the (my God!) tripsis

of boant anapaests leaping in lucent line

against the skiaphagous luculent ululant

phalanges of the foe!

Yet must we bear in mind

the hepatic ingenium of the adversary, whose

herpetic tongue knows too well how to rive
the hyaline dynamis of our archarchitect!

The rest is silence.

🕸 SCENE VI [AGON: α]

[*Enter from the house* DIONYSOS, AISCHYLOS,
EURIPIDES

EURIPIDES:
No, Dionysos, I will not give up the Chair.
I'm better than he in every branch of the art.
DIONYSOS:
Say something, Aischylos. You heard the man.
EURIPIDES:
He's going into one of his Portentous Silences.
It's a favourite trick of his to impress the audience.
DIONYSOS:
Euripides, please don't *talk* so much!
EURIPIDES:
I know him,
and I know those noble-savage heroes of his with their
raving tongues:
no restraint, no decent respect
for language, but a flood of chaotic bombast
spewed out of that doorless cave he calls a mouth!
AISCHYLOS:
'And is it thou, scion of the vegetable garden',
rag-picker, old-clothes-man, confector of
beggars, incarnate cliché? You'll get no comfort here!
DIONYSOS:
Enough, Aischylos.
'Do not o'erheat, raging, thy raging heart.'
AISCHYLOS:
Not till I have shown how this Master of the Limp
has fooled all Athens with his casts of cripples.
DIONYSOS:
A lamb, a lamb, a black lamb, slaves! Bring it quickly!
The sky is full of thunder!
AISCHYLOS:
And as for his Kretan

 arias, his idiotic filthy
 bridal-scenes (miasma of art)—
DIONYSOS:

         My dear Aischylos,
 remember your blood-pressure.

             [*To* EURIPIDES
        And you, friend, keep back.
 Do you know what a really terrible man this is?
 He's perfectly capable of knocking you on the head
 with a word that would alkalize your *Alkestis.*

               —Come,
 let's be calm. It's a shocking thing when poets
 shriek at each other like fishwives over a sale.
EURIPIDES:

 I merely ask for judgement.
 Let him attack or defend, I don't care which.
 Let him examine my dialogue, my lyric
 passages—the core of Tragedy—; let him investigate
 my *Peleus,* my *Aiolos,* my *Meleágros,* and, above all,
 my *Telephos.*
DIONYSOS:

 Well, Aischylos, will you begin?
AISCHYLOS:

           If you say.

              —And yet,
 this contest is bound to be one-sided.
DIONYSOS:

             One-sided?

AISCHYLOS:

 My poems are still on earth in the mouths of men.
 All of his are with him here in Hell. However,
 let us proceed.
DIONYSOS:

       Bring me fire, slaves, and incense.
 Before this mighty argument, I must pray
 for guidance to a right verdict.

          Friends,
 invoke the Muses in song.

     [*Burning incense is brought, which* DIONYSOS
     places upon the altar while the CHORUS *sings.*

CHORUS:
    O Nine
        O virgin daughters of Zeus
    Chaste lovers of the delicate craft of words
            Breathe now
    On these unparalleled antagonists!
      Grant one a new thunder of poetry
          Grant the other
    Increase of the subtle sweet sleights of language
        As they advance
          Toward this great duel of Art.

DIONYSOS:
    Pray to the gods, both of you, before we begin.
AISCHYLOS:
    Demêter! Goddess! Matrix of my mind!
    Grant me wisdom in these Mysteries!
              [*Censes the altar*
DIONYSOS:
    Now it is your turn, Euripides.
EURIPIDES:
           Very kind of you,
    but my gods are different.
DIONYSOS:
           You have gods of your own,
    made in your image, after your likeness?
EURIPIDES:
           Yes.

DIONYSOS:
    Then pray to your special gods.
EURIPIDES:
           O succulent Aither!
    O nimble Loquacity! Quivering quick Nose!
    Be with me now in this Confabulation!

CHORUS:
           [STROPHE
    Breathes the man with soul so benumbed by Lethê
    That he burns not when he regards these champions
    Stripped for word-play in the arena óf our
      Elegant contest?

One will strike with subtlety, one with fury.
Who will win? Rise up, O my soul, and stretch thine
Ears! The strife is mortal, the triumph doubtful—

> [*A gong-stroke*

There goes the bell now!

⟨❦⟩ SCENE VII [AGON: β]

> [DIONYSOS *seats himself on an elaborate stool,* C,
> *facing the audience.* AISCHYLOS *and* EURIPIDES
> *have plain stools at opposite sides of the stage,*
> *where they sit facing each other.*

DIONYSOS:
Let's not waste time, gentlemen. What we want is ele-
gance:
no pointless decoration, no second-hand imagery.

> [EURIPIDES *rises.*

EURIPIDES:
For myself and my poetry
I shall not speak at the moment. What I propose to do
is to show how this charlatan, this gaudy boaster,
has taken advantage of a trusting public
brought up on the plays of Phrynichos.

—This is his method:
He brings on a single actor, veiled—a Niobê, maybe,
or an Achilleus, it makes no difference—, and has him sit
in a chair. And then the audience is treated
to a long Aischylean Silence.

DIONYSOS:
Yes, I remember.

EURIPIDES:
And then his Chorus enters:
strophê, antistrophê; strophê, antistrophê: four stanzas
on the same subject. Then silence. Meanwhile the actor
sleeps.

DIONYSOS:
I like that. Too much chatter on the stage these days.

EURIPIDES:
That's because you're so easily taken in.

DIONYSOS:

I suppose I am.

But how does he manage it?

EURIPIDES:

Simply by mystification.
There you are in the audience waiting for Niobê
to get something off her mind, and she never does.
So the drama drams.

DIONYSOS [to AISCHYLOS]:

Why are you making
those hideous faces?

EURIPIDES:

He knows that I see through him.
As I was saying: After a long period of this,
about half way through the piece, the actors wake up
and begin to shout. I will say this for his diction:
it's ravine-like, hairy, mad-bull-like, crustacean,
battering, craggy, shattering,—and it makes no sense.

AISCHYLOS:

I object!

DIONYSOS:

Sit down.

EURIPIDES:

Not a man in the house
can tell what it's all about.

DIONYSOS [to AISCHYLOS]:

Stop gnashing your teeth.

EURIPIDES:

Something about Skamándrosses and entrenchments,
dragons in brass rampant on rutilant shields—
language to fry a man's brain!

DIONYSOS:

Right, by God!
'I spent a sleepless night in my naked bed'
trying to figure out what, of all possible fowls,
that 'flavescent horse-cock' of his might be.

AISCHYLOS:

A figure-head for a ship, you abysmal rustic!

DIONYSOS:

I took it for Eryxis.

EURIPIDES:

Besides, what good is a cock
in tragedy?

AISCHYLOS:

Damn you, what can *you* show us?

EURIPIDES:

Well,
I may not be so clever as you when it comes to
horse-cocks and goat-elks and the other weird beasts
you've plagiarized from the Persian; but just the same,
I have done what I could.

I inherited tragedy
from you—a flabby legacy, all puffed out
with dropsical big words and inane bluster—,
and I went to work.
I cut away the bloat; I injected tickling phrases
here and there; I prescribed gentle exercise
and a white-beet diet with a cup of gossip-juice
before each meal, and filtered book-dust. Then
I fed it softboiled monodies—

DIONYSOS [*aside*]:

With a dash
of Kephisophôn.

EURIPIDES:

This was no haphazard treatment,
no grabbing in the dark at bottles on the shelf.
Everything was planned. And at the very outset
I'd describe the source of my plot.

DIONYSOS [*aside*]:

That was better
than describing your own source, I swear by God it was!

EURIPIDES:

From the first line of the Prologue
to the end of the play there was never an Aischylean
Vacuum: everyone spoke—women, slaves,
kings, virgins, hags—

AISCHYLOS:

They certainly did,
and you ought to have been hanged for it.

EURIPIDES:

No, by Apollo!

It was the true democratic Art.

DIONYSOS [*aside, to* EURIPIDES]:

Forget it, friend.

That's not the best way in the world to plead your case.

EURIPIDES:

I taught people how to speak—

AISCHYLOS:

You did, you did,

and I wish you had burst your guts first!

EURIPIDES:

I taught them

the planes and angles of language. Taught them Seman-
tics:

that is to say,

how to think straight, see straight, plan straight, cheat
straight,

debate straight, arrange straight, hate straight, and be
straight

in any emergency.

AISCHYLOS:

No doubt about that!

EURIPIDES:

And what's more,

I brought real life to the stage, men and women
just like those out there in the audience.
This was really audacious, since the cheapest
critic could understand me and complain.
I never tried to numb them with narcotic adverbs
or scare them to death with Kyknosses and Memnons
charging about in cars drawn by bell-bedizened
bullocks!

—Influence? Consider the Aischylean school,
and then the Euripidean. He has his Phormisios
and that Megainetos person they call Snake Eyes—
the virile clique: horns and lances
and horrible howls and skin-corroding laughter.
But who are my followers?
Kleitophôn and Beau Theramenês.

DIONYSOS:

Theramenês? He's a canny bird! He's a
caution, *he* is! Say a friend of his

gets into some sort of trouble, and Theramenês is there:
just you watch how gracefully he'll leave,
with never a word to anyone!

EURIPIDES:

And thus I teach the crowd to say:
'From day to day
In every way
I'm clearly growing better.'
My verses bring them new insight:
Night after night
They think aright
On things that really matter.

DIONYSOS:

Yes. When a householder comes home
Drunk as an owl,
He's learned to howl:
'Hey, where the hell's the grub?'
Blest be Euripides's name!
Before you came,
He'd have hidden his shame
In a bedroom at his club.

CHORUS:

[ANTISTROPHE

'You have heard thé prater, Achilleus.' Answer!
But confine your answer: the storm's upon you.
Shall your ship go down in this verbal tempest?
Not by a long shot!

Set your sail ánd scoot for a placid harbour.
You, the first Greek poet t' explore these waters:
Shall this chartless charlatan win the combat?
Tell it to Thespis!

DIONYSOS:

Aischylos has the floor.

AISCHYLOS:

Wrangling of this kind
sickens me; my cup
runneth over. Still, I must reply to this verse-jockey.
Euripides, tell me:

what do you consider the chief duty of a poet?

EURIPIDES:

To speak truth for the improvement of the City.

AISCHYLOS:

And if you yourself have not done this; if your poems
have poisoned our citizens, made rascals of good men:
what do you deserve?

[EURIPIDES *is scornfully silent.*

DIONYSOS:

Death. But that is not a proper question.

AISCHYLOS:

He laughs at my legacy of tragic verse.
Let him. But can he find in any of my plays
a shirker of public duty, a clown, a pavement
cavalier, a slippery shifter, an intriguer?
He can not.
My men are truly men. They breathe crests and helms
actinic, the cuirasse-clatter, the sonant
whack of spear on spear.

EURIPIDES:

Gentlemen,
beware the hardware!

DIONYSOS:

Tell me, Aischylos:
what play are you talking about?

—And please *don't* be so noisy!

AISCHYLOS:

A play aërated by Arês.

DIONYSOS:

The title?

AISCHYLOS:

Seven Against Thebes. If you ask my opinion,
one of my best. Every man in the audience
went out and enlisted.

DIONYSOS:

Oh? So you taught the Thebans
greater manliness in war?—Sounds subversive to me.

AISCHYLOS:

You might have learned something from it yourself
if you'd been inclined that way.

—Then I staged my *Persians,*

where I prove that a man's whole life must be given up
to conquering what adversary soever.
That play had a record run.

DIONYSOS:

                       I still remember
the joy I felt when Dareios' ghost
rose up, and the Chorus all clapped their hands
and shouted 'Eeee-YOW!'

AISCHYLOS:

                These are the only themes
worthy of poetry, these high themes. Think: from the
    first
it has been the poets who have served men best.
Orpheus: he taught us to understand the Mysteries
and to hate murder; Musaios: the arts of healing
and divination; Hesiod: sowing and reaping;
and godlike Homer in his deathless chant:
did he not teach us the glory of bearing arms,
the black joy of battle?

DIONYSOS:

                If he did, Pantaklês missed it.
Just the other day I saw him leading a troop
in the Panathenaia: he'd forgotten to screw the crest
into his helmet, and was dangling it in his hand.

AISCHYLOS:

Remember rather the true men Homer has taught,
men like our hero Lamachos.
                —From these poems
I took my Patroklosses and my lionhearted
Teukrosses as examples for every man
when the trumpet sings to arms. But you will find
never a Sthenoboia in my plays,
nor a nasty Phaidra: I would not dirty my stage
with a love-drooling woman.

EURIPIDES:

                No; Aphroditê and you
never had much in common.

AISCHYLOS:

                I thank God for it.
But you and your Modernists are haunted by her:
you see her everywhere, in every possible shape.

As a matter of fact, you personally have suffered from
   her.

DIONYSOS: [*To* EURIPIDES

By God, that's true enough!
The very things that you showed other men's wives doing
your own wife did to you.

EURIPIDES:

                              Aischylos, you fraud,
how have my Sthenoboias hurt the City?

AISCHYLOS:

By corrupting the decent wives of decent men.
Those Bellerophons of yours have led them
to death by hemlock out of the shame you've taught
   them.

EURIPIDES:

I suppose you'll say *I* invented the myth of Phaidra?

AISCHYLOS:

Not at all.
But the poet's duty is to conceal the filth,
not drag it onto the stage. We have schoolmasters
for little boys; we have poets for grown men.
Let our concern be only with what's good.

EURIPIDES:

And when you howl your Lykabettos-language,
your Parnês-periods—, is that what you call teaching?
Is that your 'good'? Why not speak like a man?

AISCHYLOS:

Fool!
High thoughts must have high language. As the dress
of our actor demigods is nobler than our own,
so must their speech be nobler. I have adorned
the theatre; you have debased it.

EURIPIDES:

                              Tell me how.

AISCHYLOS:

First of all, you dress your kings in tatters
to squeeze tears out of the audience.

EURIPIDES:

                              What if I do?

AISCHYLOS:

It's a bad precedent. There's not a rich man in Athens

who will outfit a galley these days. All the millionaires
say they're too poor, and walk about in rags.

DIONYSOS:

Yes, by Demêter! And all the time they're wearing
the finest cloth underneath; and when they're done
cheating us, they head for the most expensive markets.

AISCHYLOS:

Also, you have taught bragging and silly gossip.
The gymnasiums have shut down because the boys
are scraping their buttocks thin on library benches,
learning your verses. Even the common sailors
are drunk with your clever talk, and dare answer back
to their officers. Why, in my time
all they did was chew hardtack and sing 'Yo-ho-ho!'

DIONYSOS:

Yes, and poop in the face of the oarsman beneath,
and daub the next man with dirt, and steal from the
  shops
when they got shore leave. Nowadays their brawn
is all in their tongues; they never flex their muscles.

AISCHYLOS:

What evil has Euripides
  Not brought upon the stage?
He gives us leering pimperies,
Obstetric scenes in sacristies,
Incestuous adulteries,
  'The denial of the Age'.
      He's filling the City
      With second-rate wit. He
    Founds a school of writing apes,
    Thumbs his nose, and off he trapes.

DIONYSOS:

The good oldfashioned manly ways
  Are lost, thanks to his art.
Just watch a modern relay-race:
Fat fancy fellows without grace,
Limp in the legs and green in the face,
  Outrun before the start!
      The customers grumble,
      But only a rumble

Mutters in the sagging bowels.
Quick, boy: water and clean towels!

CHORUS:

Ah the sweet rage of logomachy,   [STROPHE
The fury of the word,
When trope meets trope's hostility
With syntax for a sword!
The screams of zeugma! Howls of tmesis!
Moans of apocopé ripped to pieces!
Curses of syzygy!
What wonder that this warfare teases
Gods from the sky!

If, subtle combatants, you fear   [ANTISTROPHE
Our audience may not un-
derstand the wiles you'll practise here
Before the battle's won:
Take heart; the Newer Education
Has brought enlightenment to the nation:
We're an erudite folk:
Each member of this congregation
Has read a book.

🎝 SCENE VIII [AGON: γ]

EURIPIDES:
I should like to begin with his prologues.
                                        —I hope to show
Gentlemen, that this 'accomplished wash-out'
was a bungler from the beginning.

DIONYSOS:
                              Which prologue do you want?

EURIPIDES:
A lot. But first let's listen to the *Orestês*.

DIONYSOS:
Silence, everyone!—Begin reading, Aischylos.

AISCHYLOS:
O Hermês, Angel of the nether world,

> *Guardian of fathers, help me in my need!*
> *I come again, returning to this land.*

DIONYSOS:
Anything wrong with that?

EURIPIDES:
                              A dozen things.

DIONYSOS:
But there are only three verses!

EURIPIDES:
                              With twenty mistakes
in each.

AISCHYLOS:
             You see? the man's mad.

EURIPIDES:
                              It makes no difference to me

AISCHYLOS:
Show me a single mistake!

EURIPIDES:
                              Recite it again.

AISCHYLOS:
> *O Hermês, Angel of the nether world,*
> *Guardian of fathers—*

EURIPIDES:
                        Stop!—Orestês is speaking
at his dead father's tomb?

AISCHYLOS:
                              He is.

EURIPIDES:
                              Does he mean
that this Patron Saint of fathers merely looked on
when Agamemnon died at a woman's hands,
'murther'd in secret shame'?

AISCHYLOS:
                              Not at all. He invokes
Hermês as 'Angel of the nether world',
the Helper, in darkness working the will
of his father.

EURIPIDES:
                  Worse and worse: for if his father
makes him work underground—

DIONYSOS:

That would seem to imply
that Zeus is a grave-robber.

AISCHYLOS:

I consider that joke in bad taste.

DIONYSOS:

Give us the rest.—Euripides, watch for mistakes.

AISCHYLOS:

—help me in my need!
I come again, returning to this land.

EURIPIDES:

Brilliant Aischylos! He says the same thing twice.

DIONYSOS:

Twice?

EURIPIDES:

Twice. Just look at his words. He says
I come again and *returning to this land.*
What's the difference between 'coming again' and 're-
turning'?

DIONYSOS:

By God, you are right! It's as if I should say,
'lend me a wash-pot or a pot to wash in.'

AISCHYLOS:

Not the same thing at all, you impossible chatterer!
It's a beautiful verse.

DIONYSOS:

It is, is it? Show me why.

AISCHYLOS:

'To come again' to his country is said of the man
who has travelled and now comes home to his father's
fields.
Not so the fugitive: he both 'comes back' and 'returns.'

DIONYSOS:

A palpable hit, by Apollo!—Euripides?

EURIPIDES:

I will not allow that Orestês 'returned': he came
like a smuggler, stealing past the border guards.

DIONYSOS:

An excellent answer, by Hermês!

Though I must confess
that I don't understand it.

EURIPIDES:

> Shall we have some more?

DIONYSOS:

Yes, Aischylos, finish the passage.

AISCHYLOS:

Prostrate on this paternal mound, I beg
My father's ghost to hear me and give ear.

EURIPIDES:

There he goes again: *hear me* and *give ear.*

AISCHYLOS:

Blasphemer! Orestês is calling upon the dead!
Even our three-fold *Hail!* is not enough.

DIONYSOS:

Tell us how *you* write prologues, Euripides.

EURIPIDES:

I will. And if you find me chasing my own tail
in repetitions or padding my lines with garbage,
spit in my eye!

DIONYSOS:

> Your prologues have always enchanted me

EURIPIDES:

Once was Oidipûs a fortunate man—

AISCHYLOS:

Stop! Even in the womb he was most wretched.
The Oracle sang that he would kill his father
before he was born.

DIONYSOS:

> A precocious embryo!

AISCHYLOS:

How can you call him fortunate?

EURIPIDES:

> Let me finish.
But later became the unhappiest of mortals.

AISCHYLOS:

Wrong again! He was unhappy all his life.
Examine the evidence. The very day he was born
he was put in a jug and left out in the mountain snow
to die, so that he might not murder his father.
Later he travelled to Korinth on his swollen feet;
and later, though still young,

he married a hag who turned out to be his mother,
and then he poked out his eyes. A fortunate man!

DIONYSOS:

At least he never went into politics.

EURIPIDES:

Talk as you will, you can't talk away my prologues!

AISCHYLOS:

I certainly won't dissect them phrase by phrase;
but with God's help I think I can do for them
with a little oil.

EURIPIDES:

You said oil?

AISCHYLOS:

Just a drop or two.
This poetry of yours is such predictable stuff
that a man can tag it with almost anything:
a pinch of cobweb, an oil-jar, a sack. I'll show you.

EURIPIDES:

You really think so?

AISCHYLOS:

I do.

DIONYSOS:

Come on: begin.

EURIPIDES:

Aigyptos—so the rumour runs i' th' world—
Sailing the broad sea, landing at Argos with
His fifty stalwart sons—

AISCHYLOS:

Ran out of oil.

DIONYSOS:

Ran out of oil?—Watch out, Euripides!
Let's have a different prologue.

EURIPIDES:

Dionysos, dressed in fawn skin, he who leads
The choric revels upon high Parnassos,
Waving his holy thyrsos—

AISCHYLOS:

Ran out of oil.

DIONYSOS:

Is that so!

EURIPIDES:

        Never mind. I have a prologue here
that's oil-proof. Let's see what he can do to this:
No man is truly happy in all things.
Say one was nobly born: today he's bankrupt;
Another, of humble parents—

AISCHYLOS:

              Ran out of oil.

DIONYSOS:

  Euripides.

EURIPIDES:

        Dionysos?

DIONYSOS:

            Reef your sail.
We're in for an oil storm.

EURIPIDES:

               Do you think I care?
I'll drown him in his own oil, by Demêter!

DIONYSOS:

                  Good.
Another prologue, then. But mind what you say!

EURIPIDES:

Kadmos, Agênor's son, departing from
The citadel of Sidon—

AISCHYLOS:

             Ran out of oil.

DIONYSOS:

  Euripides, you'd better buy up that oil of his
before it stickies all your favourite prologues.

EURIPIDES:

  Never! I've all sorts of prologues left
that he can't touch. For example:
Pelops, Tantalos' son, on his way to Pisa,
Drawn by swift coursers a-gallop—

AISCHYLOS:

             Ran out of oil.

DIONYSOS:

  You see? There he is again with his old oil-jar.
—Come, Aischylos, let the son of Tantalos have it:
you can buy a better one anywhere for a penny.

EURIPIDES:

Not so fast! I haven't given up yet.
Oineus, reaping in the fields—

AISCHYLOS:

Ran out of oil.

EURIPIDES:

Let me finish. Let me finish.
Oineus, reaping in the fields the season's foison,
Sacrificed to the gods but—

AISCHYLOS:

Ran out of oil.

DIONYSOS:

While he was sacrificing? Where was the leak?

EURIPIDES:

Let me try once more.
Zeus, as Truth itself asserts—

DIONYSOS:

That's enough!
Can't you hear him saying that Zeus ran out of oil?
An unorthodox thought!
—That oil of his
dirties your verse like the droppings from your eyes.
For God's sake, take up his choruses!

EURIPIDES:

I will.
I'll prove that he's incompetent as a lyrist
and given to vacant iterati-on.

CHORUS:

What cán he do? What cán he say?
How cán he hope to damn
The finest lyrics of our day?
Am I confused? I am.

SCENE IX [AGON: δ]

EURIPIDES:

'The finest lyrics', eh? All right: I'll prove
that these marvelous songs of his

are nothing more than the tune the old cow died to.
What's more, I'll compress them all into one example.

DIONYSOS:
And I'll keep score with these pebbles.

EURIPIDES: [*Singing to flute accompaniment*
Achilleus, Laird o' Phthia,
Hear'st not the onset
of the wife-
dehonestizing, childimpaling foe?
Oh,
Praise to Hermês, inaugurator of swamp life!
Hear'st not the onset?

DIONYSOS:
Here go
two pebbles against you, Aischylos.
—Proceed.

EURIPIDES:
Son of Atreus, glory o' th' Achaians!
Thou World Federation incarnate! Bend thine ear:
Hear'st not the onset?

DIONYSOS:
Another onset. Really, Aischylos!

EURIPIDES:
Be auspicious, O ye tongues of mortal dust!
The honeybear girls
Expand the fane of Artemis.
Hear'st not the onset?
The greathearted
Heroes are gone! The glory is departed!
Hear'st not the onset?

DIONYSOS:
Merciful God, these onsets!
My knees ache, and a drowsy numbness pains
my pants, as though I needed a hot bath.

EURIPIDES:
Wait till you've heard another number of his,
composed for voice and harp.

DIONYSOS:
                              If I must, I must.
But no more onsets!

EURIPIDES:
Alas! Can it be that the doublethroned power of Hellas
        phlattothrattophlattothrát
Has yielded unto the Sphinx, that deathwhiffing bitch?
        phlattothrattophlattothrát
With hand and lance arm'd, the bombinating squallbird
        phlattothrattophlattothrát
    Cedes to the heav'nengender'd dogs
        phlattothrattophlattothrát
        The adherents of Aias-Aiantos!
            phlattothrát!

DIONYSOS: [*To* AISCHYLOS
What's all this phlatting and thratting? A battle-cry
from Marathon, maybe? or something you picked up at
        sea?

AISCHYLOS:
I found beauty, and made it more beautiful. You cannot
        say
that I worked in the Muses' fields with Phrynichos.
But this man, like a sad little whore,
took anything from anyone: a catch from Meletos,
a flute-turn from Karia, snatches here and there
of dirges and dances.
                        Bring me my lyre!
Yet why should I waste my lyre upon this buffoon?
No. Let me have a castanet girl.
                        Approach,
Euripidean Muse: embellish thy master's music!
        [*Enter a decaying prostitute, nude; she accom-
        panies the following aria on a pair of large casta-
        nets.*

DIONYSOS:
That Muse never came from Lesbos, Aischylos.

AISCHYLOS:

> Halcyons, halcyons,
> Chirruping gossipers on the spume of the wave,
> Ye roscid-wing'd!
>
> And spi-spi-spiders,
> Tangle-angle-angle-angling
> With threadlittle feet your ingle-dainty webs,
> As the dolphin darts
> Sheer from the surge,
>
> presaging
>
> Safe passage to harbour!
> Vineshoots, lacy
> Voles o' the vine!
> Kiss me, darling, I'm
> Coming!

You recognize the manner, do you not?

DIONYSOS:

I do.

AISCHYLOS:

And this man dares to laugh at me!
This man, whose poetry apes the twelve positions
of Kyrenê in her bed!
                    —Well, that was a lyric example.
Now for a Euripidean monody.
        [*Castanets and flute; the* CHORUS *mimes the fol
        lowing monody:*

> Night
> and dreaming dreamless O
> Son of sightless Night
> from
> whát dreaming dream'd
> into my spiritless spirit,
> Sable ghost,
> There is no
> speculation in those eyes:
> Claws acute!
> Beaut-
> y hurts me.
> Virgins:
> Siphon the wellsprings off and heat the water!

O friends, friends,

                    purloinèd hath been my rooster
                                        By Glykê.

        Let me wash away this dream.

                                        Oreads,

        Take her! Seize her, Susan!

                                Who's an

        Idler here? Not I!

                            Worra-worra-working,
                        Over a hot loom,
        Sp-sp-sp-spinning

                            dreamwoofs, dreamwarplets:
And off he wing'd, winging the wind with his wings,
        And left me idle in tears. I know not what they
            mean.

    O Kretans, offspring of Ida,
Bring your arrows (and bows) and invest my residence!
        And thou, young Artemis, Diktynna: have the
            sense

                        To scout thy dogs
                        Across the bogs!

                                    O Hekatê
Daughter of Zeus, ambidextrous flare-flarer,
                    Light me to Gly-Gly-Glykê's:
I propose to search her premises, and will do so.

DIONYSOS:

That's enough of the lyric style.

AISCHYLOS:

                            You are right.
The one thing left is to weigh my verse against his
in the scales. That will decide.

DIONYSOS:

                            Whatever you say.
                        [*To the* SERVANTS
Go, one of you, and bring us the cheese-scales:
they're the only thing for weighing poetry.

CHORUS:

            I admire the ingenuity   [STROPHE

Of the artistic mind.
It would not have occurred to me
That problems of this kind
Could really be
So easily
Resolved. If my own brother
Had told me so,
I'd have said: 'No,
My dear Charles, you're another!'

✵ SCENE X [AGON: ε]

[*A large pair of scales is placed on a block before*
DIONYSOS.

DIONYSOS:
Take your places by the scales.
AISCHYLOS *and* EURIPIDES:
All ready!
DIONYSOS:
Each of you hold one of the pans and recite a line,
and don't let go until I say 'Cuckoo!'
AISCHYLOS *and* EURIPIDES:
All right.
DIONYSOS:
Begin. Speak your verses into the pans.
EURIPIDES:
I would that the good ship Argo had never sailed!
AISCHYLOS:
O stream of Spercheios, where the cattle roam!
DIONYSOS:
Cuckoo! Let go!
[*They release the pans;* AISCHYLOS' *drops.*
Aischylos wins that bout.
EURIPIDES:
But why?
DIONYSOS:
Why? He tossed in a whole river,
like merchants who soak their wool to make it heavier.
Your line was winged; it flew away.

AISCHYLOS:

Try again!

DIONYSOS:

Hands on the scales!

AISCHYLOS *and* EURIPIDES:

We're ready.

DIONYSOS:

Begin, Euripides.

EURIPIDES:

Skill in speech is Persuasion's inner shrine.

AISCHYLOS:

Death is the sole god who cannot be bought.

DIONYSOS:

Cuckoo!

[AISCHYLOS' *pan drops.*

EURIPIDES:

I don't understand. What happened that time?

DIONYSOS:

He threw in Death, the heaviest of evils.

EURIPIDES:

I threw in Persuasion, and made an adorable verse.

DIONYSOS:

Persuasion's a tricky, bodiless affair.
Come, look through your plays:
You must find something solid.

EURIPIDES:

Solid? But where?

DIONYSOS:

Try this:
Dicing Achilleus rolled a two and a four.
Take it from there: it's the last chance you'll have.

EURIPIDES:

In his right hand a cudgel loaded with iron.

AISCHYLOS:

Chariot upon chariot, corpse upon corpse.

DIONYSOS:

Beaten again!

EURIPIDES:

But why?

DIONYSOS:

In a single line

he had two chariots and a pair of corpses.
A hundred Egyptians couldn't lift that verse!

AISCHYLOS:

That's enough! Let him climb into his scale
with his wife, his children, Kephisophôn, and all his plays.
I'll outweigh the whole caboodle with two lines!

> [*The palace door opens. Enter* PLUTO, *crowned,
> sceptred, escorted by interestingly infernal attend-
> ants.*

DIONYSOS:

Your Majesty *must* help me! How can I be their judge?
I can't bear the thought of either of them hating me!
Euripides is *so* sophisticated,
and Aischylos so rewarding!

PLUTO:

　　　　　　　　　Then you've wasted your trip.

DIONYSOS:

And if I give a verdict?

PLUTO:

　　　　　　　　　Take whichever one wins
back to earth with you.

DIONYSOS:

　　　　　　　　　Oh dear. Well, if I must!

> [*He turns to* AISCHYLOS *and* EURIPIDES.

Now listen carefully to what I'm going to say.
—I came down here to find a poet. Why?
To restore the splendour of Dramatic Art
to the City. And so,
whichever of you can be of more service to Athens,
he shall go back with me to the world above
Tell me, then:
What is your opinion of Alkibiadês?
Our unhappy citizens
'love him, abhor him, and would have him back.'
Tell me what you think.

> [*A pause

EURIPIDES:

　　　　　　　　　I hate a citizen
slow to aid the State, quick to undermine it,
server only of self at the public peril.

DIONYSOS:

Excellent, by Poseidon!

—Now, Aischylos?

AISCHYLOS:

The lion's whelp should not be brought up in the City;
but if it has been, the people must learn to live with it.

DIONYSOS:

I *can* not decide! One of them is deep;
the other, profound.

—Another question:
What is the surest way to rescue Athens?

EURIPIDES:

I know, and I will tell you.

DIONYSOS:

Let me hear it.

EURIPIDES:

When we put our trust in what is untrustworthy
and distrust what we should put our trust in—

DIONYSOS:

I don't understand.
Speak less gnomically, and more clearly.

EURIPIDES:

If we reject the leaders we follow today
and follow those whom we reject, we can be saved.

DIONYSOS:

Aischylos?

AISCHYLOS:

Who *are* the current leaders?
Honest men?

DIONYSOS:

Absurd! Athens always discards them.

AISCHYLOS:

She prefers bad men?

DIONYSOS:

Not really; but they're forced upon her.

AISCHYLOS:

I see no hope for a State
that cannot make up its mind between silk and hemp.

DIONYSOS:

Think of some way, if you hope to see sunlight again!

AISCHYLOS:

I will tell you as we journey, not in this place.

DIONYSOS:

No. Let the City have your advice from Hell.

AISCHYLOS:

Let Athens remember:
The Enemy's land is Athens', and Athens' land
is the Enemy's. The only safety lies in our ships.

DIONYSOS:

Yes . . . But the dicasts gobble up everything!

PLUTO:

The judgement, come!

DIONYSOS:

Judgement is yours by right;
but 'him I choose o'er whom my heart doth yearn'.

EURIPIDES:

Remember, you swore by the gods you would take me
back!

DIONYSOS:

'Sworn hath my tongue . . .'; but I choose Aischylos.

EURIPIDES:

Liar and slave! What have you done?

DIONYSOS:

What have I done? Chosen Aischylos. Why not?

EURIPIDES:

You can look me in the eye after this betrayal?

DIONYSOS:

It's no betrayal unless our audience thinks so.

EURIPIDES:

And you will leave me here among the dead?

DIONYSOS:

'Which of us can say that life's not death's twin brother',
or that breathing's not eating, or that going to bed's not
a sheep?

[*Exit* EURIPIDES *indignantly*, L

PLUTO:

And now, Dionysos, you must come into my house.

DIONYSOS [*terrified*]:

What for?

PLUTO:

For a feast before you leave.

DIONYSOS:

Oh.
—Here I come!

[*All but the* CHORUS *enter the palace.*

CHORUS:

[ANTISTROPHE 1
Thrice blessèd is the man who's found
  The true Philosophy!
Take Aischylos: he's upward bound
  To Earth's felicity.
         His sapience
         And prescience
Restore him to the sunlight.
         His own shall greet
         Him on the street
With loud cries of 'You've done right!'

How different is Sokratês   [ANTISTROPHE 2
  And his sophistic school
Of Tragic Art. There, if you please,
  The smart twist is the rule.
         The Sisters Nine,
         The craft divine,
Languish in clever phrases,
         While tasteless lips
         Pollute with quips
Our placid public places.

🌸 ÉXODOS

[*Enter from the house* PLUTO, DIONYSOS, AISCHYLOS

PLUTO:

And so, Aischylos, fare well!
Go back and save our City with your wise art.
Restore our men—there are many!—to their senses.

Here are three gifts for you to distribute in Athens:
this knife for Kleophôn, this halter for
Myrmex and Nikomachos, and this poison

for Archenomos. They'll know how to use them,
and I hope to greet them here soon. If not, they'll feel
the hot brand; yes, and I'll bind the three of them up
with Admiral Adeimantos, old Whitefeather's son,
and fry them on the hottest plates of Hell.

AISCHYLOS:
I will see that it's done.

        —Let Sophoklês have my Chair
until I come again, if I ever do.
I name him second among the serious poets.
But as for that quack Euripides,
let him never again hold the Tragic Foundation,
not even if he's elected in spite of himself.

PLUTO:
O ye Initiate: lift high your holy torches
and lead this mighty poet on his way,
singing his music to him as he ascends.

CHORUS:
O spirits of the world below!
    The poet moves up to the world of light:
May he heal the sick State, fight
The ignoble cowardly inward foe,
    And bring us peace.
        Let Kleophôn and his friends
Disrupt their own lands for their selfish ends!

GENERAL NOTES

Page

80: *Phrynichos*: A comic poet, rival of Aristophanes.

80: *son of / Juice*: Dionysos calls himself υἱὸς Σταμνίου ('son of the Jug') instead of the expected υἱὸς Διός ('son of Zeus').

81: *If only I were / a Navy veteran!*: The slaves who served at the great naval victory of Arginusai (406) were given their freedom.

82: *This lion skin! this saffron gown!*: Dionysos' costume, like his language, is a bizarre combination of the heroic and the effeminate.

84: *Many men no more are*: Parodied from the lost *Oineus* of Euripides.

85: *'Sworn hath my tongue . . .'*: A verse from the *Hippolytos* of Euripides.

86: *'. . . creep not into my mind'*: 'From the *Andromachê* [of Euripides],' says Σ; but it is not. Possibly from the lost *Andrómeda*, which has just been mentioned by Dionysos.

88: *the Initiates*: Participants in the Eleusinian Mysteries, which were celebrated once a year in honour of Demêter and Persephonê. Heraklês himself was admitted to the Minor Mysteries before undertaking his journey to Hadês.

95: *'Breathes there the man . . .'*: The Greek parodies a verse from the lost *Philoktetês* of Euripides [Σ].

96: *The other one's donkey-manure*: A beautiful but puzzling statement. In *Elektra* Sophoklês says that the Furies advance with strides of brass, and that is reason enough for attributing a brass leg to the Empûsa. Lucian reports a never-never land where the women have asses' legs. The 'manure' may be a fanciful addition on Xanthias' part or a covert reference to his master's present condition.

96: *Is there a doctor in the house?*: In the original, Dionysos turns to his own priest, who would be sitting officially in the front row of the audience, and begs him to intervene.

97: *'After the storm I see the clam again'*: The story is that the actor Hegelochos muffed a line in the *Orestês* of Euripides: instead of 'After the storm I see once more the calm,' he proclaimed—by a slip of the tongue almost imperceptible in Greek—'After the storm I see once more the polecat.' The difference is between γαλήν' and γαλῆν. 'Appositè Merry,' Van Leeuwen observes, 'emunctae naris editor narrat actoris tragici infortunium, qui cum proferret verba *il a vaincu Loth,* in subselliis joci aliquis appetens finxit se audivisse *il a vingt culottes* magnâque voce clamavit *qu'il en donne à l'auteur!* quod verbulum quantos civerit cachinnos audire nobis videmur.'

98: *What a heavenly smell of pork!*: Σ says that pigs were sacrificed to Demêter and Dionysos.

99: PÁRODOS: The *párodos* is the entrance of the Chorus into the dance-enclosure (*orchêstra*). We have already heard off stage the chanting of the accessory chorus of Frogs and a preliminary strophe and antistrophe by the Chorus itself. Now the Initiates enter, gowned for the infernal counterpart of their solemn annual procession to the earthly Eleusis. As in the *parábasis* (p. 114), to which this may be considered a detached prelude, the poet addresses the audience directly through his Chorus.

102: *A Korinthian baggomania*: According to their jealous neighbours, the inhabitants of Korinth could never forget that they lived in 'God's City.' Xanthias thinks Dionysos has a comparable obsession with baggage.

103: *Ay, and gloomhearted Styx*: *Verba tragica,* as Fielding would say. The whole passage is a glorious parody of the Inflated Manner.

104: *'Invoke the god'*: Ritual phrase in making libation.

106: *How can a deathbound slave*: Both Heraklês and Dionysos were sons of Zeus by mortal mothers. This reference to the human parent rather than to the divine is pleasantly illogical.

107: *Plathanê*: Plathanê and her unnamed friend are *pandokeútriai*—that is to say, 'hostesses' in a public place of refreshment. Since they are of low (though not servile) condition, their interests are represented by professional patrons—in Hadês the demagogues Kleôn and Hyperbolos.

110: *Ditylas, Skeblyas, Pardokas*: 'Names of barbarian archers' [Σ]. The police force of Athens was composed largely of Skythian bowmen.

112: *Look at the gorgeous cavalry!*: Obviously an attempt to twist 'Oooh! Oooh!' into a cry of delight; but the remark is inane, even for Dionysos, and I join the commentators in failing to understand it.

113: *a verse from Hipponax*: Dionysos' 'Oh Apollo!' is a cordial yelp of pain, and he tries to save the situation by tacking on a fragment of poetry. According to Σ, the verse is by Ananios, not Hipponax. Is Aristophanes confused? or Dionysos? or Σ?

113: *'Thou holding sway . . .'*: From *Laokoön*, a lost play by Sophokles.

114: PARÁBASIS: *Parábasis* is the technical term for the interlude when the poet suspends the action of his play and addresses the audience through the Chorus. It is a moment of great topical interest, though not always of great art; and like all topicalities—the joking of the Porter in *Macbeth*, for instance—it can be heavy going for readers who have lost the key. In this *parábasis* Aristophanes is concerned with the deteriorating War and the resultant political recriminations and retaliations in Athens. He urges tolerance in the face of the common danger and expresses hope for a victorious peace, but there is a sense of catastrophe throughout and the ending of the address is particularly ominous.

114: *Kleophôn on his Thracian tree*: Kleophôn's mother, at least, came from Thrace; consequently Aristophanes ridicules him as a barbarian, 'split-tongued,' and associates him with the horrible Tereus-Philomela-Prognê legend. At the time of *Frogs* Kleophôn was indeed in danger, and a year later he was convicted on charges involving his citizenship and put to death. But the reasons for Aristophanes' animosity are deeper. The demagogue had come to power in 410 after a series of convulsive governmental changes and had re-established some of the abuses of the discredited old régime. He was, moreover, immovably opposed to the repeated peace overtures of Sparta—overtures which Aristophanes perhaps regarded as offering a practical and honourable solution to a desperate problem.

114: *Phrynichos with his tricks*: This Phrynichos was a public official who had been involved in an unsuccessful attempt to restore the oligarchy of the Four Hundred. Later, because of his ambiguous attitude towards Sparta, he was formally disgraced and informally assassinated (410).

114: *peers of Plataians*: Plataia had been an ally of Athens since the Persian Wars and in 421 the Plataians were granted honorary Athenian citizenship. In 406 the Athenian slaves who fought at Arginusai were freed. Aristophanes approves of the emancipation but finds it hard that slaves should be better treated than many citizens in disfavour only for adherence to the wrong political party.

115: *'If aught of skill in augury . . .'*: Parody of a verse by Iôn of Chios [Σ].

120: *your master Dionysos*: As god of the theatre Dionysos is a logical choice for umpire.

121: *'And is it thou . . .'*: Parody of a verse from an unknown lost play by Euripides. According to his enemies, Euripides' mother conducted a vegetable-&-herb shop.

121: *'Do not o'erheat, raging . . .'*: Another parody of Euripides; the source is lost.

121: *this Master of the Limp*: Aristophanes repeatedly condemns Euripides for bringing deformed or down-at-the-heels characters onto the stage.

121-2: *his Kretan / arias*: These monodies accompanied by dancing mimes were not the invention of Euripides, but he seems to have used them to excess.

122: *alkalize your Alkestis*: Not a translation, but a pass at a comparable effect. The Greek says 'knock your *Telephos* out of your head,' the title of a (lost) tragedy being substituted for the expected word 'brains.'

125: *'I spent a sleepless night . . .'*: Parody of a passage in the *Hippolytos* of Euripides.

125: *'flavescent horse-cock'*: This strange device was a ship's figurehead in the (lost) *Myrmidons* of Aischylos.

128: *'You have heard thé prater, Achilleus'*: Σ says that this was the first line of Aischylos' *Myrmidons*.

133: *'O Hermês, Angel . . .'*: The opening of Aischylos' *Choephoroi*. The lines owe their survival to this citation by Aristophanes.

136: *our three-fold Hail!*: As part of the funeral ritual, the name of the dead was called out three times.

136: *Once was Oidipús*: Opening of the *Antigonê* of Euripides [Σ].

136: *he was put in a jug*: This jug (*óstrakon*) will surprise readers of Sophoklês. It seems to be a bit of Athenian local colour: thus, in *Thesmophoriazûsai* Aristophanes had a midwife carrying a baby in an earthen pot.

137: *Aigyptos*: From an unknown play, probably by Euripides. Σ and the later commentators are at a loss.

137: *Dionysos, dressed*: Beginning of the *Hypsipylê* of Euripides, now lost. The third line ends: 'with the Delphic virgins.'

138: *No man is truly happy*: Beginning of the lost *Sthenoboia* of Euripides [Σ]. The third line ends: 'tills the rich plain.'

138: *Kadmos, Agênor's son*: 'Opening of the second *Phrixos* of Euripides. The rest of the [second] line: "came to the Theban plain." ' [Σ]

138: *Pelops, Tantalos' son*: Beginning of the *Iphigeneia in Tauris* of Euripides. 'The rest of the [second] line is: "married Oinomaos' lass." ' [Σ]

139: *Oineus, reaping in the fields*: From the prologue to Euripides' lost *Meleagros*. The original conclusion: 'no off'ring made / to Artemis' [Σ]. Aristotle in an absent moment attributed the passage to Sophoklês.

139: *Zeus, as Truth itself asserts*: Beginning of the lost *Sage Melanippê* of Euripides [Σ]. The verse is complete.

140: *Achilleus, Laird o' Phthia*: Euripides composes an absurd 'chorus' of verses parodied from here and there in Aischylos and punctuated by a ridiculous question.

141: *Alas! Can it be*: Another kind of burlesque. This time the Aischylean lines are interrupted by the nonsense refrain 'phlattothrattophlattothrát!' which Dionysos affects to mistake for a battle slogan.

141: *in the Muses' fields with Phrynichos*: Tragic poet; a 'sweet melodist,' according to Σ. Except for fragments his work is lost, but Aischylos seems to have been indebted to him for certain ideas in *Persians* and speaks of him with reserve.

141: *That Muse never came from Lesbos*: Sappho and her girls may have been maligned, as recent scholarship contends, but the Lesbian lie is old enough to have created a perverse verb in Greek that accounts for the under-meaning here.

142: *Halcyons, halcyons*: Another choral parody, this time in the

manner of Euripides. The outlandish 'new' diction is bur-
lesqued, and the reduplicated syllables constitute an attack
upon Euripides' melodic innovations.

142: *Night*: This burlesque of the 'Kretan arias' mentioned on
p. 121 is an almost hysterically elaborated affair, as though
Aristophanes had decided to expose in one song all the hateful Euripidean tricks. The 'plot,' if any exists, seems to
concern a woman who has fallen asleep at her loom and
waked to discover that a neighbour, Glykê, has stolen a
cock.

144: *I would that the good ship Argo*: First line of the *Medea* of
Euripides.

144: *O stream of Spercheios*: 'From the [lost] *Philoktetês* of
Aischylos.' [Σ]

145: *Skill in speech*: 'From the *Antigonê* of Euripides.' [Σ]

145: *Death is the sole god*: 'From the [lost] *Niobê* of Aischylos.'
[Σ]

145: *Dicing Achilleus*: From an unknown play, probably by
Euripides.

145: *In his right hand a cudgel*: From Euripides' *Meleagros*.

145: *Chariot upon chariot*: 'From the [lost] *Glaukos* of Aischylos.'
[Σ]

148: *The Enemy's land is Athens'*: This advice, as Σ notes, is
taken from Periklês. Dionysos retorts that it is all very well
to talk about naval expansion, but the officials are bankrupt-
ing the treasury.

148: *'him I choose . . .'*: Possibly from Euripides.

148: *'Sworn hath my tongue . . .'*: See note on p. 85.

148: *It's no betrayal*: The sentiment is parodied from the lost
Aiolos of Euripides: 'What's disgrace, if our friends do not
think it so?'

148: *'Which of us can say . . .'*: 'From the *Polyïdos* of Euripides.'
[Σ] Van Leeuwen observes that the next line is absurd. He
is right.

150: *Kleophôn and his friends*: See note on p. 114.

THE BIRDS

for ROBERT FITZGERALD

ALASTOR. *Sed quid opus est triremi?* CHARON. *Ni-chil, si velim in mediâ palude rursus naufragium facere.* ALASTOR. *Ob multitudinem?* CHARON. *Scilicet.* ALASTOR. *Atqui umbras vehis, non corpora. Quantulum autem ponderis habent umbrae?* CHARON. *Sint tipulae, tamen tipularum tanta vis esse potest, ut onerent cymbam. Tum scis et cymbam umbratilem esse.*

INTRODUCTORY NOTE

The Birds was produced at the feast of the Great Dionysia of 414 B.C., and although it is certainly the most fanciful and one of the most lyrical of Aristophanes' plays, it won only the second prize. Composed during those tense months after the sailing of the Sicilian Expedition, when the disheartening war must have seemed endless in prospect and even victory a sick delusion, it is nevertheless not a war play. It is outspoken enough, particularly in its attacks upon the kind of civil neurosis that finds traitors and enemy agents in every office and that encourages, applauds and rewards the professional informer; but the attack this time is of less importance than the creation of a comic dream, the dream of Cloudcuckooland the Beautiful, that ideal commonwealth in the skies. Elaborate political reconstructions of the dream have been made—classical scholarship is ingenious and tireless—but they seem, in all their complexity, pastimes better suited to the academies of Cloudcuckooland itself than to the enrichment of our understanding. *The Birds* is not a play of escape: it is too honestly aware of its time for that; but it is primarily an entertainment, and as such, I think, it should be read and weighed.

For the *rationale* of my translation I must refer those interested to my remarks prefatory to *Lysistrata* and *The Frogs*. In general, however, I hope that I have reduced the number of liberties that were conscious on my part, and that my ignorance, not my arrogance, is to blame for the errors. At the same time, I demand a certain licence in rendering the choral passages and in handling mythological or topical references. Many difficulties can be taken care of in the Notes; but there are times when only a loose paraphrase, or maybe the incorporation of explanatory ideas into the text itself, can save the poem. And it is my faith that the poem is what matters most.

The text followed is the Budé, established by Coulon.

159

In the distribution of a few speeches I have preferred the reading of other editors, and have sometimes relied upon otherwise unreliable MSS. sources because they made better theatre sense. Once or twice I have followed myself alone, so amorous is *hybris,* and assigned a speech or two as it has never been assigned before.

For many corrections and the best of suggestions I am indebted to my colleague Alston Hurd Chase, and to the poet and Hellenist to whom this translation is dedicated.

CONTENTS

The supernumeraries include various servants and liturgical attendants, PROKNE the Nightingale wife of EPOPS, MANES a slave, and BASILEIA the bride of PISTHETAIROS.

🏵 PROLOGUE

> [*A waste region. Rocks, low bushes, a few thin trees. In the background, a steep rock face surmounted by a single tree. Enter two old men,* PISTHETAIROS *and* EUELPIDES, *followed by slaves carrying baggage.* PISTHETAIROS *has a raven perched upon his wrist;* EUELPIDES *has a jackdaw. Weariness and frustration*

EUELPIDES [*to the jackdaw*]:
Straight ahead? Over by that tree?

PISTHETAIROS [*to the raven*]:

Oh, damn your feathers!
—Euelpidês, this fool fowl keeps cawing
a retreat.

EUELPIDES:

I know. What's the use?
All this humping up and down hills,
we'll be wrecks before we find the right road.

PISTHETAIROS:

Miles and miles, walking around in circles,
all because of a brainless bird.

EUELPIDES:

Yes,
tramping my toenails off for a damned jackdaw.

PISTHETAIROS:

I wonder where we are.

EUELPIDES:

Do you think we could find our way back?

PISTHETAIROS:

Exekestidês himself couldn't find his way back.

EUELPIDES:

Hell!

PISTHETAIROS:

That's a road you'll have to go on your own.

EUELPIDES:

No, damn it, but I was thinking of that birdseller.
Nice service that was,
swearing that these two specimens would lead us straight
to Tereus, the king who turned into a Hoopoe;
selling us a jackdaw for a penny, the damned jackass,
and three pennies for that raven. What a pair!
All they can do is peck.

[*To the jackdaw*
—What's the matter now?
Forgotten how to shut your beak? Or a brilliant thought
like leading us bang up against that rock?
I don't see any road.

PISTHETAIROS:

Not so much as a path.

EUELPIDES:

Do you think that raven of yours is still conscious?

PISTHETAIROS:
I don't know. He sort of grunts, every once in a while.
EUELPIDES:
I mean, do you think he knows what he's up to?
PISTHETAIROS:
He seems to know enough to chew on my finger.
EUELPIDES:
Silly, isn't it?
Here we are, two of us for the birds,
and we can't even find the road.

[Addresses the audience
—Gentlemen:
Our trouble's just the reverse of Sakas's.
He isn't a citizen, and he's dying to become one;
but we,
native born, pure strain, citizens all our lives,
we can't get away from Athens fast enough.
Not that we don't like Athens:
it's a fine city, progressive, full of opportunities
to appear in court, citizens
happy as locusts droning in the shade—
only I must say they seem to do most of their droning
before a judge.
To come right down to it,
that's why the two of us are taking this walk,
fitted out with baskets and braziers and myrtle boughs.
We're looking for a less strenuous residence,
a City where we can pass our lives in peace;
and we thought of Tereus:
what with all the flying he's done, maybe
he'll know a nice restricted—
PISTHETAIROS:
Look! Look!
EUELPIDES:
What's the matter?
PISTHETAIROS:
The rock! Look at my raven!
EUELPIDES:
Yes, and my jackdaw sees something: his beak's
open again. I'll give you odds
there's birds around that rock. Let's do something.

PISTHETAIROS:
Why don't you go bang your foot against that rock?
EUELPIDES:
You go bang your head. It'll make twice the noise.
PISTHETAIROS:
Pick up a stone and knock.
EUELPIDES:

                  Anything you say.

—Porter! Porter!
PISTHETAIROS:

               Idiot, that's no way
to call a Hoopoe. You should say "Hoop! Hoop!"
EUELPIDES:
Hoop! Hoop!
Have I got to knock again?
Hoop! Hoop! Hoop!
          [A door in the rock face opens; enter SERVANT,
          wearing an enormous bird mask
SERVANT:

             Whoop are youp? What do you want?

PISTHETAIROS:
Holy Apollo, what a beak! It's a canyon!
SERVANT:
That's all we needed: a couple of bird-watchers!
EUELPIDES:
Not so bad as all that.

         —Come, let's think this thing through.
SERVANT:
You'd better make it good.
EUELPIDES:

              Well, first of all,
we're not really men, you see.
SERVANT:

              Then what are you?

EUELPIDES:
I am a Yellowyammer, a Libyan bird.
SERVANT:
Never heard of you.
EUELPIDES:

           Just look at the mess on my feet.

SERVANT:

 I see.—And your friend: what kind of bird is he?

PISTHETAIROS:

 A Crapulet, from Phartia.

EUELPIDES:

        For that matter,
what animal are *you*, for all the gods' sake?

SERVANT:

 A slave bird.

EUELPIDES:

     You mean you were beaten by some cock?

SERVANT:

 Not that, no. But when the Chief became a Hoopoe,
he made me turn into a bird, too, to keep him company
and do little jobs for him.

       Say he wants a mess
of sardines from Phaleron: off I run with my jug
to buy some. Or maybe it's pea soup,
and we need a tureen and a ladle: well, off I go
and arrange everything. See?

EUELPIDES:

       I'd call this bird a Kitchern.
Well, Kitch, you can do a little job for us.
Bring out Tereus.

SERVANT:

     I wouldn't think of it!
He's just had a lunch of ant and myrtle salad,
and now it's time for his nap.

EUELPIDES:

      Bother his nap!

SERVANT:

 He won't like this a bit. But if you say so,
I'll do it. It's no skin off my beak.

PISTHETAIROS:

     Get going!
       [*Exit* SERVANT
To hell with him and that chasm he calls a beak!

EUELPIDES:

 He scared away my jackdaw.

PISTHETAIROS:

     You got scared,

you mean, and let it loose.

EUELPIDES:

                              How about you?
When you were falling flat on your face over there,
didn't you let vour raven fly away?

PISTHETAIROS:

I certainly did not.

EUELPIDES:

                         Then where is it?

PISTHETAIROS:

                                        Absent.

EUELPIDES:

You can wash your hands of it now, old lion-heart.

EPOPS [within]:

Open the door. I'm going out to meet them.

            [Enter EPOPS, the Hoopoe. He is inadequately
            covered by thin drooping feathers, and wears a
            mask with a very long pointed beak and a tall
            radiant crest.

EUELPIDES:

What in the name of High Heraklês is that?
Those feathers! That tiara!

EPOPS:

                              Gentlemen,
your names, if you please? The purpose of your visit?

EUELPIDES:

The Twelve Gods seem to have visited something, friend,
on you.

EPOPS:

            You find my feathers laughable?
Remember: once I was a man.

EUELPIDES:

                              We are not laughing at you.

EPOPS:

At what, then?

EUELPIDES:

                  That damned funny beak of yours.

EPOPS:

I can't help it. It's Sophoklês' fault,
the way he misrepresented me in his plays.

EUELPIDES:

You are really Tereus? A bird, or a parody?

EPOPS:

Every inch a bird.

EUELPIDES:

What's the matter with your wings?

EPOPS:

Feathers missing.

EUELPIDES:

Some bird disease, or what?

EPOPS:

Every bird moults in the wintertime.
We get new feathers in the spring.

—But tell me:

who are you two?

EUELPIDES:

Mortal men.

EPOPS:

Nationality?

EUELPIDES:

Land of the Free. Home of the Brave.

EPOPS:

I suppose

you're jurymen?

EUELPIDES:

No; you might call us *de*

jure men.

EPOPS:

Isn't that a new crop down there?

EUELPIDES:

If you work hard enough you can grow it in some fields.

EPOPS:

Well, well.—But what brings you to this place?

EUELPIDES:

We want to integrate ourselves with you.

EPOPS:

Why?

EUELPIDES:

Because you were a man once, like us;
because you owed money, like us, and because,

like us, you hated to pay it. Now you are a bird,
with a bird's-eye view of things and a man's knowledge
of all lands under the sun, of every sea.
So we have come to you
as to an authority, meaning no disrespect,
to ask if you can tell us where to find
a soft snug woolly city
where a man can loaf and stretch and lie down in peace.

EPOPS:
A nobler city than Kranaos' town?

EUELPIDES:
Not nobler, no; but something more to our taste.

EPOPS:
More aristocratic?

EUELPIDES:
               The Social Register
pains me in a spot I needn't describe.

EPOPS:
What sort of city?

EUELPIDES:
               What I have in mind
is a place where the worst of your troubles would be
friends crowding in early in the morning
with invitations: 'Look, Euelpidês,
'I'm giving a dinner today. For God's sake,
'get a bath somewhere, pick up your wife and kids,
'come early and stay late. If you forget,
'I'll never turn to you when I need a friend.'

EPOPS:
I can see that you're fond of troubles.

                        —How about you?

PISTHETAIROS:
I feel the same way he does.

EPOPS:
               For example?

PISTHETAIROS:
I'd like to live in a town
where a friend of mine, father of a goodlooking boy,
would meet me and, 'You old bastard,' he'd say,
'what's this I hear about you from that son of mine?
'He tells me he ran into you outside the gymnasium,

'and though he was fresh from his bath
'you didn't say anything nice to him, or kiss him,
'or feel his balls or his biceps—
'Why, I thought you were a friend of the family!'
EPOPS:

It's clear that both of you want to live the hard life.
Well, this city of yours
does exist, after all. You'll find it on the Red Sea.
EUELPIDES:

And have the *Salaminia* turn up some morning
with a constable on board? Thanks, no sea for us!
Haven't you a Greek city you can recommend?
EPOPS:

How about Lepreon?
EUELPIDES:

No. I've never been there,
but the name reminds me of Melanthios.
EPOPS:

Then there's Opûs, over in Lokris.
EUELPIDES:

No.
You couldn't pay me enough to be Opuntios.
But tell me,
what is life like up here among you Birds?
EPOPS:

Not bad, take it by and large. No money, of course.
EUELPIDES:

There go most of your problems right away.
EPOPS:

As for food, we have poppy seed and myrtle,
white sesame, mint—
EUELPIDES:

It's a non-stop honeymoon!
PISTHETAIROS:

I have it! I have it!
I've just dreamed the most powerful dream in the world
for you Birds, if you only do what I tell you to.
EPOPS:

What's that?
PISTHETAIROS:

Well, first of all

I advise you to stop flying around aimlessly
with your beaks open. It isn't dignified.
Back in Athens when we see a man running around,
somebody asks 'Who's that?', and Teleas
or someone else says, 'Him? He's a hot bird, *he* is!
'Jittery, ants up his tail, all over the place, un-
'dependable type.'

EPOPS:
                                    You're right, by Dionysos!
What else do you advise?

PISTHETAIROS:
                                    I advise you to found a city.

EPOPS:
We birds? Found a city?

PISTHETAIROS:
                                    O ye of little faith!
Look down there.

EPOPS:
                                    I'm looking.

PISTHETAIROS:
                                    Now up there.

EPOPS:
                                                            I'm
looking.

PISTHETAIROS:
                    Look all around you.

EPOPS:
                                        Whatever you say.
I hope you're not trying to make me sprain my neck.

PISTHETAIROS:
Do you see anything?

EPOPS:
                            Clouds, and a lot of sky.

PISTHETAIROS:
That's the birds' sphere.

EPOPS:
                            Sphere? What do you mean?

PISTHETAIROS:
It's a space, really; but it revolves,
and everything passes through it, so we scientists
call it a sphere.

Very well. You settle this sphere,
build walls around it, and you'll have a city.
And what's more,
you can lord it over the human race as though
they were so many grasshoppers. And the gods—
why, you can starve them out like the Mêlians.

EPOPS:

How?

PISTHETAIROS:

Just as we manage these things on earth.
Suppose a man wants to consult the Oracle
at Delphoi: well, he has to get a pass
from the Boiotians, because Boiotia's on the way
to the Shrine. And so it will be with the gods:
there's all that air between earth and the top of Olympos,
so if they won't pay tribute to the Birds
you can make it illegal
for the smoke of offering to pass up to them.

EPOPS:

Oh by Earth, by Nets, by Traps, by Springes,
I never heard a cleverer idea in my life!
With you to help me, I will build that city—
that is, if we can get the other Birds to agree.

PISTHETAIROS:

Who will explain it to them?

EPOPS:

You.

I've lived with them so long that they have learned
to speak Man now instead of twittering.

PISTHETAIROS:

Can you call an Assembly?

EPOPS:

Nothing easier.
I'll just step back into the coppice here
and wake my darling wife, my Nightingale.
We'll summon them, she and I,
and they'll come racing when they hear our voices.

PISTHETAIROS:

Oh do, do! Dear Tereus, be quick!
Into the woods, wake the Nightingale!

> *[Exit* EPOPS; *presently his voice is heard singing within.*

EPOPS:

  Awake, Love, lazy sleeper,
    Awake, and pour
  The lilting glory of your golden throat
  For Itys, ours no more.
    Ah, the liquid trill
      Of the holy monody rising
  To God's house from the stillness of the woods!
    Phoibos himself, that high
  Singer, struck by your music, would sweep
  The lutestrings with his delicate fingers
   Antiphonal, and all the air along
     Lead the quiring
  Of the tireless gods responsive to your song.

EUELPIDES:

Heavenly God, what a voice that little bird has!
He is drowning the forest with honey.

PISTHETAIROS:

You!

EUELPIDES:

  What?

PISTHETAIROS:

    Be quiet, can't you?

EUELPIDES:

        Why?

PISTHETAIROS:

The Hoopoe is going to sing for us again.

> *[During the following monody, birdcalls are heard from various points behind the scene, distant and uncertain at first, but increasing in volume and in urgency until the* CHORUS OF BIRDS *enters for the* Párodos.

EPOPS [*within*]:

 Epopoí
   popoì epopopoí
  popoì
    iô
  iô
    iô

          To me,
      to
me here, here, here, O
   friends, O feathery
myriads!
          Leave your
fields now, furrows
          deep
   in seed, beak-
wielders,
              swift
   spiralers,
              melodists
of delight
   tiotiotioti
      All you
divers for stingvoiced gnats
   in dusky wet ravines,
          you
curlew, curlew crying,
      you,
   spume-guests of the halcyon
on the enchanted water:
      Come to me, come,
hear this remarkable old **man**
   whose brain
brims for our common **gain:**
      Hear him,
      come
   here, here, here,
      hear him!

CHORUS [*within*]:
          Tórotorotórotíx
              tototíx
          whit tuwhit tuwhit
          Tórotorotórotorolílilíx

PISTHETAIROS:
   Do you see any birds?

EUELPIDES:

                    Not a single bird.
There's not so much as a feather in the sky.
PISTHETAIROS:
   It seems to have done no good
   for the Hoopoe to go gargling in the glade.

🐦 PÁRODOS

> [*The* CHORUS *is composed of twenty-six persons
> dressed in stylized representation of various birds,
> each with a large beak-mask. These enter sep-
> arately from every direction, gathering about
> their leader, the Flamingo, in the* orchêstra. *The
> entrance should be complete by the end of the
> Hoopoe's catalogue.*

A BIRD:
   Torotìx torotìx.
PISTHETAIROS:
                  Look, there's one coming now!
EUELPIDES:
   What do you suppose it is? A peacock, maybe?
PISTHETAIROS:
   The Hoopoe can tell us.
                  —What kind of bird is that?
EPOPS:
   That, Sir, is a water bird; you don't see
   that sort every day.
EUELPIDES:
                  Nice colour; flame-y.
EPOPS:
   Naturally. He's a Flamingo.
EUELPIDES:
                  Oh look!
PISTHETAIROS:
   Now what?
EUELPIDES:
                  Another bird.
PISTHETAIROS:
                  I should say so!

He's a weird sister, all right, as the poet puts it.
See how he struts! I wonder what he is.

EPOPS:

We call him the Bird of Araby.

PISTHETAIROS:

Araby?
Did he come on a flying camel?

EUELPIDES:

There's another one!
By Poseidon, he looks as if he had been dyed!

PISTHETAIROS:

This is astonishing. Do you mean to say
there's more than one Hoopoe in the world?

EPOPS:

He's the son of Philoklês and a lady Hoopoe,
and I am his grandfather. It's like the formula
'Kallias : Hipponikos :: Hipponikos : Kallias II'.

EUELPIDES:

So that's Kallias II. I see he's losing his feathers.

EPOPS:

A man about town, you know, always getting plucked
by parasites and party girls feathering their own nests.

PISTHETAIROS:

Here comes one with a crest. What's he called?

EPOPS:

That one? Gobbler.

EUELPIDES:

I thought Kleonymos was the Gobbler

PISTHETAIROS:

This can't be Kleonymos: he hasn't thrown away
his crest.

EUELPIDES:

Speaking of that, why do birds
wear crests? To compete in the Armed Men's Race?

EPOPS:

It's like the Karians: crests make fighting safer.

PISTHETAIROS:

I never saw so many birds! They make me nervous.

EUELPIDES:

You said it.

When they lift their wings you can't see where you're
    going.

EPOPS:

That's the Partridge; and that's—let's see—that one's
the Francolin; the Egyptian Mallard; and that female's
a Hen Kingfisher.

PISTHETAIROS:

                        What's that in back of her?

EPOPS:

A Shavetail, of course.

PISTHETAIROS:

                    Do birds shave tails?

EPOPS:

Doesn't Sporgilos?
                    —And that's a female
Owl.

EUELPIDES:

That's an idea! Bringing Owls to Athens.

EPOPS:

Magpie. Turtledove. Lark. Warbler. Spryneck.
Pigeon. Snirt. Falcon. Ringdove. Cuckoo.
Redleg. Firepate. Purple Hatch. Kestrel.
Grebe. Bunting. Lämmergeier. Woodpecker.

PISTHETAIROS:

Birds and more birds!

EUELPIDES:

                    Even white Blackbirds!

PISTHETAIROS:

The way they chatter and screech at each other!

EUELPIDES:

Do you think they're dangerous?

PISTHETAIROS:

                        Their beaks are wide open,
and they're certainly looking hard at both of us.

EUELPIDES:

I think so, too.

KORYPHAIOS:

                Who-oo-oo called this Assembly?
Where is he?

EPOPS:

                Here I am, your tried

and trusted old friend.

KORYPHAIOS:

Spea-pea-pea-peak:
What clever new message have you to give us?

EPOPS:

A profitable one, safe, correct, ingenious.
These two gentlemen, both of them keen thinkers,
came here looking for me.

KORYPHAIOS:

Looking for you? Why?

EPOPS:

I am telling you.

—These elegant old men
have detached themselves temporarily from
the human race and brought us what I am sure
is a plan of promising proportions.

KORYPHAIOS:

I think
you have made the greatest blunder in history.
What are you talking about?

EPOPS:

Be not afraid.

KORYPHAIOS:

Why not?
What have you done to us?

EPOPS:

I have lent an ear
to two respectable bird-struck Senators.

KORYPHAIOS:

You have?

EPOPS:

I have. And I am proud of it

KORYPHAIOS:

What, in our house?

EPOPS:

As sure as I'm standing here.

CHORUS:

Oh misery!   [STROPHE
Duplicity!
Oh horror without end!

                    Who lays the snare
                    And leaves us there?
                        Our old familiar friend!
            Is this the Hoopoe of our heart,
                Copartner of our fields and skies,
            Who bids our ancient laws depart
            And sells us to our enemies?

KORYPHAIOS:
    We can take care of him later. Just now
    it's a matter of these two old fools. Look at them!
    The usual penalty is clearly in order:
    death by dissection.
PISTHETAIROS:
                        Done for, by God Almighty!

EUELPIDES:
    Your fault, your fault entirely. Why did you ever
    lead me here?
PISTHETAIROS:
                        So that you could follow me.

EUELPIDES:
    It's blood and tears for us!
PISTHETAIROS:
                            Hardly tears for you,
    once the Birds have pecked out both your eyes.

CHORUS:
                    The cock-trump sings.   [ANTISTROPHE
                    Advance both wings,
                        O army of the air!
                    The hour has struck
                    That ends the luck
                        Of this repulsive pair.
            No clouds that cluster in the sky,
                No raindark mountain peaks,
            Shall save them from the battery
            Of our insulted beaks.

KORYPHAIOS:
    Forward! Peck them apart! Flay them!
                                —Where's

that Wing Commander? Tell him to get moving
on the right!

> [*Immense confusion of movement among the*
> *Birds in the* orchêstra. EUELPIDES *and* PISTHE-
> TAIROS *confer apart.*

EUELPIDES:
> That settles that.

How do we get out of this mess?

PISTHETAIROS:
> Why not

stick around?

EUELPIDES:
> Of course. And get pulled apart?

PISTHETAIROS:

I suppose you have figured out some way of escape?

EUELPIDES:

You know I haven't.

PISTHETAIROS:
> Then listen to me.

Let them come on. We'll stand here and fight them
with these kitchen pots.

EUELPIDES:
> Pots? What good are pots?

PISTHETAIROS:

They'll keep the Owl from attacking us.

EUELPIDES:

How about those fellows with the horrible claws?

PISTHETAIROS:

Stick that spit up in front of you like a spear.

EUELPIDES:

But our eyes?

PISTHETAIROS:
> Use a couple of saucers.

EUELPIDES:
> What a mind!

You remind me of Nikias. You ought to be
on the General Staff, in charge of secret weapons.

KORYPHAIOS:

Eleleú!

Ready, beaks at the charge! Let 'em have it!
Grab! Claw! Tear! Gouge! Break the pots first!

*[Much noise on both sides, but no other activity,
the Hoopoe intervenes.*

EPOPS:
Permit me. Just a minute, please.
                         —With the best intentions,
you are behaving like besotted beasts.
What is the good of killing two harmless men,
both of them perfect strangers and, what's more,
related to my wife?

KORYPHAIOS:
                         Are you promoting
a Be Kind to Wolves week?

EPOPS:
                         Oh, come. I'll admit,
men are our natural enemies; but these men
are different, they really mean us well.
More than that,
they have a practical plan for the good of us all.

KORYPHAIOS:
A practical plan? Nonsense. Our enemies,
our fathers' enemies—what can they teach us?

EPOPS:
Why, people before this have learned from their enemies
An open mind's a weapon in itself.
It's not our friends teach us resourcefulness,
but our wise enemies. Cities and princes
have learned the use of warships and fortresses
from necessity, not from friends. Enmity saves
our homes, our children, everything that we love.

KORYPHAIOS:
You may be right.
                         At least it can do no harm
to hear what they have to say.
                         It may be
we shall take some profit even from what we hate.
       *[The Birds cluster in doubtful conference about
       the* KORYPHAIOS.

PISTHETAIROS *[apart to* EUELPIDES]:
They're coming to their senses. Easy, now!

EPOPS *[to the Birds]:*
Think over what I've said. You'll thank me for it.

KORYPHAIOS:

We have always admired the Hoopoe's intellect.

PISTHETAIROS:

Now we can breathe again.

Leave your pot there on the ground. Pick up your
    spear—

your spit, I mean—and let's walk around

and see what the place is like.

Keep this side

of the pots, and keep your eye on those Birds. Above all,

don't act as though you were nervous.

EUELPIDES:

I'd like to know:

if they kill us, where'll we get buried?

PISTHETAIROS:

I should hope,

in the National Cemetery. For a first-rate funeral

at the public expense, we'd say we fell gloriously

in combat with the common enemy

at Gettysbird.

[The Birds decide upon a truce.

KORYPHAIOS:

At case! Stack arms!

Now we must find out who these strangers are

and what they want.

Listen, Epops!

EPOPS:

I am listening.

KORYPHAIOS:

Who are these men? Do you know where they are from?

EPOPS:

Travelers from Greece, where education is general.

KORYPHAIOS:

What brings them to the Birds?

EPOPS:

Ornithophily.

They have heard of your laws and customs and they long

to live with you for ever.

KORYPHAIOS:

Is it possible?

What else do they say?

EPOPS:

                   Incredible things, transcending
utterance.

KORYPHAIOS:

           What do they ask from us?
Does 'living with us' mean living as honest friends,
or serving their own interests at our cost?

EPOPS:

    This savant speaks of benefits to you
that fairly rob me of words to describe them.
It's all for you. He will tell you so himself.

KORYPHAIOS:

    Is the man crazy?

EPOPS:

                His sanity defies
definition.

KORYPHAIOS:

        Really?

EPOPS:

              Pure fox, subtle, deep.

KORYPHAIOS:

    Then let him speak, let him speak!
 . These hints of yours have got me all a-twitter.

 AGON

            [Order is now restored. As EPOPS *takes command
            of the situation, the* CHORUS *forms itself at op-
            posite sides of the* orchêstra *to listen to the en-
            suing debate.*

EPOPS:

    You there, and you,
carry these weapons in and hang them up
in the kitchen again, next to the tripod.
Fair fortune befall them!

            *[Exeunt two Bird Servants with the pots, spits,
            and other utensils*

                     —And you, friend,
inform the Birds why I have summoned them
to this Assembly. Expound.

PISTHETAIROS:

No, by Apollo!
Not unless they promise me first
what Monk the Knifeman made that wife of his
promise *him*: no biting, no tickling, no unseemly
prodding in the—

EUELPIDES:

The arse, you would say?

PISTHETAIROS:

No;
I mean my eyes.

KORYPHAIOS:

Sir, you have our promise.

PISTHETAIROS:
Swear it.

KORYPHAIOS:

I swear it; but on condition that
this Comedy of ours win First Prize
by unanimous vote of the judges and audience.

EPOPS:
NOW HEAR THIS:
Break ranks! Every private will pick up his arms
and go back to barracks. See your bulletin boards
for further announcements.

CHORUS:

Men were deceivers ever; and it may be,   [STROPHE
Friend, that the quality of our guilelessness
   Tempts you to gull us. Nevertheless,
      Nothing risked may be gain rejected when

Truth as a Stranger comes. If you have discerned
New forces in us, talents earthed over, dis-
   used instruments of old artifice:
      Speak out. Let age edify unfledged youth.

KORYPHAIOS:
You are at liberty to say whatever you like.
You have our promise:
We shall not be the first to break the truce.

PISTHETAIROS:
I thank you.

        —Gentlemen, you will find
much to chew on in the following message.
But first, with your permission—

                       [*To a* SERVANT
                Boy, bring me
a garland and a bowl of water to wash my hands.

EUELPIDES [*apart*]:
Do you see dinner coming?

PISTHETAIROS [*apart*]:
                No; I am trying to think
of something to tell them, some enormous concept
that will knock them silly.

                —Gentlemen: My heart
bleeds—bleeds, I say—when I reflect that you
who once were kings—

KORYPHAIOS:
              Kings? Kings of what?

PISTHETAIROS:
Why, kings of everything! Kings of myself, of this
poor friend of mine, yes, kings of Zeus the King!
Before Time was, you were: you antedate
Kronos, the Titans, Earth—

KORYPHAIOS:
                Earth?

PISTHETAIROS:
                  Yes, by Heaven!

KORYPHAIOS:
That's something that I never knew before.

PISTHETAIROS:
Ignorance, acedia. There are authorities
for what I say: Aisôpos, to go no farther.
He tells us—don't you remember?—that the Lark
was the first Bird born in those chaotic times
before even Earth was thought of; and the Lark's
father died—have you forgotten?—, and because
there was no earth on Earth to bury him in,
the Lark finally laid him away in her head.

EUELPIDES:
Exactly. That's how Hyde Lark got its name.

PISTHETAIROS:

You see my point, I hope? If birds existed
before the Creation, before the gods themselves,
then you Birds must be heirs apparent: the royal power
belongs to you.

EUELPIDES:

Of course. At the same time,
they'd better keep their beaks in fighting trim:
Zeus won't give in to the first woodpecker.

PISTHETAIROS:

In those glorious days it was not the gods who ruled
over men, but the Birds. Let me cite you a few proofs.
Consider the Cock.
Long before any Dareioses or Megabazoses
the Cock was King of the Persians, and such a king
that ever since he's been called the Persian Bird.

EUELPIDES:

That's why, even now,
Cocks strut like the Shah; and of all birds living
only they have a right to the tiara.

PISTHETAIROS:

What power he had! Why, to this very day
when the Cock sings at dawn
everyone jumps out of bed and goes to work:
blacksmiths, potters, tanners, shoemakers,
grocers, masseurs, lyre-&-shield-manufacturers—
Some of them are hard at it before it's light.

EUELPIDES:

Some of them certainly are! That's how I lost
a perfectly good new Phrygian all-wool coat.
I'd been asked to a party to celebrate
naming somebody's baby. Well, when I got there
I had a couple of short ones, so I felt sleepy
and lay down for a minute; and—would you believe it?—
some damned cock began to crow, and I woke up
and thought it was morning, before the other guests
had even sat down to dinner! Well, I started out
on the Halimos road, but I'd hardly poked my nose
past the drive when, baff! somebody boffed me
with something blunt, and I went down for the count.
When I came to, my coat was somewhere else.

PISTHETAIROS:

At that same time the Kite reigned over the Greeks.

KORYPHAIOS:

The Greeks?

PISTHETAIROS:

The Greeks. That's when they learned
to prostrate themselves when the kites come back in the
spring.

EUELPIDES:

I remember I prostrated myself one day
when I saw a Kite, or I tried to, but somehow
I fell on my back by mistake and my market money
went down my throat. That day I ate no more.

PISTHETAIROS:

Then there's the Cuckoo.
Once upon a time
in Egypt and in Phoinikia the Cuckoo
was king. As a matter of fact, when the Cuckoo
said 'Cuckoo!',
all the Phoinikians went out and mowed their fields.

EUELPIDES:

'Cuckoo! Back to the furrows, you foreskinless!'
as the proverb has it.

PISTHETAIROS:

Another thing: You will find
that whenever a man managed to become a king,
an Agamemnon, say, or a Menelaos,
he would always carry a bird on the end of his sceptre
to share the royal gifts.

EUELPIDES:

That explains something.
I used to go to the theatre; and whenever Priam
came on in the tragedies, he'd have a bird
on his sceptre, just as you say. I used to think
the bird was there to keep an eye on our friend
Lysikratês when the bribes were passed around.

PISTHETAIROS:

But the best proof is that Zeus, the current King,
wears an Eagle on his head as a sign of power.
His Daughter has an Owl; his son Apollo,
as a medical man, has a Hawk.

EUELPIDES:

That's perfectly true.
Why do you suppose those gods have those birds?

PISTHETAIROS:

Why? So that when the sacrificial roasts
are offered to the gods, the birds may taste them first.
And here's something else:
In the old days men never swore by the gods,
but always by birds.

EUELPIDES:

Lampôn still does today.
He always says 'Holy Kites!' when he makes a mistake.

PISTHETAIROS:

You understand, then, that years and years ago
you were great, even holy, in the minds of men.
But now? Now you are rejects, fools,
worse than slaves, stoned
in the streets by arrogant men, hunted
down even in your sanctuaries
by trappers with nets, springes, limed
twigs, cages, decoy-
boxes;
caught, sold
wholesale, goosed, prodded
by fat fingers, denied
even the grace of wholesome frying,
but served up sleazily, choked
with cheese, smeared with oil,
sprayed with vinegar, doused
as though you were dead meat, too gamy,
in rivers of sweet slab sauce.

CHORUS

[ANTISTROPHE
Tears, and no idle tears, Stranger, distress us
Hearing your plain account of calamity.
Clearly our primeval dignity
Has lapsed in the long sliding of the years.

You, by a happy chance or some divine influence sent to guide us, have indicated

Future recovery, joy ahead.
Ourselves, our wives, our chicks depend on you.

KORYPHAIOS:

What can we do? Instruct us, since you say
you have a plan. Life's no life for us
till we win back the power that we have lost.

PISTHETAIROS:

My plan is a great City for All Birds,
a single City, with the surrounding air
and all the space between encircled by
massive brick walls like those at Babylon.

EUELPIDES:

Bring on your Giants! What a mighty fortress!

PISTHETAIROS:

Once the wall's built, you must send an embassy
to Zeus and lay your grievances before him.
If he denies them, if he temporizes,
then you should declare a Holy War
against the whole of Olympos: no more free passage
for divinities in an obvious state of erection
on their way through your land to flirt with their Alopês,
their Sémelês, their Alkmenês! No; once across the border,
each strutting member must be stamped and sealed.
That should give them something to think about!

As for Mankind,
you must send another bird to them, a herald
to announce that from now on, since the Birds are kings,
the first sacrifices must be made to them,
and then (if convenient) to the Olympian gods.
But even in sacrifices to the gods
an appropriate Bird must be adored as well:
thus, Aphroditê and a Phalarope; Poseidon
and a Duck; Heraklês and a Cormorant;
or, if the victim is offered up to King Zeus,
let the Wren, the Wren, the king of all birds, receive
the flesh of the Balled Gnat.

EUELPIDES:

What price gnat-flesh?
Let the Good Gosh bounce thunderballs in the sky!

KORYPHAIOS:
What if men refuse to treat us as gods?
What if they say, 'Them? Jackdaws, that's all,
'flying around up there with their silly wings'?
PISTHETAIROS:
I can't believe you are serious. Why, good Lord!
Hermês has wings, and he flies; yes, and Nikê,
she has wings; and Erôs—all sorts of gods
fly, don't they? Why, even Iris,
the one that Homer refers to as 'Trembling Dove'—
Iris has wings, Iris flies.
EUELPIDES:
                          Speaking of wings,
what if Zeus drops one of his wingèd bolts on us?
KORYPHAIOS:
But what if Mankind is so unregenerate
that only the regulars of the Olympos clique
are recognized?
PISTHETAIROS:
                          We'll draft a regiment
of Sparrows and march them off to steal the seeds
in the new-planted fields. Demêter can set up
a Farm Program to fend off starvation.
EUELPIDES:
Demêter will also find a thousand ways
to get around any program that she sets up.
PISTHETAIROS:
If the Sparrows fail, we'll send some Elite Crows
to the grazing lands and have them bite out the eyes
of herdsmen and herds. Let Apollo cure them:
he's a doctor, he gets paid.
EUELPIDES:
                          Let me know in advance:
I'll want to sell my yoke of oxen first.
PISTHETAIROS:
But if they sense the indwelling divinity
of the Birds, as they should, knowing that you are **God,**
and Life, and Earth, and Kronos, and Poseidon—
then everything will end as they would have it.
KORYPHAIOS:
Everything? What do you mean?

PISTHETAIROS:

For example,
locusts will not touch their budding vines:
the Hawks and Owls will see to that. Then, too,
a single platoon of indoctrinated Redwings
will be assigned to keep the gall-flies and emmets
from chewing up fig-shoots.

KORYPHAIOS:

But how shall we manage
money? Men seem to set great store by money.

PISTHETAIROS:

The Auspice birds will show them where rich mines
lie in the earth. The Augurs, too, will learn
the secret of quick returns. Shipwrecks will end—

KORYPHAIOS:

How so?

PISTHETAIROS:

They'll consult the Birds before each voyage:
'Is it safe to sail?' 'Not today; a storm's blowing up.'

EUELPIDES:

I'll invest in a boat. Yo-ho for the briny deep!

PISTHETAIROS:

Then, of course, there are those buried pots
of treasure. The Birds know. Haven't you heard
'A little bird told me where to look for it'?

EUELPIDES:

I'll sell my boat. Me for the buried pots!

KORYPHAIOS:

But what about health? That's the gift of the gods.

PISTHETAIROS:

When business is good, health takes care of itself.

EUELPIDES:

I never heard of a bankrupt whose health was good.

KORYPHAIOS:

How will they ever live to reach old age?
Surely that's an Olympian dispensation.
Or must they die in the cradle?

PISTHETAIROS:

Not at all.
The Birds will add three centuries to their lives.

KORYPHAIOS:
  Where will they get three centuries?
PISTHETAIROS:

From themselves.

  The poet says:
  'One crow caws down five generations of man'.
EUELPIDES:
  Almost thou persuadest me to be a bird.
PISTHETAIROS:
  Why not be birds? They demand no marble temples
  intricate with golden doors; their shrines
  are the ilex, the sparkling shrubs. Their highest gods
  live in the sanctuary of olive trees.
  We need no Delphoi or Ammon for this worship,
  but at home, on our own ground,
  in peace among our own familiar flowers,
  we can raise hands full of grain to them in prayer,
  invoking their dear aid:
  and when our words fly up, they will be answered
  in blessings that fall upon the scattered grain.
KORYPHAIOS:
  Dearest of old men, you have won me utterly
  to your cause. From this hour your words are my words.

CHORUS:

  My mind applauds.
  Swear faith to me,
  And I will swear
  Death to the gods.
  The fight is fair:
  Sing Victory.

KORYPHAIOS:
  We are ready to do whatever must be done.
  The plans and stratagems we leave to you.
EPOPS:
  Action, quick action. By God, this is no time
  for taking naps or dawdling like Nikias!
  But first, gentlemen,
  this is my nest, a poor thing of twigs and straw,

but my own. Will you permit me to entertain you
inside? And will you tell me who you are?

PISTHETAIROS:
Of course. Pisthetairos is the name. That one's
Euelpidês; comes from Kriôa.

EPOPS:
                              Very happy
to meet you both.

PISTHETAIROS:
                  Not at all.

EPOPS:
                              Will you please step in?

PISTHETAIROS:
After you.

EPOPS:
              Right this way.

PISTHETAIROS:
                              There, I almost forgot!
Tell me, how can a couple of men like us
live with birds? You can fly. We don't know how.

EPOPS:
I see.

PISTHETAIROS:
        And speaking of Aisôpos again,
he has a fable about a fox and an eagle.
The fox lost.

EPOPS:
                  Really, it's no problem at all.
There's a useful little herb. You nibble it
and, presto!—you sprout wings.

PISTHETAIROS:
                              That's fair enough.
—Here, Xanthias, Manodôros: pick up the baggage.

KORYPHAIOS:
Hi! Epops! Before you go—

EPOPS:
                          What's the matter?

KORYPHAIOS:
You'll invite our venerable guests to dine, of course;
but the Nightingale,

the Muses' love, sweet cataract of song—
will you send her out and let us play with her?

PISTHETAIROS:

A sound idea, by God, and I second it.
Ask the delightful bird to step this way.

EUELPIDES:

Yes, just for a minute. You can't imagine how long
- we've longed, my friend and I, for a nightingale.

EPOPS:

You are too kind.
                              —Proknê, Proknê,
come here and show yourself to our noble guests.
              [*Enter the Nightingale: a flute-girl, nude except
              for her mask and wings*

PISTHETAIROS:

God of our fathers, what a heavenly little bird!
So soft, so white—
How I should like to get between those thighs!

EUELPIDES:

The gold, all the gold, like a bride on her wedding day!
I can't help it; I am obliged to kiss this young woman.

PISTHETAIROS:

Stupid, don't you see the little spikes on her beak?
You'll get hurt.

EUELPIDES:

                              No, I shan't. It's like opening an egg.
Tap her on the head, the shell falls away,
and there's my kiss.

EPOPS [*indicating the door*]:
                              Gentlemen.

PISTHETAIROS:

                              Let's go in.
                                                            [*Exeunt*

🏵 PARÁBASIS I

              [*In the* orchêstra *the* CHORUS *turns to face the
              audience; the Nightingale accompanies the lyric
              passages on her flute.*

CHORUS [*a solo voice*]:

> Tawnythroat, Partner   [KOMMATION
> In song, dark
> Muse, dearest of Birds:
> Come, let the curving long
> Line of your fluting
> Fall, sparkling
> Undersong to our words.

KORYPHAIOS:

[PARÁBASIS

Come now, let us consider the generations of Man,
Compound of dust and clay, strengthless,
Tentative, passing away as leaves in autumn
Pass, shadows wingless, forlorn
Phantoms deathbound, a dream. Let Men turn
To the Birds, aerial philosophers of
Forever, safe from age, from change, from death.
Let them be humble and learn from us
The truth of Being, the essential germ,
The Bird, first Cause of Gods and Rivers,
Of Erebos, and of the great Void of Chaos.

Here is the absolute Theogony:
Professor Pródikos can lecture somewhere else.

CHAOS and NIGHT: that was the start of it,
And black Erebos, and the long nothing of Tártaros;
No Earth as yet, no Air, no Heaven. There,
In the untried lap of Erebos, sombre Night
Laid a wind-egg, whence, with the circling year,
Erôs was hatched, golden Erôs, wind-swift
Love, the world's longing. His was the sleight
Joined Night and wingèd Chaos in that first
Tartarean marriage and brought the race of Birds
To the shores of light. It was Erôs
Created the line of Gods also, mixing
The urgent elements in adorable ways
To make the Sky and Sea and Earth and all
The Blessèd Ones.

So it appears that we

Are móre ancient than these same Blessèd Ones,
Older in the line of Love. What I say is clear
In a thousand proofs:
                    We are wing'd, and so is Love.
Love is our art: how many a handsome boy
Has armed his heart with scorn, only to yield
His proud thighs to the persuasion of the Birds,
Won by a gift of quail, or geese, or cocks!

And birds are good to men in numberless ways.
We lead in the seasons. The clanging Crane
Flies towards Libya, and the sowing begins;
She it is who tells the mariner
When it is time to take his winter sleep,
The unshipped rudder hanging against the wall.
This same Crane
Inspires our friend Orestês of the Alleys
To knit himself a shirt against the cold,
Thus winning the gratitude of citizens waylaid
Who otherwise would shiver in nudity.
Later, the Kite brings back the brilliant Spring
And you barber your sheep; and then the summer
        Swallow
Suggests bargains of thin dress at the shops.

We are Ammon, Delphoi, Dodôna, Phoibos Apollo.
Are you not always taking the advice of birds
In matters of business, of marriage, of daily life?
You see Bird in everything: your rumours are what
A small Bird told you; your sneeze is a Bird, your chance
Hello in the street's a Bird; a stranger encountered;
An ass on the road: all Birds, all signs of Birds.
Are we not right to call ourselves your Apollos?

        Therefore confess us gods, for so   [MAKRON
        We are, to you; and you shall have
        Feathery Muses to foretell
        The winter wind, the summer breeze.
        We will not perch like Zeus, at ease
        In some remote cloud-citadel,
        But live with you and with your sons,

Your sons' sons, and their sons as well,
Bringing you gifts of youth and peace,
Love, laughter, wealth, new dances, brave
Festivals, more than the human tongue
Can tell, more than the heart can know.
This is our pledge, this is our song.

CHORUS:

Woodland Muse   [ODE
   tiotiotinx tiotinx
      Lucency
Darting voice
     Valley
Wanderer, circling flight
   tiotinx tiotiotinx
     on the bright hills:
    My singing
Spills
     duskiness into the light
For Pan
     and thou hearest
         For
The Great Mother, Mountaindweller,
  tótotototótotototinx
     and thou
     hearest
In air
   on the heights
        fields
   where Phrynichos
Tastes the ambrosial finality
   tiotinx
        of song.

KORYPHAIOS:
             [EPIRRHEMA
If any gentleman in the audience is interested
In a pleasant life, he should get in touch with us.
We practise what your laws forbid: You would like to beat
Your father? Good. According to your code
It's an off-colour pastime and, moreover, illegal.

All right; but if you were one of us Birds,
You'd just walk up to the old man, tap him
On the snout, and say: 'Put 'em up, if you want to fight!'
Or say you're on the lam, branded and all that: here,
We'd refer to you as a Mottled Francolin, and forget you.
You're a sub-asiatic type like Spíntharos?
Here you'd be a Migrant Finch, Philêmon species.
Even a creeping calamity like Exekestidês
Can hatch ancestors up here and become respectable.
Why, if Peisias' son himself
Should take after the old man and cohabit
With subversives by the dozens, we'd only say
'What a clever bird he is, always drumming up trade!'

CHORUS:

                    So the wild Swans   [ANTODE
                        tiotiotínx tiotínx
                            calling
                    Above the roar
                    Of their great wings,
                                                cry
                        tiotínx tiotiotínx
                            'Apollo!'
                        on the Hebros
                    Shore:
                            The company
                    Of spotted wood-beasts fly
                            for dread,
                    The sea
                            hearing
                        tótotototótototínx
                            falls
                            hearing
                        and is still:
                    Olympos
                        is hushed
                                    The Graces
                        shriek back against
                    The liquid instancy
                        tiotínx
                                of song.

KORYPHAIOS:

[ANTEPIRRHEMA

There is nothing more practical or more enjoyable
Than a pair of wings. Suppose you go to the theatre
And find it's some Tragedy or other: well, of course
You're bored, and hungry, so off you fly home,
Take care of your belly, and get back for the last act.
Or say you develop a sudden case of the runs.
Do you sit there and spoil your suit? No. You simply
Zoom up into the air, do your job, fart twice,
Catch your breath, and coast back to your seat again.
Or maybe you're an Adulterer, of all things, and there's
Your girl's husband in the front row gawking at the
     Chorus.
A flap of the wings, and you're off you know where; and
     when
You've laid the lady—a flap of the wings, and you're back
Wings? There's nothing like them!
Look at Dieitrephês, if you want a good example:
Those wicker wing baskets he manufactures got him
A captaincy, then a colonelcy, and now, rags to riches,
He's a full-fledged Horsecock in a yellow uniform!

🎜 SCENE

[Re-enter PISTHETAIROS and EUELPIDES. Both are
now absurdly feathered, winged, and beaked.

PISTHETAIROS:
So far, so good.
EUELPIDES:
                    By God, it's the funniest thing
I ever saw in my life!
PISTHETAIROS:
                    What is?
EUELPIDES:
                    You,
with those pinfeathers. Know what you look like?
PISTHETAIROS:
You look like a cut-rate reproduction
of an unsuccessful sketch of a goose.

EUELPIDES:
Do I?
You look like a blackbird tonsured in the dark.
PISTHETAIROS:
These similes are futile. Remember the poem:
'I shot an arrow into the air . . .'
KORYPHAIOS:

Next business?

PISTHETAIROS:
First we must find
a name for our City, a glorious name;
and then we must sacrifice to the gods.
EUELPIDES:

You said it.

KORYPHAIOS:
Let's get busy. What shall we call this City of ours?
PISTHETAIROS:
Shall we go in for a touch of Lakonian *je ne sais quoi*
and name it New Sparta?
EUELPIDES:

I want no part of Sparta.
Gosh, I wouldn't tie a name like that
to a flop-house bunk!
PISTHETAIROS:

Well, have you any ideas?

EUELPIDES:
Somewhere, what with all these clouds and all this air,
there must be a rare name, somewhere . . .
PISTHETAIROS:

How do you like
'Cloudcuckooland'?
KORYPHAIOS:

That's it! That's it!
What a name, what a jewel of a name you've thought of!
EUELPIDES:
Cloudcuckooland. Isn't that the place
where Aischinês and Theogenês rent castles?
PISTHETAIROS:
Yes: and it's where the Giants met the Gods
and got themselves bluffed off the battlefield.

KORYPHAIOS:
Cloudcuckooland's a city with a future!
What god or goddess shall we choose for Patron?
EUELPIDES:
Why not Athêna?
PISTHETAIROS:
In a City with a Future,
'what boots a mailèd warrior goddess in arms',
since Kleisthenês tends to the weaving?
KORYPHAIOS:
But the Akropolis?
Who will guard the Pelargic Wall?
PISTHETAIROS:
A bird.

KORYPHAIOS:
One of us? What kind?
PISTHETAIROS:
Something Persian, I should say,
something with a reputation for ferocity.
An Arês-chicken, maybe?
EUELPIDES:
Hail, Arês, Master Cluck!
He's used to uncomfortable roosts, at any rate.
PISTHETAIROS: [To EUELPIDES
But now,
off you go into the air! See what the builders
are up to. Make sure they have enough stones.
Get plenty of tubs. Make the mortar yourself. (Better
strip first.) Carry the hods up—
EUELPIDES:
And fall off the ladder.

PISTHETAIROS:
Bank the fires. Post sentries in the right places.
Make the round of the guards at night—
EUELPIDES:
And take a snooze.

PISTHETAIROS:
Send out two heralds, one to the gods above,
one to mankind below.
When you have done this, report back here to me.

EUELPIDES:
  And here you'll be on your back! I wish to God
  you'd do some of the work.
PISTHETAIROS:
                                    Friend, that's not like you.
  We all depend on you to get things done.
  I shall be busy too:

                                              [*Exit* EUELPIDES
  I must arrange for the dedication service
  and collar a priest to recite the liturgy.
  Boy!—You, boy!—Bring me the basket and the lavabo.

CHORUS:
                  Inevitably right! My mind   [STROPHE
                    Melts in your mind's embrace.
                  High rituals of any kind
                    Are proper in this place.
                  Here let our piety devote
                  To the blest gods one skinny goat.

                  So may they look down from above
                    Upon our sacred feast,
                  Accept our sparsely offered love,
                    And overlook the rest.
                  Sing one, sing all! Sing deaf, sing mute!
                  Chairis, assist us with your flute.

PISTHETAIROS [*to the* Fluteplayer]:
  You, there, stop that futile tooting!
  What a man! I swear by my God, I've seen
  strange sights in my life, but this is the first
  crow I ever saw with a leather beak-rest.

                                              [*Enter a* PRIEST
  Holiness, get busy. Sacrifice to the gods.
PRIEST:
  I would fain do so.
                  —Where is my acolyte?
  LET US PRAY:
  TO HESTIA NESTIARCH, TO THE HIGH HAWK
    OF THE HALL, TO ALL OLYMPIAN BIRDS AND
    BIRDETTES—

PISTHETAIROS:

Hail Storkissimo! Hail, Super of Sûnion!

PRIEST:

—TO THE PYTHODELIAN SWAN, TO LETO
CORNCRAKE, TO ARTEMIS SISKIN—

PISTHETAIROS:

That's a pretty association of ideas!

PRIEST:

—TO SABAZIOS THE PHRYGILLATOR, TO THE
GREAT OSTRICH MOTHER OF GODS AND
MEN—

PISTHETAIROS:

Lady Kybelê, Ostrichess, Mother of Kleokritos!

PRIEST:

THAT THEY MAY VOUCHSAFE HEALTH AND
LENGTH OF DAYS TO ALL CLOUDCUCKOO-
LANDERS, and also to the Chians—

PISTHETAIROS:

My heart leaps up when someone mentions the Chians!

PRIEST:

AND TO ALL HERO BIRDS AND BIRDSONS OF
HEROES: MORE ESPECIALLY TO THE POR-
PHYRION, THE WRY PECKER, THE PELICAN,
THE PYROPHLEX, THE RUDDY GUINEA, THE
PEACOCK, THE MAJOR OUSEL, THE TEAL, THE
BANDED BITTERN, THE HERON, THE DISTEL-
FINK, THE BALMY PETREL, THE PIPIT, THE
GOATGREEN TITMOUSE, THE—

PISTHETAIROS:

Birds, birds, birds! Enough! Why, what a man
you are, to summon all those vultures and sea-eagles
to our Eucharist! Can't you see that a single hawk
could take our entire victim at one gulp?
Go away, and take your portable altar with you.

[*Exit* PRIEST

I'll finish the service myself.

CHORUS:

      If that is so, it seems that I   [ANTISTROPHE
        Must tune my voice again
      In sacramental hymnody

Of even deeper strain:
O Gods, and thou our Patron's God,
Exact no more from us than laud.

Behold our sacrificial beast,
    Sick bones and stringy hair:
If you partake of the thin feast,
    How shall we laymen fare?
Reject our poor oblation, then,
And feed your worshippers. Amen.

PISTHETAIROS:
    Let us propitiate the Feathery Gods.

                            [*Enter a* POET, *singing*

POET:
    Cloudcuckooland, my happy home,
        Sung by the Muses Nine—
PISTHETAIROS:
    How did this one get in?
                            —Who are you?
POET:
    Who am I? A honeythroated bard,
    a 'willing slave of the Muse', as Homer puts it.
PISTHETAIROS:
    A slave? With that haircut?
POET:
                            You misunderstand.
    I am a poet. All we poets are
    'willing slaves of the Muse', as Homer puts it.
PISTHETAIROS:
    That cloak of yours has seen service, willing or not.
    Speak, O Bard: What catastrophe brings you here?
POET:
    In honour of Cloudcuckooland, that great City,
    I have composed the following lyric items:
        a] a batch of cyclic verses
        b] a few simple virginations
        c] some odes in the manner of Simonidês.
PISTHETAIROS:
    God forbid. When did you start writing them?

POET:

Long have I meditated on this City, long.

PISTHETAIROS:

Impossible. Why, only a minute ago
I was dedicating the place, giving it a name!

POET:

Ah, swift is the speech of the Muses,
Yea, swifter than swivelling steeds!

Mark me, man:

Thou Author of Aitna, Father,
At whose dire doom do foregather
All the high hierarchs—
Och! wad
Thy nod
Some giftie gi'e me:
I don't care what, just a token of your regard.

PISTHETAIROS:

He'll be around all day if we don't pay him off.
Here, you in the new overcoat:
take it off and give it to this lyric has-been.

—Put it on. You look as though you were catching cold.

POET:

Thy, Sir, high gratuity
Compels gratitudinity.
Brace yourself. I will now address you
in the vein of Pindar.

PISTHETAIROS:

It's a vein I can do without.

POET:

Ill fares the man amid the Skythian spears,
Beset by Nomads, who no 'pparel wears.
Nil is his number, nameless is his name,
Who hath no garment to refúge his shame.
Do you get me?

PISTHETAIROS:

I get the idea that you want some underwear.
—Take that off too, man, and let him have it.

He's a poet, after all.

              —There you are. Get out!

POET:

    Out, out, poor poet!

       Sing, O Muse in gold enthroned,
          This chilly City!
       Naked in many a snowbank have I moaned,
          Which seems a pity.
            But still I'll chant, where'er I roam,
            Cloudcuckooland my happy home.
   Alalai!

                                  [*Exit* POET

PISTHETAIROS:

    God, what a nuisance! I hope I never meet
    another one like that. How did he hear so soon
    about our City? Well . . .

                    —You, there:
    Go around again with the holy water.

                 [*Enter a* TRAVELLING PROPHET
DEARLY BELOVED: WE GATHER TOGETHER
    IN—

PROPHET:

          Silence!
    Begin not the sacrifice of the goat!

PISTHETAIROS:

    Who says so?

PROPHET:

               I; an Expounder of Oracles.

PISTHETAIROS:

    Expounders be damned!

PROPHET:

                   Tut. We mustn't blaspheme.
    I come to reveal an oracle of Bakis
    that bears directly on Cloudcuckooland.

PISTHETAIROS:

    In God's name, why did you wait to reveal it
    until I'd gone and founded Cloudcuckooland?

PROPHET:

    God moves in a mysterious way.

PISTHETAIROS:

He does.

Well, since you're here, let's have your revelation.

PROPHET:

WHAT TIME WOLVES AND WHITE CROWS
CONFECT BUNGALOWS
'TWIXT SIKYON AND KORINTH—

PISTHETAIROS:

It's a lie! I never had any dealings with Korinth.

PROPHET:

That is Bakis' way of referring to the Air.

Now listen:

TO PANDORA THIS DAY
A WHITE RAM THOU MUST SLAY,
AND TO WHOSO DIVINES ME THOU SHALT
NOT REFUSE
A WARM WINTER SUIT AND A PAIR OF NEW
SHOES.

PISTHETAIROS:

Does it say shoes?

PROPHET:

Look in the book.
PLUS A GENEROUS CUP,
PLUS A SLICE OFF THE TOP—

PISTHETAIROS:

A slice off the top, hey?

PROPHET:

Look in the book.
AND IF, GODLY INFANT, THOU DOST AS I SAY,
A HEAV'N-KISSING EAGLE SHALT THOU BE
TODAY,
NOT SO MUCH AS A TITTYMOUSE IF THOU
SAY'ST NAY.

PISTHETAIROS:

Is that there too?

PROPHET:

Look in the book.

PISTHETAIROS:

Strange. It's so unlike the oracle
I took down from Apollo's dictation.

PROPHET:

What was that one?

PISTHETAIROS:
> BUT IF BY ILL HAP A CHEAP ORACLE-MONGER
> DISTURBETH THE SERVICE WITH LIES BORN
>   OF HUNGER,
> THOU SHALT BASH IN HIS RIBS—

PROPHET:
> I don't believe it says that.

PISTHETAIROS:
Look in the book.
> AS FOR HEAV'N-KISSING EAGLES AND ARSE-
>   KISSING SEERS,
> TO HELL WITH THEM ALL. END OF MESSAGE.
> [LOUD CHEERS]

PROPHET:
Is that there too?

PISTHETAIROS:
> Look in the book.
> *[Suddenly losing patience*
Damn you, get out of here!
> *[Strikes him with his staff*

PROPHET:
> Ouch! I'll go! Ouch!
> *[Exit* PROPHET

PISTHETAIROS [*calling after him*]:
Peddle your damned oracles somewhere else!

> *[Enter* METON, *wearing a saffron gown em-*
> *broidered with geometrical figures*

METON:
My aim in coming here—

PISTHETAIROS:
> Another headache!
What's your project? And, above all,
why that absurd costume?

METON:
> I have come
to subdivide the air into square acres.

PISTHETAIROS:
May I ask who you are?

METON:
> You may. My name is Metôn.

The word's a commonplace in Greece and Kolonos.
PISTHETAIROS:
What's that you've got with you?
METON:

An aerial straight-edge.
Observe:
The conformation of the air, considered as
a total entity, is that of a conical damper.
Very well. At the apex of this cone we apply
the ruler, bracketing in the dividers to allow
for the congruent curve. Q.E.D.
PISTHETAIROS:

Q.E.D.?

METON:
We calculate the declination by cathexis
according to the sine. Thus we square the circle.
In the centre we postulate a forum, the focus
of convergent streets that, stelliform,
subtend the radii extended from this point.
Q.E.D.
PISTHETAIROS:
Q.E.D.! The man's a Thalês!
Metôn.
METON:
Yes?
PISTHETAIROS:
I admire you. I really do.
Take my advice and subdivide somewhere else.
METON:
Why? Is it dangerous here?
PISTHETAIROS:
Yes, here and in Sparta.
You know how they're treating aliens these days:
nasty demonstrations in the streets.
METON:
You apprehend
seditious manifestations in Cloudcuckooland?
PISTHETAIROS:
God forbid.
METON.
Then what?

PISTHETAIROS:

Well, we've passed a law
that charlatans shall be whipped in the public square.

METON:

Oh. Then I'd better be going.

PISTHETAIROS:

You're almost too late.
Here's a sample, God help you!

[Knocks him down

METON:

My head! My head!

PISTHETAIROS:

I warned you. On your way, and be quick about it!

[Exit METON; enter an INSPECTOR, elegant in full
uniform, carrying two urns for balloting

INSPECTOR:

Summon the Consuls.

PISTHETAIROS:

Who's this Sardanápalos?

INSPECTOR:

My good man, I am a legally designated
Inspector, empowered to investigate
the civic status of Cloudcuckooland.

PISTHETAIROS:

Your warrant?

INSPECTOR:

This illegible document
endorsed by Teleas.

PISTHETAIROS:

My dear Inspector,
it seems a pity to waste your valuable time.
Suppose you collect your pay and go right home?

INSPECTOR:

A first-rate idea! As a matter of fact,
I ought not to have left Athens at all.
There are certain sensitive foreign affairs—you know?—
that Pharnakês leaves to me.

PISTHETAIROS:

Is that so?

Here's your pay.

[Slaps his face

INSPECTOR:

Sir, I demand the meaning of this.

PISTHETAIROS:

It's a sensitive foreign affair.

INSPECTOR:

I make formal protest
that you have assaulted and battered an Inspector.

PISTHETAIROS:

Take your voting-jugs and get out of my sight!
It's an outrage:
Inspectors before there's a City to inspect!

[The INSPECTOR *withdraws, but hides behind one
of the Acolytes; enter a* DECREE-VENDOR, *who begins to read from a scroll*

DECREE-VENDOR:

'AND IF ANY CLOUDCUCKOOLANDER WHATSO-
EVER SHALL CAUSE INJURY OR DISTRESS TO
ANY ATHENIAN CITIZEN WHATSOEVER—'

PISTHETAIROS:

Another one! A walking law-book this time.

DECREE-VENDOR:

Your Honour, I am a dealer in the latest decrees.
Satisfaction guaranteed.

PISTHETAIROS:

As for example?

DECREE-VENDOR:

'VOTED: THAT FROM THE DATE HEREINUNDER
SUBSCRIBED ALL WEIGHTS MEASURES AND
STATUTES WHATSOEVER OF CLOUDCUCKOO-
LAND SHALL BE IDENTICAL WITH THE SAME
OBTAINING IN OLOPHYXOS.'

PISTHETAIROS:

That ought to fix us.

—Look here, you!

DECREE-VENDOR:

What's the matter with you? Something you ate?

PISTHETAIROS:

Go back where you came from with your silly laws,
or you'll get some rough and ready legislation.

[*Strikes him; exit* DECREE-VENDOR *hurriedly; the* INSPECTOR *reappears.*

INSPECTOR:

I charge Pisthetairos with felonious assault,
returnable April Session.

PISTHETAIROS:

How did *you* get back?
[*The* DECREE-VENDOR *re-enters.*

DECREE-VENDOR:

'AND IF ANY MAN SHALL SCUTTLE A MAGIS-
TRATE AFTER THE NAME OF SAME HAS BEEN
POSTED ON THE PILLAR IN ACCORDANCE
WITH THE LAW—'

PISTHETAIROS:

Holy God! You too?

[*Drives him away with blows*

INSPECTOR:

I'll have your license! This will cost you a cool thousand!

PISTHETAIROS:

I'll smash those jugs of yours in a thousand pieces!

INSPECTOR:

Do you remember the evening you polluted the pillar?

PISTHETAIROS:

Go pollute yourself!
—Grab him! That's it!

[INSPECTOR *escapes.*

Let's hope that's the end of him.
—Gentlemen:

If we're going to sacrifice our goat at all,
I'm afraid we'll have to do the job inside.

[*Exeunt; manet* CHORUS

🎖 PARÁBASIS II

[*The* CHORUS *again addresses itself to the audience.*

CHORUS:

We are Lords of Earth and of all upon it,   [ODE
Marking all, all-knowing, in tireless session

Guiding, weighing, judging the varied drama.
  Come and adore us!

Guardians of young fruit in the open orchards,
Our swift beaks transfix the insect marauder,
And he falls, struck down by the feath'ry ictus
  Whirring from heaven.

KORYPHAIOS:

[EPIRRHEMA

You see CRIMINAL WANTED notices everywhere:
'Whoever kills Diágoras the Mêlian',
So much reward; 'Whoever kills
'A dead tyrant or so,' still more
Reward. Well, then, I proclaim:
'Whoever kills Philókratês the Birdseller,
'One talent, cash; whoever brings him in
'Alive, four talents'—twice as much
As for poor old Diágoras. This Philókratês
Hangs bullfinches on hooks in his shop
And sells them at cut rates; he inflates thrushes
With air pumps and exposes their abused puffy
Bodies for sale; he mutilates blackbirds; he
Stuffs live pigeons into nets and makes them
Act as decoys. That's Philókratês for you!
                                   —And
If any members of this audience
Maintain a bird in a gilded cage at home,
We beg you let it go. Refuse, and you'll see
How quickly the Birds will make decoys of you!

CHORUS:

Joy of birds! In summer the long thick sunlight   [ANTODE
When the locust drones in the trance of noontime:
Mad with sun we shout, and the forest dances
  Heavy with music.

Wintertime is sun on the tropic headlands
Where the Nymphs play counterpoint to our singing;
Spring is myrtle, pang of the pink sweet prickling
  Buds of the Graces.

KORYPHAIOS:

Now for a word or two, Judges, about   [ANTEPIRRHEMA
This Competition. If you give us the Prize,
We'll pay you better for it than Prince Paris
Was paid by the Goddess. First of all,
The Owls of Laureion will never desert you:
They'll be everywhere in your houses, nesting
In your purses, maniacally producing
Miniature Owls. Judges are fond of Owls.
More than that, we'll add new wings
To your houses: you'll dream that you dwell
In marble halls, and you'll be right.
                                        If your jobs
Are slow pay, if your fingers begin to itch,
We'll send you a little confidential Hawk
To perch on your wrist. For state dinners you can have
The loan of a bird-crop to solve capacity problems.
But if we lose the Prize,
Take portable canopies with you on your strolls,
Or your new white robes will suffer
Avine criticism dropping from the skies.

🏵 SCENE

                    [*Re-enter* PISTHETAIROS *with his attendants*

PISTHETAIROS:

The omens are favourable, I'm glad to say.
Strange that we've had no news
about the wall.
                —But here comes a messenger now,
puffing like an Olympic sprinter.
                            [*Enter* FIRST MESSENGER, *wildly*

MESSENGER:

Where is he? Where is he? Where is he?

PISTHETAIROS:

                                        Where is who?

MESSENGER:

The Chief. Pisthetairos.

PISTHETAIROS:

                    Here.

MESSENGER:

Great news! Great news!
Your Wall is finished!

PISTHETAIROS:

That *is* great news.

MESSENGER:

Oh how
shall I describe the splendour of that Wall,
the apocalyptic hugeness? Take two chariots,
hitch four fat Wooden Horses to each one,
let Theogenês and old Proxenidês
of Belchertown meet head-on—, they'd pass each other
without a scratch. It's that big.

PISTHETAIROS:

Holy Heraklês!

MESSENGER:

And tall? Look, I measured it myself:
it stands six hundred feet!

PISTHETAIROS:

Merciful Poseidon!
What workmen could build a wall as high as that?

MESSENGER:

Birds, only birds. Not a single Egyptian
hodcarrier or stonemason or carpenter
in the gang; birds did it all, and my eyes
are popping yet.
Imagine thirty thousand Cranes
from Libya, each one with a belly full of stones
for the Rails to shape up with their beaks; ten
thousand Storks, at least,
all of them making bricks with clay and water
flown up by Curlews from the earth below.

PISTHETAIROS:

Mortar?

MESSENGER:

Herons with hods.

PISTHETAIROS:

How did they manage it?

MESSENGER:

That was a triumph of technology!
The Geese shovelled it up with their big feet.

PISTHETAIROS:

Ah feet, to what use can ye not be put!

MESSENGER:

Why, good Lord! There were Ducks to set the bricks,
and flights of little apprentice Swallows
with trowel tails for the mortar in their bills.

PISTHETAIROS:

Who wants hired labour after this?
—But the joists and beams?

MESSENGER:

All handled by birds.

When the Woodpeckers went to work on those portals
it sounded like a shipyard!

—So there's your Wall,
complete with gates and locks, watchfires burning,
patrols circling, the guard changed every hour.

But I must wash off this long trek of mine.
You'll know what to do next.

[*Exit* FIRST MESSENGER

KORYPHAIOS:

Surprises you, hey? That quick job on your Wall?

PISTHETAIROS:

Surprises me? Why, it's a lie come true!
But here's another non-stop messenger,
and this one looks like trouble.

[*Enter* SECOND MESSENGER: *tragic manner*

MESSENGER:

Alas! Alas! Alas!

PISTHETAIROS:

What's the matter with *you*?

MESSENGER:

Confusion now hath made his masterpiece!
One of the gods, I do not know his name,
has invaded our air and slipped through the gate
right under the beaks of the Jackdaws on day duty.

PISTHETAIROS:

Murther and treason!

—What god did you say?

MESSENGER:

Identity not established. But he has wings,

we know that.

PISTHETAIROS:

Alert the Air Cadets!

MESSENGER:

Cadets! We've alerted everything we have.
Ten thousand mounted Arrowhawks,
to say nothing of claw-to-claw raiders
of every calibre: Kestrels, Buzzards,
Kites, Vultures, Nighthawks, Eagles—
every mortal inch of air
they've ploughed up with their wings, looking for that
    god.
He won't get away,
he's somewhere around here; I feel it in my feathers.

PISTHETAIROS:

Slings and arrows, slings and arrows! All of you,
here: get shooting, quick! Give me my bow!

CHORUS:

War to the end,   [STROPHE
Inexpressible war,
God against Bird!
Arm to defend
Our fathers' Air!
Olympos' host
Must not get past
Our border guard!

KORYPHAIOS:

Each one of you keep watch on every side.
I hear, or seem to hear, an ominous clack
of wings, as though some Deity were descending.

> [*The goddess* IRIS *appears from above, suspended
> in the* machina; *she has broad static wings and
> wears a large rainbow around her head and
> shoulders.*

PISTHETAIROS:

Heave to! Let go halyards! Lower the flaps! Easy all!

> [*The* machina *stops with a violent jerk.*

Who are you? Where are you bound? What's your home
    port?

IRIS [*tragic tone*]:
I come to you from the Olympian gods.
PISTHETAIROS:
Your name? Are you sea-going, or a flying
hat-rack?
IRIS:
Fleet Iris am I.
PISTHETAIROS:
Deep sea or
inland waters?
IRIS:
What *are* you talking about?
PISTHETAIROS:
Some of you birds had better get on the ball
and board this crate.
IRIS:
Board me? I never
heard such a thing!
PISTHETAIROS:
Well, you heard it now.
We'll give you something to squawk about.
IRIS:
Well, really!
PISTHETAIROS:
All right, all right. What gate did you come through?
IRIS:
How should I know? Gates mean nothing to me.
PISTHETAIROS:
Oh. So that's the way it is.
—Well, then,
did you report to the Chief Jackdaw? Say something!
Did you get your passport countersigned by the Storks?
You did not?
IRIS:
Are you in your right mind?
PISTIIETAIROS:
Not a single
bird there punched your card for you?
IRIS:
No, or punched
anything else for me, you poor idiot.

PISTHETAIROS:

So

you're flying over foreign territory
without any papers.

IRIS:

How else should gods fly?

PISTHETAIROS:

Good God, how should I know?

But they can't do it here!
I don't care if you're a whole fleet of Irises;
you've committed a violation, and the penalty
for that is death.

IRIS:

Mortal, I am immortal.

PISTHETAIROS:

Death just the same!

Things have come to a pretty pass
if we set up a system of border controls, only to have
you gods flying back and forth whenever you feel like it.
But tell me:
What was the destination you had in mind?

IRIS:

Destination? I am about my Father's business.
He has commanded me to remind mankind
that they must sacrifice to the eternal gods,
smiting the hornèd beasts upon their altars
and filling their streets with the smoke of immolation.

PISTHETAIROS:

What do you mean? Sacrifice to what gods?

IRIS:

Why, to us gods in Heaven.

PISTHETAIROS:

So you are gods too?

IRIS:

Can you think of others?

PISTHETAIROS:

I am thinking of the Birds.
So far as mankind is concerned, Birds are now gods.
It's they must have sacrifices—not God, by God!

IRIS:

Alas, deluded worm, think not to stir

the guts of wrath eterne: else heavenly Justice,
with Zeus's pitchfork arm'd, drops from on high
to man's undoing and leaves not a rack
behind. Fried and consumèd shalt thou be,
as i' th' Euripidean Tragedy!

PISTHETAIROS:
Madam, wipe the foam from your mouth,
and do stop quivering so. Am I a slave,
some Lydian or Phrygian slave, that you imagine
you scare me with talk of this kind?

                                   As for Zeus:
you can inform your Zeus
that if he gets in my way I'll burn him out,
yea, I will blast him in Amphíon's hall
with eagles lightningbeak'd that heed my call.
Notify him furthermore
that I command a squadron of six hundred
sky-scaling porphyrion birds in panther skin.
That will hold him, I think: a single Porphyrion once
kept him busy enough.

                       —And if *you* get in my way,
Iris or no Iris, messenger or whatever you are,
I'll just hoist up your legs and get in between:
then, by God, you can tell your wondering friends
how you met an old battleship with a triple prow!

IRIS:
No gentleman would address a lady so.

PISTHETAIROS:
On your way! Scat!

IRIS:
                        I shall certainly tell my Father.

PISTHETAIROS:
Next time, consume someone your own age!

                        [*Exit* IRIS *in the* machina

CHORUS:
                    My word is sure: [ANTISTROPHE
                    Children of Zeus,
                    No entrance here!
                    And it shall stand.
                    Let no man dare

Cajole the skies
With ritual brand
Or sacrifice.

PISTHETAIROS:

Speaking of mankind, I am worried about our herald.
It's strange that his commission should keep him so long.

[*Enter a* HERALD, *in haste*

HERALD:

O Pisthetairos! O Blessedest! O Sagaciousest!
O Superlativest! O Sagaciousest! O Perspicaciousest!
O Thrice Blessedest! O And-so-forth!

PISTHETAIROS:

Did you speak?

HERALD:

I crown you with this golden crown, the gift
of your admiring public.

PISTHETAIROS:

I thank you.
Tell me: Why does mankind admire me?

HERALD:

O Pisthetairos, mighty father of
Cloudcuckooland the Beautiful, how slight
your skill in understanding human thought
if you must ask that question!

What is man?
Or, rather, what was man before your triumph?
An abject Spartomaniac—long hair,
infrequent baths, bad honest food, knobbly
accessories, the Sokratês pose.

What is man now?
Mad about birds! Birds, birds, from the moment
they get out of nest in the morning: eggs and birdseed
for breakfast, and then bird business,
reeding and piping till clucking-off time.
They even affect bird names:
'Partridge' is any man gone in one leg;
Menippos is 'Swallow'; Opûntios,
'Monocle de Mon Oncle'; Philoklês
is 'Lark'; Theogenês, 'Gypsy Goose'; Lykûrgos,
'Ibis'; Chairephôn, 'Bats'; Syrakosios, 'Jaybird';

and Meidias, of course, is called 'Goon Quail'—
one look at that bashed-in face of his
will tell you why.
                         As for song-writing,
you can't so much as buy a hearing unless
you stuff your lyrics with assorted wild ducks
and swallows, or doves, or geese, or maybe
a few last feathers from a cast-off wing.

That's what it's like down there. And mark my words:
you'll soon be getting visitors by the thousands,
all sorts of men begging to be fitted out
with wings and beaks and claws. Take my advice
and lay in a pile of pinions.

PISTHETAIROS:
                         Heavens, yes!
I can see we'll be busy.
                         —Quick, you:
                                   [*To a* SERVANT
fill every last basket you can find with wings
and tell Manês to bring them out to me here.
I want to be prepared for these gentlemen.

CHORUS:
          My City is Cloudcuckooland,   [STROPHE
            And men of every nation
          Confer on us, I understand,
            Ecstatic approbation.

PISTHETAIROS:
          And surplus population.

CHORUS:
          What wonder though it should be so?
            Here Love and Wisdom dwell,
          And through the streets the Graces go,
            And Peace contrives her spell.

PISTHETAIROS:
          The servant problem's hell!

CHORUS:

[ANTISTROPHE

Manês, awake! New wings, new beaks!
Surely there never was
A slower slave. Your master speaks!
The precious moments pass!

[*Enter* MANES *emptyhanded*

PISTHETAIROS:
This Manês is an ass.

[*Exit* MANES

CHORUS:

Wings make the man; let each man wear
The crest that suits his bent:
Musician, merchant, privateer,
Cleric, or laic gent,

[*Re-enter* MANES *as before*

PISTHETAIROS:
Or slave of snail descent.

Manês, I swear by All Hawks, I'll haul you
hairless if you don't get busy! Come on; service!
[*General confusion.* MANES *and other servants ap-
pear and reappear carrying wings of all shapes
and sizes. These are arranged on a bench.*
PARRICIDE [*within, singing*]:
'Ah that the eagle's eager wings were mine,
To gyre above the waste of bloomless brine!'
PISTHETAIROS:
That messenger seems to have been right.
Here comes somebody singing about eagles.

[*Enter a young* PARRICIDE
PARRICIDE:
Here we are!
I vow, there's nothing like flying.
—Sir,
I'm mad about birds, I'm
always up in the air. More than that,

I apply for citizenship under your laws.

PISTHETAIROS:

What laws? We Birds have many laws.

PARRICIDE:

All of them; especially that glorious statute
that gives Birds the right to strangle their own fathers.

PISTHETAIROS:

We *do* consider it a sign of manliness
when a chick stands up to his father and faces him down.

PARRICIDE:

Exactly my own motive in emigrating:
I propose to throttle the old man for his property.

PISTHETAIROS:

At the same time we have an ancient decree
(you'll find it in the Book of Storks) that says:
STORKLINGS CARED FOR BY THE STORK THEIR
    SIRE
AND BY HIM TAUGHT TO FLY SHALL IN THEIR
    TURN
CARE FOR THE STORK THEIR SIRE IN HIS OLD
    AGE.

PARRICIDE:

What was the use of my coming all this distance
if I've got to support my father after all?

PISTHETAIROS:

Come, it's not so bad.
You obviously mean well, and we'll make
a decent orphan bird of you yet, young man.
But first
permit me to recite a useful thought
        'that was given me
        at my mother's knee':
Sons, don't beat your fathers. It's unkind.

> [*During the following speech* PISTHETAIROS *arms
> the* PARRICIDE *with a toy sword, shield, and hel-
> met.*

Stick out your hand: receive this bright cock-spur.
Your other hand: receive this shining wing.
Stick out your neck: receive this crested helm.
Now you're in the Army, cock.
Keep awake on guard duty, live on your pay, and let

your father alone. If you feel like fighting,
take a trip to Thrace: there's always a war on there.
PARRICIDE:
You're right. I'll do it, by God!

                                          [*Exit*

PISTHETAIROS:

                      By God, you'd better!

                    [*Enter the dithyrambic poet* KINESIAS
KINESIAS [*singing*]:
    'Lifted aloft on wings of song,
        Towards high Olympos winging—'
PISTHETAIROS:
This man needs wings if ever a poet did!
KINESIAS [*singing*]:
    'Pure in mind, in body strong,
        Ever of thee, love, singing—'
PISTHETAIROS:
Kinêsias, as I live. Old limpety-lop,
why did your limping feet bring you up here?
KINESIAS [*singing*]:
    'I aim, nor shall my purpose fail,
        To be a Neo-Nightingale.'
PISTHETAIROS:
Damn your aim. I suppose you can talk sense?
KINESIAS:
Oh, ay. Enwingèd, man, by thee I'd be,
that from the gravid clouds I may charm down
a meed of music for my sacred soul,
    'Batter'd by ev'ry wind that blows,
    And snow'd upon by snowing snows.'
PISTHETAIROS:
This meed of music: you find it in the clouds?
KINESIAS:
Yea, i' the clouds my Muse doth perch and preen.
Wottest thou not that th' dithyrambic gene
burns in the air, most dark, and bright with gloom?
Plastic with pinions, too.
                          I'll give you an example.
PISTHETAIROS:
Never mind.

KINESIAS:
>No trouble at all. For instance,
here's a description of the upper air:
>*Pteroid shapes*
>*Thro' th' aether traipse,*
>*Longneck'd wrynecks—*

PISTHETAIROS:
Hard alee!

KINESIAS:
>*Zigging upon the zagging blast,*
>*Free in the vast anemoplast—*

PISTHETAIROS:
By God, I'll free your blast!

KINESIAS:
>*Free to fly at the wind's behest,*
>*Now north, now south, now east, now west:*
>*Furrowing with my feather'd feet*
>*Those fields where eagles eagles meet,*
>*Praying a blessing on thy name,*
>*Old Architect, for this high game.*

PISTHETAIROS:
Stop and put on your wings, damn it, your wings!
>*[A brief scuffle about the stage*

KINESIAS:
And is it thus thoudst serve a modern poet?
A poet to whom so many tribes lay claim?

PISTHETAIROS:
Let Leotrophidês claim you to train his squabs!

KINESIAS:
Thou mockest me, proud Patriarch. Farewell.
These wings I'll flap, high water come or hell.
>*[Exit* KINESIAS. *Enter an* INFORMER, *singing, un-
>noticed at first in the confusion of the poet's
>departure*

INFORMER:
>'What birds are these whose patchwork dress
>Reveals that they are penniless?
>O Swallow, Swallow, tell me.'

PISTHETAIROS [*aside*]:
That Kinêsias was a rough customer.
>—And, by God,
here comes another one!

INFORMER:
 'O Swallow, Swallow, tell me.'
I repeat.

PISTHETAIROS:
  He seems to be singing about his coat.
Can't blame him: it would take more than one swallow
to make that bearable.

INFORMER:
    A little service, please!
Who's distributing wings here?

PISTHETAIROS:
     Just step this way.
Now then: what do you want?

INFORMER:
     Wings, man, wings.
You deaf?

PISTHETAIROS:
  I suppose you're in a hurry
to get to a clothier's.

INFORMER:
    Wrong. Plumb wrong.
I am a process-server for the Islands.
Also an Informer.

PISTHETAIROS:
   Thanks for the information.

INFORMER:
Also a professional accuser. So I need some wings.
Great thing for this Island Circuit. Big business.

PISTHETAIROS:
A pair of wings will make your business bigger?

INFORMER:
Couldn't. But the pirates, you know: always hanging
  around.
With wings I could fly right over them like a crane,
belly full of lawsuits for ballast.

PISTHETAIROS:
    Of course you could.
Tell me: are you good at spying on aliens?

INFORMER:
Well, a man's got to live. I never learned how to work.

PISTHETAIROS:
Aren't there enough honest jobs in the world,
that a healthy man like you
must pick up money selling false information?

INFORMER:
Wings I came for, not sermons.

PISTHETAIROS:
I just gave you wings.

INFORMER:
The devil you did. All you've done is talk.

PISTHETAIROS:
Haven't you ever heard of 'wingèd words'?

INFORMER:
Wingèd words?

PISTHETAIROS:
Yes, or wingèd actions?
Say you go into a barber's. Well, they're all
sitting around there, swapping lies
about their sons and grandsons. 'I swear to God,'
one of them says,
'I don't know what to make of that boy of mine.
'The horses have got him. Can't keep his feet on the
     ground.'
Another one says, 'That's nothing.
'Mine wants to take a flier at writing plays.
'The tragic bug's bitten him.'

INFORMER:
So you think
words can make wings?

PISTHETAIROS:
That's it exactly.
Words heighten concepts; words raise a man
out of himself. You came to me for wings:
all right, you can have them; and, what's more,
I'll throw in a word or two of good advice
about getting a job that you won't have to blush for.

INFORMER:
No good. No good at all.

PISTHETAIROS:
Why not?

INFORMER:
  Family pride. Can't let the old name down.
  There's been Informers in our family
  since I don't know when.
                              —But come:
  give me a couple of good swift wings, I don't care
  what model, and I'll get back,
  denounce a few aliens, get them indicted here,
  and then I'm off.
PISTHETAIROS:
                        You mean you'll have these men
  indicted before they get a chance to appear?
INFORMER:
  You said it.
PISTHETAIROS:
                        And while they're on their way to court
  you'll swoop down on the Islands and grab their goods?
INFORMER:
  You get the idea. I'm busy as a top.
PISTHETAIROS:
                        [Takes a long whiplash from the bench
  Top? Here's something to make tops spin:
  first-class goods from Korkyra.
INFORMER:
                              Put it away!
PISTHETAIROS:
  Call it a pair of wings. By God, it'll send *you*
  into a nose-dive!
                                      [*Lashes him*
INFORMER:
                    Stop it! Police! Stop it!
                              [*Exit* INFORMER
PISTHETAIROS:
  All of a flap, hey? Can't wait around? Too bad!
  You sneaking patriot,
  this time you pay the court costs!
                              [*To his attendants*
                    Come,
  let's gather up these wings and go inside.
          [*Exit, followed by attendants carrying the bench,
          wings, and the rest of the paraphernalia*

🎴 CHORIKON: CHORAL INTERLUDE

CHORUS:

Numberless are the world's wonders, and we   [STROPHE
Have roosted on most of them. In wicked Thrace
There grows the remarkable Kleonymos tree,
Immense, heart-rotted, that in summer yields
Informative fruit; but in winter time its grace
Forsakes it, and its boughs shed unused shields.

And we have seen a region of the dead   [ANTISTROPHE
Where men with Heroes dine before nightfall,
But where the reveller walks home in dread
Lest from the shades a new Orestês come,
Accost him at the turning of the wall,
Strip him, beat him, and leave him bare and numb.

🎴 SCENE

> [*Enter* PROMETHEUS, *muffled from head to foot
> in a red and yellow cloak and carrying a large
> black open umbrella*

PROMETHEUS:

I hope to God Zeus can't see me!
>   —Pisthetairos!

Where's Pisthetairos?
>   [*Re-enter* PISTHETAIROS

PISTHETAIROS:
>   What's going on here?

Who are you in the blankets?

PROMETHEUS:
>   Look:

is any god following me?

PISTHETAIROS:
>   God? No.

Who are you?

PROMETHEUS:
>   Can you give me the correct time?

PISTHETAIROS:
  Noon. Maybe a little later. But who
  are you?
PROMETHEUS:
            Noon, you said?
PISTHETAIROS:
                  Oh, for God's sake!
PROMETHEUS:
  What's the weather like?
PISTHETAIROS:
                  Hey?
PROMETHEUS:
                  I said, 'What's
  the weather like?'
PISTHETAIROS:
            Go to hell!
PROMETHEUS:
                  Splendid. I'll just
  take off these cerements.
            [*Throws off the cloak and stands revealed in
            scarlet tights*
PISTHETAIROS:
                  Well, I'll be damned! Prometheus!
PROMETHEUS:
  Sh, sh, keep your voice down!
PISTHETAIROS:
                  What's the matter?
PROMETHEUS:
  Just don't mention my name. If Zeus finds me here
  he'll scalp me. You don't know the half of it.
  I'll tell you; only,
  please hold this umbrella over my head
  so the gods can't look down and see me from up there.
PISTHETAIROS:
  The same old Prometheus! All right; get under,
  and begin to talk.
PROMETHEUS:
  Listen.
PISTHETAIROS:
        I am.
PROMETHEUS:
        Zeus is through.

PISTHETAIROS:

Since when?

PROMETHEUS:

Since you organized Cloudcukooland.
There's not been so much as a sniff of sacred smoke
coming up to us from a single human altar.
I swear, we're hungrier
than a Thesmophoria fast-day; and, what's worse,
the damnedest lot of starving yowling gods
from the back country are talking about revolt
if Zeus doesn't manage to get a decent consignment
of sacrificial cuts to keep us going.

PISTHETAIROS:

Do you mean to tell me the Barbarians
have gods of their own?

PROMETHEUS:

What about Exekestidês?
Doesn't he have to pray to something?

PISTHETAIROS:

I see.
But these godforsaken gods: what are they called?

PROMETHEUS:

Triballians.

PISTHETAIROS:

Tribal totems.

PROMETHEUS:

I suppose so.
—But this is what I have come down to tell you:
Zeus and these Triballians
are sending a delegation to look into
what's going on here. Take my advice:
laugh at every offer they make to you
until they swear to restore the Birds to power
and give you Basileia for a wife.

PISTHETAIROS:

Basileia? Who is this Basileia?

PROMETHEUS:

She's the prettiest girl you ever saw:
manages Zeus, takes care of his thunderbolts
and all the rest of his weapons—sagacity,
legislation, rearmament, ideology, ultimatums.

revenue officers, jurymen—

PISTHETAIROS:

She does all that?

PROMETHEUS:

That's only an outline. When you get Basileia,
you've got everything.

I thought I ought to tell you:
I have a certain stake in humanity.

PISTHETAIROS:

A well-broiled one, thanks to your foresightedness.

PROMETHEUS:

And I hate the gods.

PISTHETAIROS:

And the gods hate you.

PROMETHEUS:

Yes. I'm a regular Timôn.

—But it's late.
I must be getting back.

Give me my umbrella:
Zeus will think I'm a Virgin of the Escort.

PISTHETAIROS:

Take this footstool with you; it will make a better effect.

[*Exeunt*

🎴 CHORIKON: CHORAL INTERLUDE

CHORUS:

There is a mystic river   [STROPHE
In the land of the Shadowfeet
Where Sokratês the Bathless calls
The souls of men to meet.

There Chickenheart Peisandros
Made sacrifice one day
To conjure up his own dim soul
And hear what it would say.

Odysseus-like he cut the throat
Of a kind of camel-cat;

But all he raised was the squeaking ghost
Of Chairephôn the Bat.

🦢 SCENE

> [*Enter the Ambassadors from Olympos:* POSEIDON,
> HERAKLES, *and a* TRIBALLIAN GOD. *The first wears
> a sea-weed crown, a cloak embroidered with
> large horse-heads, and carries a trident and a
> rigid stuffed fish; the second wears a lion skin
> and carries a club; the third, blackface, wears a
> stovepipe hat and is desperately entangled in a
> multicoloured cloak.*

POSEIDON:
So this is Cloudcuckooland. Very well,
let us proceed to act like a Delegation.
> [*To the* TRIBALLIAN
You, there,
what are you up to now? Don't you know better
than to drape your cloak on the left side? Look,
you celestial rustic, it ought to hang on the right,
gracefully, like this. Do you want these people
to take you for Laispodias? Hold still,
can't you? There!
Democracy, what sins are committed in thy name!
Damn it, of all the barbarous gods I've met
you're the barbarousest.
> —What's your plan, Heraklês?

HERAKLES:
You heard what I said. Just cream the guy
what shut the gods out with this here Stone Curtain.

POSEIDON:
Yes, my good fellow; but we're supposed to discuss peace.

HERAKLES:
All the more reason for creaming him, I say.
> [*Enter* PISTHETAIROS *attended by various birds in
> kitchen costume; he elaborately disregards the
> Ambassadors.*

PISTHETAIROS:
> Quick, now,

let's have the cheesegrater. Where's the horseradish?
Grate that cheese, somebody. Keep the fire hot.

POSEIDON:

In the name of the Divine Authority,
three gods greet thee, O Man.

PISTHETAIROS:

> The horseradish.

HERAKLES:

Say, Mac, what kind of a roast is that?

PISTHETAIROS:

Bird roast. Subjects condemned for subversion
of the Authority of the Birds.

HERAKLES:

> And you use

horseradish?

PISTHETAIROS:

> Why, it's Heraklês! Good

afternoon, Heraklês.

POSEIDON:

> The Divine Authority

empowers three gods to consider conciliation.

A COOK:

Oil's out. What do I do now?

HERAKLES:

> No oil?

Damn bad. You can't barbecue without oil.

POSEIDON:

Regarded disinterestedly, this war
subserves no aim of the Divine Authority.
Similarly, your Delegates should reflect
how much you have to gain from a friendly Olympos:
I instance only
fresh rain water for your swamps, and halcyon days.
Shall we initiate talks?

PISTHETAIROS:

> I don't see why.

In the first place, we were not the ones
who started hostilities. But let that pass.
As for peace, we are perfectly willing to agree
if the gods will meet our terms. We demand
restoration of our ancient sovereignty

and the return of the sceptre to the Birds.
Let Zeus accept that much, and I'll invite
all three of you to dinner.

HERAKLES:

I vote Yes.

POSEIDON:

You gastric monomaniac, would you vote away
your own Father's crown?

PISTHETAIROS:

That's a silly question.
Do you gods imagine that you will be losing power
by delegating the imperium of the skies?
Surely you know that all over the earth
men are hiding under clouds and breaking your laws
with impunity. Suppose you had the Birds
on your side: then if a man swore
by Zeus and the Crow, say, and broke his oath,
we'd simply have a Crow swoop down upon him
and peck out his right eye.

POSEIDON:

Good, by Myself!

HERAKLES:

I think so too.

PISTHETAIROS [to TRIBALLIAN]:

What do *you* say?

TRIBALLIAN:

Wockle.

HERAKLES:

The poor fish says Yes.

PISTHETAIROS:

And here's something else.
Suppose a man promises an offering
to some god or other, and maybe greed
gets the better of him, and he thinks: *Well,
the gods are used to waiting:*
we birds
will know how to handle him.

POSEIDON:

How? Instruct me.

PISTHETAIROS:

Well, say that man's

sitting in his office some day, counting his money,
or say he's in the tub enjoying a nice hot bath:
down comes one of the Kites when he isn't looking
and zooms off to Olympos with a couple of his sheep.

HERAKLES:

I say it again: give the Birds what they ask for.

POSEIDON:

What do *you* think?

PISTHETAIROS:

Speak, you divine Mistake.

TRIBALLIAN:

Treeballs beetee gnaw ouch, Glapp.

HERAKLES:

He says Yes.

POSEIDON:

If you say so. I suppose I must say so too.
Very well. Divine Authority cedes the Sceptre.

PISTHETAIROS:

Hold on! I nearly forgot.
The Birds are prepared to confirm Zeus' right to Hêra,
but in return
they insist upon my having Basileia.

POSEIDON:

I can see that you are not interested in peace.
Good-bye.

PISTHETAIROS:

It makes no difference to me.
—Now this gravy, cook: see that it's thick enough.

HERAKLES:

Hey, damn it, Admiral, hold on, what the hell?
Who wants to fight a war for a damn woman?

POSEIDON:

What else can we do?

HERAKLES:

Damn it, make peace!

POSEIDON:

Idiot, can't you see he's trying to ruin you?
And you walk right into the trap.
Think a moment: if Zeus
gives the Birds what they ask for, and then dies—
Where are you then? Where's your inheritance?

PISTHETAIROS:
   Heraklês, don't listen to the man.
   Every word he speaks is a delusion.

[Beckons him aside
   Step over here a minute.
                    —My poor fellow,
   that Ancient Mariner is just leading you on.
   You inherit from Zeus? You couldn't, not a penny.
   You, being a bastard—
HERAKLES:
                    Me, a bastard?
   Say, listen, you—
PISTHETAIROS:
                    Well, your mother
   was an alien, wasn't she? Besides, Athêna
   is heir apparent, and how could she be that
   if she had legitimate brothers?
HERAKLES:
                    What if the Boss
   says I'm his heir, bastard or no bastard?
PISTHETAIROS:
   Illegal. And suppose he does:
   Poseidon will be the first to contest the will,
   as the decedent's brother.
                    Here is the law,
   straight from Solôn:
   A BASTARD SHALL NOT INHERIT IF THERE BE
      LEGITIMATE ISSUE. IF THERE BE NO LEGITI-
      MATE ISSUE, THE PROPERTY SHALL PASS TO
      THE NEXT OF KIN.
HERAKLES:
   So I can't get nothing out of the Old Man's estate?
PISTHETAIROS:
   Nothing at all.
                    —For that matter,
   has your Father enrolled you yet?
HERAKLES:
                    No. I guess I know why.

PISTHETAIROS:
   Come, what's the use of snapping at empty wind?
   Join the Birds:

you'll live like a king and feed on pie in the sky.

> [*They return to the others.*

PISTHETAIROS:

About that dame we were beating our gums about:
I said, and I say it again: Give him what he wants.

PISTHETAIROS:

You, Poseidon?

POSEIDON:

> No.

PISTHETAIROS:

> Then the Triballian
must break the tie. Vote, heavenly Hayseed!

TRIBALLIAN:

Quiffing gamsel cockitty, gotta tweet tweet.

HERAKLES:

He says Yes.

POSEIDON:

> I doubt very much if he says Yes
or anything else that matters. But let it pass.

HERAKLES:

He's ready to pass her over, anyhow.

POSEIDON:

Have it your way, you two. Make your peace,
and I'll hold mine.

HERAKLES:

> These here top-level talks
are all over, and we say he gets the green light.
Come on, man, you got a date up in the sky
with Basileia and any other damn thing you want.

PISTHETAIROS:

It's a lucky thing that I had these roasts ready.
They'll do for the wedding.

HERAKLES:

> You birds run along:
I'll stick around here and keep an eye on the cook.

POSEIDON:

Can't you rise superior to food? You come with us.

PISTHETAIROS:

And somebody bring along my wedding clothes.

> [*Exeunt omnes; manet* CHORUS

🕮 CHORIKON: CHORAL INTERLUDE

CHORUS:

Phonéya is that far country   [ANTISTROPHE
Where the Englottogasters dwell:
They plough the fields there with their tongues
And sow and reap as well.

Oh blest Englottogasters!
And yet we need not roam
In search of tongues as versatile—
They twitch for us at home:

The tongue that tells for ready cash,
The slimy tongue that smiles,
The paid, applauded, patriot tongue
That guards us, and defiles.

🕮 ÉXODOS

[*Enter* THIRD MESSENGER

MESSENGER:

Thrice happy generation of Birds, O winged
with joy beyond words' contriving: receive
your great Prince in his palace of delight!
His glory burns: no star
flames brighter in the wheeling vault, no sun
has ever blazed so pure. He comes,
and beauty walks beside him crowned
with lightning from God's hand, his divine
Bride, veiled i' th' smoke of incense rising.
Your King, your Queen!
Sing them a song of the Nine Sisters' devising.

[*Re-enter* PISTHETAIROS, *splendidly gowned, with
newly gilded wings; he is accompanied by* BASI-
LEIA, *in cloth of gold, crowned, her face hidden
by a veil.*

CHORUS:

Back!

Make way there!

Circle them!

Dance!

Beat on the bright ground with quick feet
For the Prince of Luck, for his Bride—
Oh sweet! Oh fair!—
Dance, dance the marriage in the air.

KORYPHAIOS:

Dance in the sky,

joy in the sky!

Dance in the reign of the Birds,

dance in

The augury of his polity:
Dance Hymen

the wedding chorus

dance

CHORUS:

When heavenly Hêra was the bride   [STROPHE
Of Zeus in his high hall,
The Fatal Ladies danced and sang
This for their festival:
Round the royal pair we go:
Hymen O! The wedding O!

Erôs flicked his golden wings   [ANTISTROPHE
To be their charioteer,
And through the swaying skies their car
Darted in sweet career.
Round the royal pair we go:
Hymen O! The wedding O!

PISTHETAIROS:

For your songs, for your good wishes, thanks:
I am gratified, and I am sure
that I speak for my wife as well. I should be
even more gratified to hear you perform
two or three odes in honour of my triumph
over the dangerous thunderbolts of Zeus,
the difficult lightning.

CHORUS:

O fire lancing the black night,   [EPODE
  O rage of voices under ground,
Thunder, hurly of rain, bright
  Tempest of sound:
Sing, sing his audacity
  Who draws down from God's throne
God's Basileia, Sovereignty,
  And crowns her his own.
Round the royal pair we go:
Hymen O! The wedding O!

PISTHETAIROS:

Follow the bridal, follow, fortunate friends,
to the high lands of God, to the happy bed.
And oh my darling, take
my wings in your shining hands, and I
will lift you, lift you above the sky
in the Birds' dance, the whirring dance.

CHORUS:

Ió! Ió!
   Iê Paián! Alalaí!
  See the conquering hero go!
  Hymen O! The wedding O!

GENERAL NOTES

Page

Persons Represented: The Protagonist's name is in doubt. 'Peisthetairos', attested by most of the MSS., is unsatisfactory; of various other forms, 'Pisthetairos'—'trusty friend'—seems to be the best.

163: The scene is deliberately vague. Although Pisthetairos and Euelpidês have come on foot from Athens, the site of the future Cloudcuckooland seems neither terrestrial nor aerial: a dream region, suitable for a dream city. If the transformed King Tereus has chosen to remain in the country that he ruled as a man, the location is Thrace—northward, at any rate, in the direction of witchcraft and delusion.

164: Tereus was a king of Thrace who violated Philomelê, the sister of his wife Proknê, and tore out her tongue so that she should not tell. The sisters avenged themselves by cooking Itys, Tereus' infant son, and serving him up to his father at dinner. The gods' criticism of this Faulknerian episode took the form of changing all three agonists into birds: Tereus became a Hoopoe, Proknê a Swallow, and Philomelê a Nightingale. It is worth noting that A. follows the variant that transforms Proknê, not Philomelê, into the Nightingale. Moreover, she seems to have forgiven Tereus for his affair with her sister, and Tereus has forgotten the dreadful business about Itys. The Nightingale and the Hoopoe are on exemplary domestic terms with each other.

165: A losing war is hard on the national nerves, but A.'s grievance against Athens is that of any intelligent citizen whose government has yielded to fanaticism and public hysteria. Certainly there were traitors and dangerous malcontents in Athens, working for Sparta or for their own interests, but it is also true that the inevitable Informer was providing harmless citizens and defenceless aliens with all too many 'opportunities / to appear in court' on 'loyalty' charges. After the scandals that attended the sailing of the Sicilian

244

Expedition (415 B.C.) professional patriotism had become a golden racket.

168: *The Twelve Gods*: Zeus, Hêra, Poseidon, Demêter, Hephaistos, Arês, Athêna, Artemis, Aphroditê, Hestia, Apollo, Hermês.

168: *It's Sophoklês' fault*: The reference is to the *Tereus* of Sophoklês, a play no longer extant.

171: *the Red Sea*: 'He means Arabia Felix,' says Σ. Actually he means Cockaigne or Arcady, Bali or Boston, or whatever your personal Eldorado may be.

171: *It's a non-stop honeymoon!*: Bridal wreaths were made of mint leaves and myrtle-berries. Poppy seeds dipped in honey were esteemed as an aphrodisiac and eaten at weddings. The sesame plant was associated with Aphroditê.

176: *gargling in the glade*: The word (ἐπῷῆε) is unexpectedly harsh. Pisthetairos is disappointed by the Hoopoe's apparent failure to attract an audience.

176: The *Párodos* is the formal entrance of the Chorus into the *orchêstra*, and in *Aves* it is almost entirely spectacle. There is relatively little singing for the Chorus, and the chief interest lies in the costumes of the individual Birds and in the commenting dialogue. Here, as throughout the play, the Koryphaios is spokesman for the Chorus as a whole.

177: *Bird of Araby*: This is the Cock, the Persian Bird, here called *Mêdos*, 'the Median'. (The phallic pun is the same in Greek as in English.) My 'Araby' is a licence, intended to make the 'camel' more assimilable.

177: *'Kallias : Hipponikos :: Hipponikos : Kallias II'*: The names are *ad hoc*, for illustrative purposes. In ordinary circumstances the grandson takes his grandfather's name. The Hoopoe is explaining the presence on stage of a younger Hoopoe, whom we may call Hoopoe II. Philoklês was a tragic poet of unsavoury reputation [Σ] who plagiarized the *Tereus* of Sophoklês: that is to say, the monstrous cohabitation of Philoklês with Sophoklês' 'Lady' Hoopoe produced Hoopoe II. Kallias, grandson of Kallias I, was a real enough person: dissolute and wasteful ('always getting plucked'), he is best remembered for Plato's making his house the scene of the *Protágoras*.

178: *Magpie*, &c. Some of A.'s birds, in this list and later, are no longer identifiable—'a bird of some sort,' says Σ—; and the translation reflects this uncertainty.

181: *They'll keep the Owl from attacking us*: Athêna invented pottery; hence the Owl, sacred to her, will not attack pots.

182: *related to my wife*: Proknê was the daughter of King Pandiôn of Athens, hence of the same 'tribe' as Pisthetairos and Euelpidês.

183: *National Cemetery*: Here were buried those Athenians who died in battle for their country. The reservation was called Kerameikos, which is 'Pottersville' rather than 'Potter's Field'.

183: *Gettysbird*: The bloodless one-day siege of Orneai (416 B.C.); hence, no one died in that battle. The Greek name makes the pun inevitable.

185: *Monk the Knifeman*: From the disorderly gossip of Σ we gather that this was one Panaitios, a grumpy ugly cutler who had an actively amorous wife. The general purport seems to be: 'You lay off me, and I'll lay off you'. Panaitios' nickname was Pithêkos, 'Monkey'.

186: *Do you see dinner coming?*: Pisthetairos, in accordance with correct procedure at the beginning of an address, has asked for the ceremonial wreath and the lustral water. Euelpidês affects to mistake this for preparation for a formal dinner.

186: *Hyde Lark*: The Greek says that when the Lark's father died he was encephalated, or hidden in the Lark's head— an absurd allusion to the gestation of Athêna. Euelpidês sees a chance for a joke about the place-name Kephalai, which means 'heads'.

188: *to prostrate themselves*: Probably a genuflection [Σ]. At any rate it is to be taken literally: the Kite was so greeted as the harbinger of spring. Euelpidês, carrying his market money in his mouth, seems to have genuflected too vigorously.

188: *'Cuckoo! Back to the furrows . . .'*: The meaning of the proverb is obscure; *sed latet,* as the Commentators happily remark, *spurci aliquid.*

189: *'Holy Kites!'*: Lampôn, possibly because he didn't want to be bound by his oracles, used to confirm them with this diluted oath; or maybe he was one of those mistaken persons who think that 'My Cow!', or something of the sort, avoids the profanity of 'My God!'

190: The attendant or surrogate birds are appropriate. Aphrodite's phalarope is suggested by *phallos*; as a sea god,

Poseidon should have a water bird; cormorants, like Her-aklês, are greedy; and it has always been the wren, not the eagle, who is King of the Birds.

190: *the Good Gosh*: Not a softening, like Lampôn's oath noted above, but a whimsical variation: *Zan* for *Zeus*.

193: *'One crow caws down . . .'*: A parody of a line of Hesiod (Frag. 50): 'Nine generations lives the cawing crow'. [Σ]

193: *A poor thing of twigs and straw*: The Hoopoe's nest is proverbially filthy, Proknê being a career musician rather than a housewife.

195: PARÁBASIS: At this point the action of the play is suspended while the author, speaking through the Koryphaios, addresses the audience. The Parábasis proper begins as a parody of the Theogonies, the philosophical accounts of the origin of the gods and the creation of the world; but this tone, which is precariously balanced between the solemn and the bantering, passes into mild topical satire.

196: *Laid a wind-egg*: This is an unfertilized egg, appropriate for the genesis of Love. Σ obscurely alludes to the Ledaian egg from which the Heavenly Twins, Kastor and Polydeukês, were hatched.

197: *Orestês of the Alleys:* This hoodlum with the glorious nick-name, who is mentioned again on p. 231, seems to have im-pressed A. rather deeply. He must also have had a sense of humour, for there is something comic, to the non-par-ticipant, in his habit of stripping his victims of all their clothes after robbing them.

197: *You see Bird in everything*: Birds as omens, a fashionable fad.

200: *a full-fledged Horsecock*: An unhappy Aischylean compound, which A. ridicules again in *Frogs*. Aischylos intended it as a kind of heraldic beast, half fowl, half horse, a figurehead for a ship.

201: *'I shot an arrow . . .'*: Pisthetairos quotes a verse from the lost *Myrmidones* of Aischylos, where a wounded eagle recog-nizes his own feathers on the shaft of the arrow that struck him.

202: *'what boots a mailèd warrior goddess'*: The whole speech parodies a passage from the lost *Meleagros* of Euripidês.

202: *the Pelargic Wall*: This was a part of the fortifications of the Akropolis. The more common name was 'Pelasgic';

'Pelargic', however, has the advantage of meaning 'Stork [Wall]'.

202: *And fall off the ladder*: There is no authority for assigning this interpolation and the next one to Euelpidês, but surely the conjecture is allowable. Incorporated in Pisthetairos' speech they have no comic force at all.

203: *a leather beak-rest*: The Crow, as *auletês*, or flute accompanist for the singing, would be wearing a leather lip-guard.

204: *Artemis Siskin*: One of the mystical names of Artemis was Kolainis [Σ]. The *Akalanthis* is a bird, the siskin. This is straining for a pun; but a pun of sorts emerges.

206: *Author of Aitna*: The Poet's lyrics are a farrago of imperfectly remembered fragments from the standard poets. Here he is mutilating a Pindaric ode on Hiero, Tyrant of Syracuse and founder of the town of Aitna.

215: *Owls of Laureion*: Coins begetting smaller coins; see Index of Proper Names *s.v.* LAUREION.

216: *Egyptian hodcarrier*: A. is thinking of the accounts—Herodotos, for example—of the building of the Pyramids by the slave workmen of Cheops.

216: *Cranes from Libya*: Because of their improbable shape, cranes were supposed to need a ballast of stones in order to fly.

217: *Ah feet . . .*: A proverb; but Pisthetairos substitutes 'feet' for the 'hands' of the original.

221: *Euripidean Tragedy*: 'In the [lost] *Likymnios* of Euripides, somebody or something gets struck by lightning'. [Σ]

221: *some Lydian or Phrygian slave*: A parody of Euripides: *Alkestis* 675, Pherês to Admêtos.

222: *An abject Spartomaniac*: It is curious that in a long war it should become fashionable among certain people to ape the manners of the enemy.

222: *the Sokratês pose*: Here, as in the *chorikon* on p. 234, A. reveals his inability to admire the Great Martyr. The full-dress attack takes place in *Clouds,* but even in these minor skirmishes the animus is apparent, and only by shutting our minds to the plain sense of words can we conclude that this is a friendly raillery.

224: *'Ah that the eagle's . . .'*: Σ notes that these verses are quoted [in parody?] from the lost *Oinomaos* of Sophoklês.

225: *a decent orphan bird*: A male war-orphan would be educated by the State. There are vestiges of a dim ornithological pun.

226: *'Lifted aloft . . .'*: Kinêsias enters singing a love-poem by Anakreôn.

226: *Oh, ay. Enwingèd . . .*: The absurd diction parodies the manner of the dithyrambic poets, but there is a serious criticism implied: the poetry of Kinêsias is 'wingèd' not because of its exaltation, but because of its vain triviality (πρὸς τὸ κοῦφον, says Σ).

227: *so many tribes*: Although there may be a comic allusion here to the many cities that claimed Homer as a native son, the central irony is more topical. The office of Choragos. or Trainer of the Chorus for the dramatic festivals, was important and much sought after. A. suggests that Kinêsias, a vapid poet, would be much in demand among the various tribes competing at the festivals, but that no one could have a better claim to his services as Choragos than Leotrophidês, himself a silly unsubstantial dramatist.

227: *'What birds are these . . .'*: Parody of a song by Alkaios of Mytilenê.

228: *the Islands*: The Greek Islanders, not being Athenians. would be easy prey for the Informer.

228: *belly full of lawsuits*: For the cranes' ballast, see note on p. 216.

229: *I never learned how to work*: See Luke 16:3: *Ait autem vilicus intra se: Quid faciam quia dominus meus aufert a me vilicationem? fodere no valeo, mendicare erubesco.*

231: CHORIKON: In this short ode the Birds begin to describe the strange places that they have seen in their migrations. The Thracian tree stands for the recreant bully Kleonymos, the shed 'unused shields' representing his own shield, disgracefully thrown away in battle. Kleonymos made part of his living as a paid informer: the money would come in during the summer sessions, slack off during the winter. The Antistrophe, which at first sight seems to change the subject, actually pursues it. Kleonymos is being equated with the notorious bandit Orestês (see note on p. 197), while, at the level of myth, he becomes a kind of burlesque Aigisthos accosted by Agamemnon's avenging son: the double allusion enforces a shift in the point of view. Σ explains 'numb' by recalling that a chance encounter with a Hero (the bandit had an heroic nickname) was supposed to paralyze one's side.

233: *Basileia*: Her name means Sovereignty, Imperium. She has no place in the official Pantheon, but is an *ad hoc* creation to provide Pisthetairos with a mate equivalent to Zeus' Hêra. The final mockery of this drama, of course, is the apotheosis of the bungling Hero.

234: *A well-broiled one*: Prometheus first taught men the use of fire.

234: *Take this footstool*: At the Panathenaia Festival the daughters of Athenian aristocrats were attended by wealthy girls of foreign ancestry who carried ceremonial footstools and parasols. Prometheus hopes that Zeus, looking down from Olympos, will mistake him for one of these attendants.

234: CHORIKON: The Birds' travel lecture proceeds. The Shadowfeet were a remarkable tribe, said to live in Libya, who enjoyed feet so large that they could be used as parasols during siesta time. This is a fit setting for the deplorable Sokratês, who is represented as 'leading the souls of men'— leading them, that is to say, as Odysseus did the souls in Hadês, but also misleading them by perverse teaching, a charge that A. constantly makes against this philosopher. The Strophê is a comic *Nekuia,* parodying the eleventh book of the *Odyssey.* The fainthearted Peisandros, having lost his own soul, goes to the land of the Shadowfeet to conjure it back.

235: *the Ambassadors from Olympos*: This theophany seems outrageous to us, but our ideas of what constitutes blasphemy are different from the Greeks', who would find A. brilliantly but conventionally comic.

235: *Democracy, what sins . . .*: Zeus, to be fair, has decided that even the Barbarians should be represented in this embassage.

236: *The horseradish*: Literally, *silphion.*

237: *by Myself!*: Poseidon swears 'By Poseidon!'

237: *Wockle*: The Triballian speaks a murky language rather like that of Muta and Juva in *Finnegans Wake.* Much needless ingenuity has been expended by Professors attempting to reduce it to sense.

238: *Who wants to fight a war for a damn woman?*: As the Trojan War was fought for Helen.

239: *has your Father enrolled you yet?*: In the register of citizens; as the illegitimate son of a foreign woman, Heraklês would be ineligible.

240: *pie in the sky*: The Greek phrase was 'birds' milk', but this seems too esoteric.

241: CHORIKON: The travelogue resumed. The Englottogasters, 'men who live by their tongues', are nearer home than the Shadowfeet: they are to be found wherever men make money by informing on their fellows, and are particularly flagrant in times of political uncertainty.

241: ÉXODOS: The conclusion of the play is dictated not only by dramatic appropriateness—the marriage and deification of the Hero—, but by ritual inheritance. Comedy culminates in marriage, and the final scene (*cf.* the *Peace* and, though slightly different in vein, the *Lysistrata*) has overtones of an ancestral fertility rite. The Chorus sings of the wedding of Zeus and Hêra, thus equating Pisthetairos and Basileia with the King and Queen of Heaven. The ordinary man has found Cloudcuckooland, his Utopia, and now becomes God. Like God, he insists upon the recital of his own meritorious exploits.

243 *Iê Paián!*: The play ends with a volley of ritual phrases, among which rings the Athenian battle-cry, *Alalai!*, which had been *Eleleú!* among the Birds.

LADIES' DAY

for CORNELIA

Τὼ Θεσμοφόρω δ'
ἡμῖν ἀγαθήν
τούτων χάριν ἀνταποδοῖτον.

INTRODUCTORY NOTE

Thesmophoriazúsae was first produced in Athens at the Great Dionysia of 411 B.C. The unwieldy title is even more awkward in translation, for we should have to say something like 'The Women Keep the Thesmophorian Festival', which is clear enough, but not particularly stimulating. It is one of the three plays—the others being *Lysistrata* and *The Women's Parliament*—in which Aristophanes handles the idea of women interfering in men's affairs, and this may be a reason why the comedy did not take first prize at the Dionysia. Another reason may be the fact that so much of the play is literary parody. There is action enough: some of the rough-&-tumble is as hearty as anything in the comic theatre; but it must be confessed that an extended burlesque of any poet, even a Euripides, lacks popular appeal. Nevertheless there is great vigour here, of a heady kind, and even this special kind of fun has overtones that reach us across the centuries.

When the infamous and vivid Publius Clodius disguised himself as a woman and intruded upon the rites of the Bona Dea in Julius Caesar's house, he was, consciously or not, reënacting the plot of our comedy. The Thesmophoria, the annual Feast of Demêter and Persephonê, was sacred to women. What the rites were, the holy mysteries, we do not know; we can suppose that they were awful enough, and that the men-folk had their own ribald conjectures as to what went on; and we can be sure that the presence of a male was unthinkable, a kind of profanation. Clodius paid for his indiscretion, and Caesar's poor wife paid even more; but our hero Mnesilochos, who not only invades the forbidden precincts but has the temerity to speak up in open meeting, gets off with a few bruises, a great deal of humiliation, and a broad education in what might be called the Early Stanislavski Method. It is not given every old man to play, in one afternoon, the rôles of Helen of Troy and the princess Andrómeda *vis-à-vis* the Author himself; and we can believe that Mnesilochos is as glad as anyone in the house to hear the final words of the Chorus: 'It is late, and we have been playing long enough.' He is a scandalous old man, and Euripides is not much better; but they have beheld the Mysteries, made their point, and got off free.

The play is a friendly attack upon Euripides. (Another and minor poet, Agathôn, is less amiably handled in the Prologue, but it is Euripides who is the principal butt.) Why Euripides? First of all, because he was a shock: his innovations outraged authority and threatened the established conventions of the tragic stage, and his iconoclastic treatment of religious and social questions had already identified him with the new science, the new philosophy. Euripides, like Ibsen, was one of those germinal artists who both enchant men and make them think. Artists of this kind are never welcomed by the guardians of social order. An aristocrat and conservative—and Aristophanes was both —will distrust them instinctively. Add the petty but exacerbating flames of literary intrigues, the interminable cliquish squabblings of writers and artists among themselves, and you have reason enough for an attack upon Euripides. The wonder is that it is so good-humored; for while it is true that the dramatist takes a merciless drubbing at the hands of Aristophanes, it is also true that the very magnitude of the attack, the documentation itself, must be accounted a compliment of the most flattering kind. Such brilliant parody implies admiration, however qualified that admiration may be.

It also poses a problem for the translator. When Mnesilochos, ridiculous in his saffron gown, starts chanting the verses of the Ethiopian princess chained naked on the seashore rock, and Euripides, equally ridiculous in the stage device that lifts him above the scene, begins to intone the lines of Perseus, son of God—that is visual parody, and it can be managed. The verses themselves are a different matter. When a Euripidean original survives, as the *Helen* does, we can see what changes the parodist has made— generally they are not in the direction of verbal caricature —and estimate their effect upon an audience already familiar with the original. When the original has been lost, like the *Andrómeda*, we can only speculate. What we can not do, however, is to achieve the same effect in English by using the same means: quiet verbal parody no longer serves, and the only solution that I have been able to find is caricature and burlesque. The *disjecta membra* of Shakspere, the Border Ballads, popular tear-jerkers, and badly remembered passages from various devotional works, are far from being thoughtless or accidental: they are one way of suggesting the hundreds of quotations, misquotations, and overt and hidden allusions with which Aristophanes has salted this extraordinary poem.

It remains to be said that for my translation I have used the Budé text established by Victor Coulon, with aberrations whenever I have been attracted elsewhere by Rogers and the Oxford editors.

CONTENTS

MNESILOCHOS
EURIPIDES
SERVANT TO AGATHON
AGATHON
A WOMAN HERALD
FIRST WOMAN (MIKA)
SECOND WOMAN (KRITYLLA)
KLEISTHENES
A MAGISTRATE
A POLICEMAN
CHORUS OF ATHENIAN WOMEN

The supernumeraries include MANIA a slave, FLEURETTE a dancing-girl, TEREDON a fluteplayer, and various servants and attendants.

The scene is Athens: before the house of Agathôn, in the Prologue, and thereafter in the Thesmophorion, the temple of Demeter and Persephonê.

✨ PROLOGUE

[*Before the house of* AGATHON. *Enter the tragic poet* EURIPIDES *and his father-in-law* MNESILOCHOS. *Both are quite bald, patriarchally bearded, and richly dressed. They seem apprehensive, and* MNESILOCHOS *is obviously exhausted.*]

MNESILOCHOS:
'If winter comes', they say . . . Yes, but this winter
has been riding herd on me ever since dawn,
and I'm a wreck.
                    —For God's sake, Euripides,
before my guts give way entirely,
tell me where we're going.

261

EURIPIDES:

Never seek to hear

what soon you will behold with your own eyes.

MNESILOCHOS:

How's that? Say it again. 'Never seek to hear'?

EURIPIDES:

What you're destined to see.

MNESILOCHOS:

And never seek to see—

EURIPIDES:

What you're destined to hear.

MNESILOCHOS:

I wish you would explain.

You seem to be trying to make sense. Do you mean
I do not need to hear what I do not see?

EURIPIDES:

Right. The acoustic and the optic faculties
are distinct by nature.

MNESILOCHOS:

Not seeing and not hearing

are different things?

EURIPIDES:

That's exactly it.

MNESILOCHOS:

How did that happen?

EURIPIDES:

It goes back to the Creation.

When Æther sifted out the first elements
and brought the seeds of living things to light,
he invented Vision, an eye round like the sun,
and for Hearing he sunk a shaft right through the head.

MNESILOCHOS:

And this is the shaft I neither see nor hear with?
How charming is divine Philosophy!

EURIPIDES:

Stick around me and you'll learn all sorts of things.

MNESILOCHOS:

I don't doubt it for a minute. Maybe you'll teach me
how to become suddenly lame: I'm sick
of this endless trotting around.

EURIPIDES:

                       Step over here
and lend me your ears.

MNESILOCHOS:

                    You have them.

EURIPIDES:

                            Do you perceive
that little door?

MNESILOCHOS:

               I do. At least, I think so.

EURIPIDES:
Hush!

MNESILOCHOS:
          Hush that little door?

EURIPIDES:

                    And hear.

MNESILOCHOS:
Hear that little door hush?

EURIPIDES:

                 That little door
leads to the studio of Agathôn
the tragic poet.

MNESILOCHOS:

           Which Agathôn would that be?
You mean the one that looks like a gypsy,
the big guy?

EURIPIDES:

          No, the other one.

MNESILOCHOS:
I've never seen him. The one with all the whiskers?

EURIPIDES:
You've never seen him?

MNESILOCHOS:

             Damned if I have—at least,
so far as I know.

EURIPIDES:

        And yet you've laid him. But there,
I suppose it didn't make much of an impression.
        [The house door is opened from within.
Let's step aside for a moment.

Here's one of his servants coming out with hot coals
and branches of myrtle: an offering, probably,
to the difficult Muse of Poësy.

[*Enter* SERVANT *from the house*

SERVANT:
Let each mortal tongue keep silence.
Bound no more, O bounding Ocean.
Still thy breath, O silent Æther.
The ninefold sisterhood of Muses
roosts beneath my Master's roof.

MNESILOCHOS:
Crap!

EURIPIDES:
        Be quiet.

MNESILOCHOS:
                What's he talking about?

SERVANT:
Let the feathered generations
seek their nests; in the forest
stray no more, ye footed fauna.

MNESILOCHOS:
Crap and double crap!

SERVANT:
                        Sweet-singing
Agathôn this day is going—

MNESILOCHOS:
To get screwed?

SERVANT:
                Whose voice assails me?

MNESILOCHOS:
Silent Æther's.

SERVANT:
                —to construct the
keel of a poetic drama.
He will twist the arching word-ribs,
whirl them on the wheel, conglutinate them, inspissate with meaning,
tropify them, cerify them,
drill them and cylindrify them—

MNESILOCHOS:
Whorify them.

SERVANT:

What sad scoffer

dares invade the Master's precincts?

MNESILOCHOS:

A scoffer with a cylindrical drill for you
and that sweet singer of yours,
a scoffer ready to arch your precincts and
conglutinate your inspissation.

SERVANT:

Is that a fact?

You must have been a card, a century or two ago.

EURIPIDES:

Never mind him, my good man. Just step inside
and tell Agathôn we're calling.

SERVANT:

Why bother?

He'll be coming right out, anyway.
He's begun a new poem, and these November breezes
congeal his imagery. He needs some sun.

EURIPIDES:

And what do we do meanwhile?

SERVANT:

Why, you wait.   [Exit

EURIPIDES:

Ah, what hath God in store for me this day?

MNESILOCHOS:

Exactly! I wish to heaven you'd tell me
what this business is all about. What's
the matter with you? Why these groans? Must you
keep your secret from your own father-in-law?

EURIPIDES:

Carking calamity crawls on my horizon.

MNESILOCHOS:

Be specific.

EURIPIDES:

This day, this dreadful day,

Euripides is doomed to live or die.

MNESILOCHOS:

I don't see why.
There are no courts in session, and the Assembly's
adjourned for the holidays.

EURIPIDES:
That's why I am doomed.
For years and years
the women of Athens have been laying for me,
and today they are having a meeting
over there in the Shrine to bring the plot to a head.

MNESILOCHOS:
What's their grievance?

EURIPIDES:
They pretend that I libel them
in my tragedies.

MNESILOCHOS:
That's no pretence, by Poseidon!
But haven't you some trick to save your skin?

EURIPIDES:
Yes. I have thought of asking this poet Agathôn
to sneak into the Shrine somehow.

MNESILOCHOS:
I see. And then?

EURIPIDES:
I want him to assemble with the Assembly and
plead my cause, if he has to.

MNESILOCHOS:
In disguise?

EURIPIDES:
In disguise, of course.

MNESILOCHOS:
As a woman?

EURIPIDES:
Naturally.

MNESILOCHOS:
I find that a charming idea.
Really, Euripides,
when it comes to subtlety, you take the cake!

EURIPIDES:
Hush!

MNESILOCHOS:
Now what?

EURIPIDES:
Here comes Agathôn.

MNESILOCHOS:
   Where, where?

EURIPIDES:
                    There on the revolving porch.

MNESILOCHOS:
   God, I'm going blind! All I can see
   is that whore Kyrenê.

EURIPIDES:
                    For goodness' sake, be quiet!
   He's going to sing.

MNESILOCHOS:
                    Runs and roulades, do you think,
   or something in the more majestic line?

> [*The revolving stage has brought out* AGATHON
> *lying on a couch, holding a lyre. In this position*
> *he recites the strophes of the following Litany;*
> *but for each responsory* [R̸] *he rises, turns*
> *towards where he has been reclining, and per-*
> *forms as his own Chorus.*

AGATHON:
   I summon a glory of torches whirled
   In a maenad rout for the Spirits of Earth.
   Dance freedom, maidens, dance happiness!
     R̸ *For whom shall we dance? For whom shall we*
        dance?
   Lord Phoibos first, the golden Archer,
   Builder of fair Simoïs' ramparts.
     R̸ *Apollo, Victor in art! Apollo,*
        Laurelled with eternal music!
   Artemis also, Huntress immaculate,
   Wanderer of the mountain woodlands.
     R̸ *O Lêto's Daughter, thou pure flame,*
        Artemis, Maid inviolate!
   Strike sweetness from the Asian lyre:
   Circle the goddess, O Phrygian Graces!
     R̸ *Holy harp, O spring of song,*
        Male art joined with woman's voice!
        Her eyes are intolerable fire
        As we rejoice
        Singing the Artemis dance, the Apollo dance.

[AGATHON *resumes his couch. Attendants cluster
about him with incense, fans, bottles.*

MNESILOCHOS:

By the gods and goddesses of copulation,
that was a delightful melody!
All womanish along the tongue and kissy, I swear,
it went straight to my arse.

      —Young man,
whoever you are, permit me to address you
in the style of Aischylos:
 'What woman, or what man, or both
 Combinèd, with cosmetic art
 Bewrays the stigma of his youth
 I' th' costume of a virile tart?'
I understand the lyre, of course; but what
are you doing with a hair-net? A bottle
of gymnasium oil, yes; but why the girdle?
Why a hand-mirror and a sword at the same time?
What are you, you recumbent paradox? A man?
Show me; or, if that makes you blush,
where are your Spartan boots, your cavalry cloak?
Or are you a woman? If so, where are your breasts?
No answer. Bashful. If I want to find out,
I suppose I'll have to read your *Collected Poems.*

AGATHON:

Greybeard, greybeard, your malicious envy
bombards my ears, but I heed it not at all.
However, if you must know,
I wear this particular costume by design.
A dramatist embarked upon his art
should prepare for the voyage; and since my best plays
are female, my manner suggests the Heroine.
Do you follow me?

MNESILOCHOS:

     More or less. I take it
You're barearse when you go to work on a *Phaidra.*

AGATHON:

Again, a male rôle calls for male properties.
Thus art makes up for natural defect.

MNESILOCHOS:

Remember me when you write a satyr play:

I've a fundamental art that will enchant you.

AGATHON:

Furthermore, who wants a hairy poet?
Bah, these rugged artists!
                No, let me have
Ibykos—there's a writer for you!—or Anakreôn
or Alkaios, all of them simply a-swim with music.
Those boys liked pretty hats and pretty manners,
and that's the reason their songs are pretty, too.
Or take Phrynichos—you've heard of him, surely:
he was a fancy poet with a fancy taste,
and his fancy poems go fancing down the ages.
It's a law of nature:
Art is the perfect mirror of character.

MNESILOCHOS:

Is that why Philoklês writes horrible trash,
and Xenoklês writes filth, and that man Theognis,
cold as a haddock, writes frozen monodies?

AGATHON:

Obviously. And that, my dear sir, is why
I spend such loving care upon my person.

MNESILOCHOS:

Balls for your loving care!

EURIPIDES:

                Oh let him alone.
I was like that myself when I began writing.

MNESILOCHOS:

Really? I suppose that explains a great deal.

EURIPIDES:

Let's change the subject.
                —My dear Agathôn,
allow me to tell you why I'm here.

AGATHON:

                    Tell me.

EURIPIDES:

Brevity, someone has said, is the soul of wit.
I will be brief.
             —Agathôn, you perceive here
a suppliant with an unheard-of problem.

AGATHON:

What problem?

EURIPIDES:

Women, as usual.
They're meeting in the Thesmophorion today,
and the single dreadful purpose of that meeting
is to ruin Euripides. They say I've insulted them.

AGATHON:

What could I do?

EURIPIDES:

You could do anything;
but what I have in mind is
that you get yourself into the meeting (it's easy enough
for you to pass as a woman) and make a speech
for me at the proper time. That would save my life.
Will you do it? After all,
I could hardly find a more appropriate spokesman.

AGATHON:

Why not go and make the speech yourself?

EURIPIDES:

I'll tell you. First of all, they know me;
secondly—well, I'm not so young as I was,
silver threads among the gold, you know, and this beard
is fairly long. But you're handsome and smoothcheeked
with a ladylike voice and delicate way. You'd do.

AGATHON:

Euripides.

EURIPIDES:

Yes?

AGATHON:

Do you remember once writing:
'You love the sun; do you think your father does not?'

EURIPIDES:

I wrote it.

AGATHON:

And now you propose to shove off your problems
onto me. Do I look crazy? No, no, I tell you,
calamity must be met with guts, not guile.
You've got to bear your own bad luck.

MNESILOCHOS:

You'll bare
that arse of yours, and that's no figure of speech.

EURIPIDES:
What are you afraid of?
AGATHON:
I'd be even worse than you.

EURIPIDES:
How so?
AGATHON:
The women would think
that I had come with Lesbian intentions.
MNESILOCHOS:
Your intentions are all *a posteriori*, friend.
Just the same, it's a reasonable excuse.
EURIPIDES:
For the last time:
Will you do it?
AGATHON:
What do *you* think?
EURIPIDES:
Then farewell,
a long farewell to all Euripides' greatness!
MNESILOCHOS:
O friend! O relative! Be not dismayed.
EURIPIDES:
Why not?
MNESILOCHOS:
Forget about this Agathôn.
Here I am. Take me. Do what you like.
EURIPIDES:
You mean it?
Off with that cloak, then!
MNESILOCHOS:
Off it goes. What next?

EURIPIDES:
Well, those whiskers of yours; and lower down.
MNESILOCHOS:
If you say so. Might as well go the whole hog.
EURIPIDES:
Agathôn, you're always shaving: will you lend us
a razor?
AGATHON:
You'll find one over there in the box.

EURIPIDES:
   Kind of you.
            —Now, father-in-law, sit down here
   and stick out your cheek.
MNESILOCHOS:
                          Ouch!
EURIPIDES:
                                 What's the matter?
   Have I got to gag you?
MNESILOCHOS:
                          Ouch! Suffering God!
EURIPIDES:
   Come back here! Where are you off to?
MNESILOCHOS:
                                    A sanctuary.
   By God, I'm not going to stay here and get carved.
EURIPIDES:
   They'll laugh at you with half your face shaved clean.
MNESILOCHOS:
   Let them laugh.
EURIPIDES:
            Oh come now, for heaven's sake,
   think of me for a change.
MNESILOCHOS:
                          I have no character.
   All right. Go ahead.
EURIPIDES:
                     Sit down.
                          —Stop fidgeting.
   Puff your other cheek out.
MNESILOCHOS:
                          Woof.
EURIPIDES:
                     What do you mean, 'woof'?
   —There! That's a handsome job, if I do say so!
MNESILOCHOS:
   Who said a soldier's bearded like the pard?
EURIPIDES:
   Never mind that. I think you're dazzling.
   Would you like to look at yourself?

MNESILOCHOS:

                               Hand me that glass.
—My God, I'm looking at Kleisthenês!

EURIPIDES:

                                    Stand up.
Bend over. Here goes the rest of the foliage.

MNESILOCHOS:
Stop! Must I be singed like a pig on a platter?

EURIPIDES:
Bring a torch, boy, or a lamp to put under him.
—Stoop over. There. Keep your tail out of the flame.

MNESILOCHOS:
I certainly will.

                 —Water! Water!
Ring the alarm! There's fire down below!

EURIPIDES:
Keep cool.

MNESILOCHOS:

            When my poop's a howling holocaust?

EURIPIDES:
Don't worry. The worst is over.

MNESILOCHOS:

                        I believe you.
The crater's full of soot.

EURIPIDES:

                     We'll sponge it out.

MNESILOCHOS:
God pity the man who sponges *that* abyss.

EURIPIDES:
Agathôn, you won't lend yourself, but you might
let us have a dress and a brassière, at least,
for his costume. Don't tell us you can't.

AGATHON:

                    Take what you need.

EURIPIDES:
Let's see. Which gown?

AGATHON:

                 Why not that saffron one?
It's simply darling.

MNESILOCHOS:

              It smells darling, all right.

Now where's that breast gadget?

EURIPIDES:

                                    Here you are.

MNESILOCHOS:

Is my slip showing?

EURIPIDES:

                        You're all right. Now
something ribbony for your head.

AGATHON:

                                    This precious toque.

EURIPIDES:

Toqué!

MNESILOCHOS:

            Does it suit me?

EURIPIDES:

                        It's a dream.
Now a fur stole.

AGATHON:

                There's one on the divan.

EURIPIDES:

                                        And slippers?

AGATHON:

Take the ones I'm wearing.

MNESILOCHOS:

                        They'll fit me?
I know you like things loose.

AGATHON:

                                They'll fit to a T.
—And now, if you have everything you want,
I think I'll have myself wheeled back inside.
            [*The inner stage revolves, carrying off* AGATHON
            and his ménage.

EURIPIDES:

Well, my dear hermaphrodite,
I hope you'll remember to speak like a woman in there.

MNESILOCHOS:

Goodneth me, I'll do my betht.

EURIPIDES:

                        I'm sure of it.
Well, let's be going.

MNESILOCHOS:

Not yet, by Apollo!
Not until you swear—

EURIPIDES:

Swear what?

MNESILOCHOS:

That if the worst
happens, as it probably will, you'll do *your* best
to rescue *me*.

EURIPIDES:

I swear it by the Æther,
the house of Zeus on high.

MNESILOCHOS:

You might as well
swear by that sty of Hippokratês's.

EURIPIDES:

I swear by all the heavenly gods at once.

MNESILOCHOS:

Remember,
it is your heart, and not your tongue, that swears.
I insist on the distinction.

EURIPIDES:

We must hurry.
They've raised the signal on Demêter's shrine.
I'm off. Good-bye, good luck!

[Exeunt separately

🏵 PÁRODOS

*[The Thesmophorion, or Temple of Demêter
and Persephonê. Women of all ages are assem-
bling about a central altar behind which, on a
platform, is the speakers' rostrum.* MNESILOCHOS
*enters mincingly, addressing an imaginary maid-
servant. At the end of his speech he attempts to
lose himself in the group nearest the rostrum.*

MNESILOCHOS:

Thratta, Thratta, keep close to me, Thratta,
over this way, Thratta. Mercy, all that lamp-smoke!
And the crowds! I declare,

I never saw anything like it, Thratta.

                                  —But

I ought to be saying my prayers:

                                  Loveliest Goddesses,

hear me, be gracious to me now, and when I get home.

—Look in the basket, Thratta:
I want the little holy cake to offer
to the Goddesses.

                        —O Demêter, august Lady,
and thou, Persephonê: grant that I
may bring my gifts to you time and time again,
or at least that no one recognize me this time.
Grant that little Pussy, my dear dear daughter,
may find a rich young man to marry her,
yes, and a silly young man, too; and grant
my dear son Jock a modicum of horse sense.
Amen.

                  —Goodness me, where's the best place to sit?
—You run along home, Thratta. It isn't right
for servants to hear the things we ladies say.

                      [*A* WOMAN HERALD *mounts the rostrum.*

WOMAN HERALD:
Silentium! Silentium!

Let us pray:
To Demêter and Persephoneia Givers of Law; to Plûtos
    and to Kalligeneia; to Mother Earth Nourisher of
    Youth; to Hermês; to the Graces also: That the de-
    liberations and enactments of this Assembly be crowned
    with success for Athens and for the Women of Athens;
    and that what woman soever this day thinks clearest
    and speaks best may triumph in the cause for the which
    she pleads.
Iê Paián! Iê Paián! Iê Paián!

Lift up your hearts.
KORYPHAIOS:
Let us pray to the blest Gods.

[*The following passage is Versicle (solo voice)*
with choral Responsory.

CHORUS:

℣ Zeus, thou Name of Awe, hear us.
℟ Zeus, thou Name of Awe, hear us.
℣ Regent of holy Dêlos, god golden-lyred:
℟ Apollo, hear us.
℣ O mighty Maiden whose flashing eyes and lance of
gold blaze in high Athens:
℟ Athêna, hear us.
℣ O Huntress, golden Lêto's Child,
O thou of many names:
℟ Artemis, hear us.
℣ Thou Lord of the fish-thronged ways of Ocean:
℟ Poseidon, hear us.
℣ O all ye Water Nymphs, Daughters of Nêreus: and
ye, Oreadês, Nymphs of the mountain reaches:
℟ Hear us, be near us.
℣ May the Golden Lyre
inspire our song.
℟ May our noble Assembly
conclude in joy.

KORYPHAIOS:

In the name of the Gods and Goddesses of Olympos:
in the name of the Pythian Goddesses and Gods:
in the name of the Gods and Goddesses Delian: and in
the name
of all other Divinities:

Hear our Commination:

CHORUS:

℣ Cursèd be he who shall conspire
against the Council of Women:
℟ Cursèd be he.
℣ Cursèd be he who shall consort with the Persians
or with Euripides:
℟ Cursèd be he.

℣ Cursèd be he who shall work to restore the Tyranny,
 or shall think to make himself Tyrant:
℟ Cursèd be he.
℣ Cursèd be he who shall betray
 the suppositiousness of any woman's child:
℟ Cursèd be he.
℣ Cursèd be any confidential handmaid
 who shall betray her mistress to her master:
℟ Cursèd be she.
℣ Cursèd be any slave who shall misrepresent
 a message sent to a lover:
℟ Cursèd be she.
℣ Cursèd be any exasperated old woman
 who shall attempt to buy a young man's love:
℟ Cursèd be she.
℣ Cursèd be any lover
 who shall seduce with promises, and break them:
℟ Cursèd be he.
℣ Cursèd be any young woman
 who shall take a lover's treat, and deny her body:
℟ Cursèd be she.
℣ Cursèd be any bartender or barmaid
 who shall falsify measures of wine, be they pints or
 quarts:
℟ Cursèd be he or she.
℣ Let all such wretches wither at the root:
℟ Yea, let their house and household perish for ever.
℣ As for us, may the high Gods bless us
 and keep us in comfort all the days of our life.

℟ Seeing that all they stand accurst
  Who stood in need of cursing,
 Heav'n grant that we avoid the worst
  Of what we've been rehearsing.

 The women's laws enacted here
  Shall not by us be broken;
 We'll whisper in no hairy ear
  What, woman-like, we've spoken.

 We'll not connive against the peace
  For all the Great King's treasure;

The dramas of Euripides
Shall stir in us no pleasure.

As women, we have known abuse;
As women, we'll persever.
To women grant thy strength, O Zeus,
And smile on our endeavour.

AGON: α

WOMAN HERALD:
The meeting will please come to order
in accordance with the following Resolution:

'MOVED AND VOTED BY THE JUNTA OF WOMEN:
'To call an Assembly for the morning
'of the Middle Day of Thesmophoria,
'when women have least to do,
'to consider the case of Euripides
'and what action should be taken in it:
'it being the sense of this meeting
'that the activities of said Euripides
'render him liable to general censure.
          TIMOKLEIA, *Presiding Officer*
          SOSTRATE, *for the Motion*
          LYSILLA, *Secretary*'

Does any lady desire the floor?
FIRST WOMAN:
                    I do.
WOMAN HERALD:
Assume the garland before you begin to speak.
          [FIRST WOMAN, *garlanded, mounts the rostrum.*
KORYPHAIOS:
Silence! No talking, please. Lend her your attention.
She clears her throat like one who has much to say.
FIRST WOMAN:
Ladies:
          I call the Two Goddesses to witness
that it is not personal vanity that obliges me

to address you today. No; I have long
viewed with alarm the reprehensible conduct
of the vegetable dealer's son Euripides.
The vicious
contumely he has indulged in, dragging us
through the cloacine seepage of his mind!
Evil? Can you think of any evil
that he has left unsaid? Give him some actors,
a Chorus, an audience, and there he goes
proving that women are good-for-nothings, incarnate
wine-jugs, walking sinks of lust, deceivers,
babblers, fly-by-nights, knives in the flesh
of honest men. And what is the result?
You know perfectly well. When those husbands of ours
come home from one of his plays,
first they look at us queerly, and then,
why, they simply tear the house apart
hunting for lovers hidden in some closet.
It's no use,
we can't do things we've been doing all our lives
but they get suspicious, thanks to Euripides
and his Advice to Husbands.
                                    Suppose a woman
buys a flower for her hair: that means she's in love.
Or she drops a pot or two on the way to the kitchen:
immediately her husband finds significance
in the broken crockery, and he quotes Euripides:
The trembling hand betrays th' adult'rous guest.
Or say a girl gets sick,
here comes big brother with his Euripides:
This morning greenness augureth no maid.
Bad enough;
but these men are into everything! Why, if a woman
can't have a baby and wants to buy one—you know—,
she hasn't a chance in the world, because there's her
          husband
camping out in front of the house. And that isn't all.
Think of the rich old men that used to marry
young girls. Do they do it any more? No. Why?
Because of Euripides and his wretched nonsense:
What's wedlock but enslavement to the old?

Do you see? And what's worse still,
our bedroom doors must now have special locks
and special keys, to keep us safe! And our houses
must be full of great growling wolfhounds from
    Molossos—
to keep us safe, and scare our lovers to death!
It's come to the point that we're no longer mistresses
in our own homes; we don't even control
our flour, our wine, any of our provisions.
These ridiculous men
have taken to using the horridest little keys
from Sparta, things with three teeth, hopeless
to try to cope with. The silliest penny ring
was good enough once to fake a seal on the door;
but now this family curse, this Euripides,
has taught our men to use fussy private signets
that you simply can't copy—and, what's worse,
they carry them around on chains hitched under their
    ears.

Ladies, I could say much more; and, with your permis-
    sion,
I shall extend my remarks in the official Minutes.
Meanwhile, in view of the abuses that I have mentioned,
I move that Euripides be taken care of
in some permanent and unpleasant way: poison,
perhaps, or a more subtle medium.
                              Ladies, I move
the abolition of Euripides!

CHORUS:

              Oh woman's tongue! Persuasion,   [STROPHE
                  Conviction, honest sense!
              What masculine evasion
                  Can twist her evidence?
              She disentangles fact from lie
              And puts to blush male sophistry.

              Now Justice laughs victorious
                  At grunting Error's frown.
              What man, however glorious,

Can talk a woman down?
Xenoklês himself would seem
An elocutionist's dry dream.

[*The* SECOND WOMAN *has taken her place at the rostrum.*

SECOND WOMAN:
Ladies, unused as I am to public speaking,
I do want to put my little oar in. Everything
the last lady said was absolutely correct,
but I have a personal complaint.
       —My man
got himself killed on Kypros, and that left me
with five little mouths to feed. Well, I managed
to make out, more or less, in the holiday wreath line
over in the myrtle market, you know, until
this person U. Ripides came along. He's in
the writing line himself, they tell me; and what
does he do but sell the carriage trade the idea
that there aren't any gods!
       No gods! I ask you!
You can guess what happened to the wreath business
  then:
cut in half, it was.
      Well, what I say,
this highbrow writer's dangerous, a wild man—
no wonder:
he was brought up on wild vegetables—and I say
he ought to be stopped.
      Well, that's it.
That's all I have time for. We got an order
for twenty wreaths this morning, festival type,
and back to the old grind for yours truly. 'Bye now!

CHORUS:

    Her complex eloquence   [MESODE
    Sways the sense
    Even more
    Than the rhetoric before.
    No fuss,
    No animus.

Pure passion, that's all.
Euripides, here's check-
mate: on your neck
Let the great axe fall.

[MNESILOCHOS *timidly mounts the rostrum.*

MNESILOCHOS:
Ladies, permit me to begin by saying
that I thoroughly sympathise with your grievance
against the so-called poet Euripides.
The mother's heart o' me burns—burns, I say—
with hatred for that reprobate. Damned if it doesn't.
However,
what I want to say is—just among us women,
no one listening in—, we've got to be awfully sure
we know what we're doing.
                              And, well, *are* we?
I mean, we let ourselves get all worked up
over this cad because he's told two or three home truths
about us, but when you come to think of it,
he hasn't said a word about the hundreds
and hundreds of things that we get away with
every day of our lives.
                         —Take me, for instance.
I won't speak for the rest of you, but I know
there's a lot of funny business on my conscience.
For example: It's
three days after the wedding, with my husband
snoring beside me. Well, I had a lover—
a sweet boy he was, too: made me a woman
on my seventh birthday—
and this night I'm talking about, he gets overcome
with emotion, and the first thing I know
I hear him scratching at the front door. Well,
I slip out of bed, just as easy as easy,
and all of a sudden up pops my husband's head.
'Where *you* going?' he says. 'Where?' says I,
all innocence, 'Why, *you* know where.
'I got a cramp. Something I ate.' 'Go ahead,' he says,
and damned if he doesn't get up too and start
boiling up a juniper-and-anise recipe

for that cramp!
                Well, I get down to the door,
pour some water on the hinge to kill the squeaking,
and sure enough, there's the boy friend out in the street.
Well, I grab hold of the doorway shrine with one hand
and the laurel bush with the other, and bend over.
And that's the story.
                   But Euripides never told it.
As a matter of fact,
he's never mentioned the times we put ourselves out
to be nice to slaves and muledrivers when we can't find
anything better. He's never explained
how we chew garlic after a really hard night
so that when our husbands come home from guard duty
they won't smell what we've been up to.
                       —Isn't that your
experience, madam?
                —And what if he does libel Phaidra?
What's Phaidra to us? At least he didn't tell
on the woman who stretched her cloak out at arm's length
to let her husband see how pretty it was,
while her lover was crawling out the window behind it!
No, or that other woman
pretending to have her pains for ten whole days
until she could buy a baby to fob off on her husband,
and all the time the poor man
running around town trying to find some medicines
to bring it on, till finally the midwife
smuggles a brat in—in a pot, with a gob of wax
down its gullet, to muffle the yells; and then,
when she gives the sign,
the wife moans: 'Darling, no men allowed! But this time
'I think I can promise you a son and heir.'
Exit husband. And then the old hag hauls the wax
out, pinches the papoose—and what a howl!
Reënter husband. The old fraud grins like a cat
and puts the evidence in the poor fish's arms:
'A lion!' she says, 'a regular little lion!
'The spitting image of you, sir, right down
'to his little acorn!'
                  —No. We have our faults, Ladies,

I swear to Artemis we have. Should we really blame
Euripides, when we're so naughty ourselves?

CHORUS:
> Can I believe my twó eárs?   [ANTISTROPHE
>> Who let this woman in?
> What are we going to do, dears?
>> How can we ever win
> If this untutored female's spite
> Brings all our little sins to light?

> The current generation
>> Has lost all sense of shame.
> Unhappy is the nation
>> When women women blame!
> *Each stone* (the proverb says) *conceals*
> *A friend*—who'll smile, and sting your heels.

KORYPHAIOS:
Both ways from the girdle do the fiends inherit.
Your woman is a catastrophic spirit.

FIRST WOMAN:
Are you out of your mind? So help me Aglauros,
you've been hypnotized, or something else awful
has happened to you. This silly woman,
are we going to let her walk away with the meeting?
                              [*To the audience*
Is there a gentleman in the house
who will help us?
                    —I see there is none; we'll have
to help ourselves. Come, tell the servants
to collect a pan of hot coals: a little singeing
in the proper place will make this person remember
her duty to speak well of other women.

MNESILOCHOS:
Oh not in the proper place, Sisters, not
in the proper place! Do I deserve
depilation? Never! What if I did say
some neutral things about Euripides?
This is a closed session, we have
freedom of speech, I only said what I thought.

FIRST WOMAN:

Freedom of speech? To defend Euripides?
You are the only one here
shameless enough to stand up for this man
whose one delight is the slander of womanhood.
Oh, he's a real artist when it comes
to painting your Phaidras and your Melanippês,
but he'll never never have a kindly word
for a solid citizen like Penelopê.

MNESILOCHOS:

There's a good reason for that. You won't find
a single Penelopê alive today,
only Phaidras and Phaidras and daughters of Phaidra.

FIRST WOMAN:

Do you hear her, Ladies? The slut
sums us all up and damns us with one word.

MNESILOCHOS:

Mercy, I haven't told
the millionth part of what we're capable of.
Do you want me to go on?

FIRST WOMAN:

                    You couldn't.
You've poured out all the filth you know.

MNESILOCHOS:

                                     Not
the millionth part of it! Shall I tell
how we use our strigils to siphon off the grain—

FIRST WOMAN:

Damn your grain!

MNESILOCHOS:

                   Or how we give our go-betweens
the food and drink saved up for festival days,
and blame it on the cat?

FIRST WOMAN:

                  Atheistical communism!

MNESILOCHOS:

Shall I tell about the woman
who chopped her husband up with a hatchet? No.
Or the one who drove her husband crazy with drugs?
No. Or the other one, that Acharnian—

FIRST WOMAN:

Stop it!

MNESILOCHOS:
—who hid her father's body under the bathtub?

FIRST WOMAN:
Shut up!

MNESILOCHOS:
Shall I tell them how you yourself
switched new-born babies with one of your own slaves
in order to get a boy instead of a girl?

FIRST WOMAN:
No, by the Goddesses, you needn't. But I'll
tell you what I have in mind: I'm going
to snatch you baldheaded!

MNESILOCHOS:

You and who else?

FIRST WOMAN:
Come on, you!   [*She strips for action.*

MNESILOCHOS:
Come on, you!

FIRST WOMAN:

Hold my dress, Philistê.

MNESILOCHOS:
Touch but a hair of this grey head, by Artemis,
and I'll—

FIRST WOMAN:
You'll what?

MNESILOCHOS:

I'll pound the breakfast out of you!

KORYPHAIOS:
Ladies, ladies, this debate is unpleasant.
Besides, there's a woman coming. What a haste
looks through her eyes! Let us compose ourselves
and hear what she has to say.
            [*Enter* KLEISTHENES, *elegant in dress, affected and*
            effeminate in speech

KLEISTHENES:
Darlingest ladies, what *is* going on?
I've been hearing the awfullest things
down in the Agora, something about a perfectly
horrid practical joke.

                         You know—
I don't have to tell *you*—how close I feel
to you. I've been mad about women all my life,
and your little problems are mine. So I am here
this bright morning to warn you to look out
for a too too *nasty* surprise.

KORYPHAIOS:

                         What surprise, dear boy?
I hope you don't mind my calling you 'dear boy':
those sweet smooth cheeks . . .

KLEISTHENES:

                         What they're *saying* is
that Euripides has sneaked a vile old man,
some relative of his, into your Assembly.

KORYPHAIOS:
Why would he do that?

KLEISTHENES:

                         To spy on you.
It seems he's worried about your intentions.

KORYPHAIOS:
A man unnoticed among all these women? Absurd.

KLEISTHENES:
Darling, he's *shaved* and *plucked*! Also dis*guised*!

MNESILOCHOS:
I never heard such a silly story. Really!
No man would ever let himself be plucked.
I don't believe a word of it.

KLEISTHENES:

                         Do you think I'd invent
a thing like that? My information comes
from usually reliable sources.

KORYPHAIOS:

                         This is dreadful!
Quick, everyone, look around for this man,
sniff him out wherever he is, the old rogue
spying on us!
                         And you, Kleisthenês,
if you want to increase our obligation to you,
help us to find him.

KLEISTHENES (*to* FIRST WOMAN):
                         You, madam: who are you?

MNESILOCHOS:
> !

KLEISTHENES:
> You, I said. I've got to begin *some*where!

MNESILOCHOS:
> !

FIRST WOMAN:
> I'll have you know, sir,
> my husband's name's Kleónymos.

KLEISTHENES:
> Does anyone vouch
> for Mrs Kleónymos?

KORYPHAIOS:
> Mercy, yes. Known her for years.
> Try someone else.

KLEISTHENES:
> Who is that fat woman
> with the unattractive baby?

FIRST WOMAN:
> My nurse, stupid!

MNESILOCHOS:
> Well, I must be running along.

KLEISTHENES:
> Just a moment, madam.
> Where are you off to?

MNESILOCHOS:
> Oh sir, spare my blushes . . .
> The Little Girls' Room, you know . . .

KLEISTHENES:
> Oh. Well, hurry up.
> [MNESILOCHOS *moves towards exit, is blocked by*
> *the crowd, and conceals himself behind a pillar.*
> I'll wait till you come back.

KORYPHAIOS:
> Keep your eye on her.
> She's the only woman here that we don't know.

KLEISTHENES:
> What's the matter in there? Have you fallen in?

MNESILOCIIOS:
> Be patient.

You can't imagine, sir, what an obstruction . . .
It must be that cress I ate.

KLEISTHENES:

Cress? I'll cress you!

[*Pulls him out from behind pillar*

Come over here!

MNESILOCHOS:

This is no way to handle
a woman in a delicate condition.

KLEISTHENES:

I want the truth, madam. Who is your husband?

MNESILOCHOS:

Husband? Oh, you mean my husband . . . Why, Whoozis.

From Kothôkidai.

KLEISTHENES:

Who's Whoozis?

MNESILOCHOS:

Whoozis? He's,
well, Whoozis . . . Son of Whoozis . . . You know . . .

KLEISTHENES:

Sounds evasive to me.

—Tell me: Have you ever
been here before?

MNESILOCHOS:

Heavens, yes. Every year.

KLEISTHENES:

Who was your roommate last year?

MNESILOCHOS:

Whoozis was.

KLEISTHENES:

Madam, I think you lie.

FIRST WOMAN:

Step aside, Kleisthenês,
and let me do the questioning. There are some things
a man shouldn't hear.

—Now, tell me, you:
What was the opening ceremony last year?

MNESILOCHOS:

We had a drink.

FIRST WOMAN:
> And after that?

MNESILOCHOS:
> We had
another drink.

FIRST WOMAN:
> Somebody must have told you.
—Then what happened?

MNESILOCHOS:
> I remember Xenylla
asked if anyone had a mixing-bowl:
there weren't any chamber-pots.

FIRST WOMAN:
> Wrong. Utterly wrong.
—Kleisthenês, here's your man.

KLEISTHENES:
> What shall I do?

FIRST WOMAN:
Undress him, naturally.

MNESILOCHOS:
> I beg you on my knees,
would you undress the mother of nine sons?

KLEISTHENES:
You revolting reprobate!

FIRST WOMAN:
> Strip him, strip him!
—What too too sullied flesh!

KLEISTHENES:
> What muscle!

FIRST WOMAN:
> What breasts!
They're not in the least like ours.

MNESILOCHOS:
> That is because
I have never known the joys of motherhood.

FIRST WOMAN:
Well really! What about those nine sons of yours?

KLEISTHENES:
Stop hunching over. Where are you trying to hide
that appendage?

FIRST WOMAN:

> Look, it's peeking out behind.
Isn't it cunning?

KLEISTHENES:

> Behind? I don't see it.

FIRST WOMAN:
Now it's in front again.

KLEISTHENES:

> No.

FIRST WOMAN:

> Now it's back here.

KLEISTHENES:
That's a sort of isthmus, friend, between your legs.
It's better travelled than the Korinth Portage.

FIRST WOMAN:
The hateful beast! No wonder he stood up
for Euripides.

MNESILOCHOS:

> This is embarrassing.
It's also my own fault.

FIRST WOMAN:

> What shall we do now?

KLEISTHENES:
Keep an eye on him. He's slippery. I'm going
to take this business straight to the City Council.

> [*Exit* KLEISTHENES. *Two burly women seize*
> MNESILOCHOS *and hustle him to one side of the
> rostrum, where he stands guarded.*

🏵 CHORIKON: CHORAL INTERLUDE

KORYPHAIOS:

Light your lamps, throw off your long cloaks, belt
your tunics tight like men, and search the Pnyx,
the aisles, each corridor, each cell. If another man
is hidden here, he must not get away.

CHORUS:

> Lightly, silently,
> A-tiptoe, swift,

Dancing the deft search,
Circle and drift,
Drift and recircle,
Rondel and round again,
Here a man, there a man,
Catch-as-catch-can a man,
Left to right, right to left,
Silently, lightly.

KORYPHAIOS:
Let the chorus hearten the hunter!

CHORUS:

If any wretched prying man   [STROPHE
   Is lurking in this place,
Let him consider, while he can,
   His imminent disgrace.

Let him reflect that Némesis
   Is the bleak wage of error,
And let him curse that pride of his
   That brings him down in terror.

His naked punishment shall be
   A paradigm of shame,
And sinners in their infancy
   Shall sicken at his name.

Accurst in living, in his death
   Accurst, beneath all pity,
His tale will not be wasted breath,
   For it shall serve the City,
Proving to each frail citizen
   That God will not be mocked. Amen.

🎜 AGON: β

KORYPHAIOS:
We seem to have looked everywhere. It's safe to say
there's not another man in the place.

[MNESILOCHOS *snatches a baby and takes refuge
at the altar.*

FIRST WOMAN:

Stop thief! Stop thief!
No, over here, look! This filthy old man
has torn my precious babe from its mother's breast.

MNESILOCHOS:

You said it. And you won't feed this brat again
until I get out of here.
*Sluiced by my steel, the infant blood
Shall dye with its empurpling flood
The holy antependium.*

FIRST WOMAN:

Oh what shall I do?
Friends, friends, will you not help me?
Must I be ravish'd of my only joy?

KORYPHAIOS:

Arise, black goddesses of vengeance dire!
Have you ever known such an outrage?

FIRST WOMAN:

Dreadful.

SECOND WOMAN:

Horrid.

KORYPHAIOS:

Alas, what more than bloody deed is this?

MNESILOCHOS:

It's simply a method of restoring balance.

SECOND WOMAN:

Makes a woman think twice, a thing like this does.

MNESILOCHOS:

Precisely my motive, Ladies. I *want* you
to think twice.

SECOND WOMAN:

You barbarian!

FIRST WOMAN:

You barefaced
baby-snatcher!

CHORUS:

Unblushing monster! Infamy   [ANTISTROPHE
Incarnate! Beast accurst!
What tongue can tell your cruelty?

MNESILOCHOS:
>You've yet to see my worst.

CHORUS:
>You hope this trick will serve your need?
>You plan to slip away?
>By Heaven, we'll have you fricasseed!

MNESILOCHOS:
>You're wrong; or so I pray.

CHORUS:
>Though you invoke celestial Power,
>>You'll find no help in that.
>No god descends in a saving shower.

MNESILOCHOS:
>Meanwhile, I have the brat.

CHORUS:
>Now by the Holy Two I swear,
>>Your tide of luck is turning.
>Fortune frowns, that once was fair,
>>And you are ripe for burning.
>The flame that fries your blasphemies
>Shall dry this weeping mother's eyes.

KORYPHAIOS:
>Go, some of you, bring lots of wood,
>and let's get down to broiling this abomination.

FIRST WOMAN:
>A thoroughly sound idea! Manía, get some wood.
>—You brute, I'll barbecue you to a crisp.

MNESILOCHOS:
>Kindle, parboil, scorch, roast—whatever you say.
>It's all the same to me.
>>>>—But you, poor child,
>unhappy sacrifice to maternal pigheadedness:
>off with these lendings, your tiny
>shroud, illstarred darling, and—
>>>>>But what's this?
>>*[Fumbling under the wrappings, he has discov-*
>>*ered only a leather wine-bottle.*
>The baby skin you love to touch has become

a dimpling wineskin—yes, with booties attached!
O fiery woman, O hydroptic salamander,
marvel of intemperate ingenuity!
These are the tricks that destroy us, bringing
delight to the winemerchant, cobwebs to the hearth,
oblivion to the principles of domestic science.

FIRST WOMAN:
Be sure you stick in plenty of kindling, Manía.

MNESILOCHOS:
Stick it all in.
　　　　　　　—But first, a question or two.
You assert that this infant is yours?

FIRST WOMAN:
　　　　　　　　　　　　　Nine long months
I carried it.

MNESILOCHOS:
　　　　　　Carried it, eh?

FIRST WOMAN:
　　　　　　　　　　Yes, by Artemis!

MNESILOCHOS:
How much did it weigh? About a pint and a half?

FIRST WOMAN:
What are you up to? Why, you inhuman pervert,
you've taken its clothes off! It'll catch cold, it's so
teeny-weeny.

MNESILOCHOS:
　　　　　　Teeny-weeny indeed. How old is it?
Three or four libations, I dare say.

FIRST WOMAN:
　　　　　　　　　　　　About that,
counting from last Dionysia. —Give it back to me.

MNESILOCHOS:
I will not, by Apollo!

FIRST WOMAN:
　　　　　　　We'll burn you, then.

MNESILOCHOS:
Burn away. But this innocent must bite the blade.
　　　　　　　　　[He draws an enormous knife.

FIRST WOMAN:
I beg you, no! Do with me what you will,
but spare my baby girl!

MNESILOCHOS:

Ah, mother-love!
Nevertheless, this teeny-weeny must bleed.
                    [*He slashes the bundle. Wine pours out.*

FIRST WOMAN:

My child! My child!
Quick, Manía, pass me the ritual bowl
and let me catch the holy blood of my babe.

MNESILOCHOS:

Hold it lower down. I'll do this much for you.

FIRST WOMAN:

Damn you, you selfish, wasteful he-harlot!

MNESILOCHOS:

To the priestess belongs the victim's tegument.

FIRST WOMAN:

What are you talking about?

MNESILOCHOS:

                    This. Catch!
                    [*Tosses her the wineskin*

SECOND WOMAN:

O Mika, Mika, what a deflowering!
—Has something happened to your baby, dear?

FIRST WOMAN:

There is the murderer. Ask him.
                    For that matter,
keep an eye on him while I get Kleisthenês
to make another complaint at Town Hall.   [*Exit*

[*The women gather at the rostrum, leaving
MNESILOCHOS alone with his two bored guards.*

MNESILOCHOS:

What exquisite trick, what access of inspiration
will save me now? Come, brain,
excogitate deliverance.
                    —It was Euripides
got me into this trouble, and where he is now
I do not know. Well, I must send to him.
Yes, but how?
                    Let me think.
                    He himself
has something in that *Palamedês* of his . . .

A hero in distress
should take an oar and carve the salient facts
on the flat of the blade, and cast it into the sea.

Good. But I have no oar.
There is not a single oar in this sanctuary.
An oar?
　　　　Let's not be bound by precedent.
Why not use one of these votive tablets
hanging on the wall? They're wood; they're flat;
they'll float.
　　　　[*He tears down several wooden plaques from
　　　　around the altar.*

　　　　　　　O hands of mine, awake!
　　　　　　　Salvation is at stake!
　　　　　　　Write! Write!

　　　　　　　　　　[*He scratches busily with his knife.*
Agh! Literary composition! That infernal R
sprained my wrist.

　　　　　　　Lie still,
　　　　　　　Ye missive shingles: feel
　　　　　　　My incisive chisel chace
　　　　　　　Disgrace upon your face.

That does it! A masterpiece of calligraphy!
　　　　[*He hurls the tablets wildly in every direction.*

　　　　　　　Depart, be off, I say,
　　　　　　　This way, that way, every way,
　　　　　　　　　　　NORTH
　　　　WEST　　　　　　　　　　　　EAST
　　　　　　　　　　SOUTH
　　　　　　　Points between:

　　　　　　　　　　[*He sits down at the base of the altar.*

End of the *Palamedês* scene.

[*The* CHORUS *turns to face the audience for the*
Parábasis.

✿ PARÁBASIS

KORYPHAIOS:
The PARÁBASIS at last! A chance to endorse our own praises.

[PARÁBASIS

—You will hear men, this one and that, dredging up the old lies
About women, calling us the calamity of mankind, the source
Of tiffs, quarrels, sedition, riot, war itself;
Which makes us reflect, sometimes, 'Well, if we're so calamitous,
'Why are you men so fond of marrying calamity?'
And you not only marry it: you keep it hoarded up
In your houses, never letting it so much as stick out its head
For a breath of air. Is this how you cope with calamity?
Or say a poor woman steps out for a moment, and you come home
And find she's gone. What do you do? Rage! Throw things! Kick
The cat! Whereas if you really meant what you say,
You'd be down on your knees praising God and offering up libations
For your happy deliverance from calamity.

Or say
We get bored with all the connubial hilarity and decide
To spend a night or two at a girl friend's house: you
Absurd men crawl under the beds and creep into the closets
Looking for calamity. Why, if one of us leans out of a window,
There's a whole platoon of you gawking at calamity,
And when she pops back in, overcome by all this attention,
You can hardly wait until calamity reappears.

It seems probable, then, that there's something about us you like.

You say we're the frail sex. We say you are. Well, let's
    examine
The evidence. It might be useful to begin with our
    names.
'Victoria' is better than 'Elmer', you can hardly deny that,
And 'Gaby' is clearly more delicious than 'John Thomas',
And it's been a long time since any of you men have
    dared
Stand up to a 'Gloria'; and as for 'Prudence',
Is there a single Assemblyman in the whole roster
Who can look her in the eye? After that meeting last
    year,
Even you would be ashamed. The frail sex? You don't
    see women
Embezzling thousands out of the public funds and then
    riding
Around town bragging about the friends they've bought.
It takes a man to do that. No, when we women steal,
It's some little tiny thing, maybe a peck of wheat or so,
And we steal it from our own husbands; and you'll find
We more than pay it back the very day it was stolen.

                                              [MAKRON
    Can you say as much for yourselves? What
    Dinner-table strategists you are, what
    Suave operators, crumbsnatchers, what
    Gifted exploiters of slaves! (They're more
    Helpless—aren't they?—than women.)
    We know about warping and woofing, we
    Know where our pots and pans are. You
    Men, can you lay your hands on
    Any essentially male implement—
    A spear, say, or a buckler? No.
    You've mislaid it; or you threw it
    Away on some battlefield.

                                              [EPIRRHEMA
Complaints against you? We have many, but one's
Particularly important: the way you treat us in public.
Surely the woman who produces a valuable son—

A general or a top sergeant—should be honoured by the
  State.
She should have a special place at the Stênia
And the Skira and all the other public festivals.
Similarly, if it's a coward she's borne, some
Navy grafter or some incompetent pilot,
They should give her a salad-bowl haircut and make her
  sit
In the back row. It's a scandal, a civic disgrace,
To seat brave Lamachos's mother side by side
With Hypérbolos's, that awful woman with her white
  gown
And her silly hair-do, financing cheap deals
At outrageous rates! Rates? She should get
No interest at all from anyone fool enough
To deal with her. She ought to be confiscated,
Frozen, immobilized, with the notation:
'No interest allowed for your interesting son.'

  [*The* CHORUS *resumes its place.*

🏵 SCENE

MNESILOCHOS:
  This waiting for Euripides
  has got me cross-eyed. Where can he be?
  Maybe his *Palamedés*
  bores him now. I should think it would.
  Which one of his plays will bring him, I wonder?
  I have it! I'll try that new hit of his,
  the *Helen*. At any rate, I'm dressed for the part.
SECOND WOMAN:
  What are you up to now? What are you batting
  them big brown eyes at me for? You behave,
  or you'll get Helen all right when the Chief comes.
MNESILOCHOS:
  All hail, ye virgin waves of Nilus' flood,
  Hail, holy stream, that with moist inundation
  Dost annually drench white Ægypt's sod
  And dosify with black th' Ægyptian nation!

SECOND WOMAN:

In the name of Hekatê, what's the matter with you?

MNESILOCHOS:

Sparta my native land, no óbscure soil;
Old Tyndareus the father is of me.

SECOND WOMAN:

He is, is he? Old Phrynôndas, more likely.

MNESILOCHOS:

Helen my name—

SECOND WOMAN:

Listen, are you turning
woman on us again? You aren't through paying
for the first time.

MNESILOCHOS:

—and all for love of me
On sad Skamandrian strand braw heroes died.

SECOND WOMAN:

It's a damn pity you didn't die yourself.

MNESILOCHOS:

Here lost and lorn I lope, and Menelaos,
My hapless husband, cometh not to me.
He cometh not, I say. Why then, alas,
Do I persist in living?

SECOND WOMAN:

That's a fair question.

MNESILOCHOS:

But what sweet vision swims into my ken?
Delusive God, mock not my hopeful heart!

[*Enter* EURIPIDES *in dripping rags tangled with seaweed*

EURIPIDES:

What prince inhabits this impressive pile?
Speak: of his courtesy will he provide
For mariners shipwrack'd on the salt sea?

MNESILOCHOS:

'Tis Prôteus rules these rafters.

SECOND WOMAN:

You're a liar!
Protéas has been dead a good ten years.

EURIPIDES:

What realm is this to which my barque hath come?

MNESILOCHOS:

'Tis Ægypt, sire.

EURIPIDES:

Alack, how have I strayed!

SECOND WOMAN:

Friend, you mustn't believe a thing this fool
tells you. This here's the Thesmophorion.

EURIPIDES:

Lord Prôteus, is he within, or is he without?

SECOND WOMAN:

You must be still feeling the sea, stranger.
I just got through saying Protéas is dead.

EURIPIDES:

'Las, is he dead? Where then is his sepulchre?

MNESILOCHOS:

This is his tomb upon the which I park.

SECOND WOMAN:

Well, I'll be damned! And so will you, damn you,
calling this here altar a damn tomb!

EURIPIDES:

O thou adorning this sarcophagus,
Tell me, why is thy visage thus enveil'd?

MNESILOCHOS:

Th' insensate force of local circumstance
Drives me to share the couch of Prôteus' son.

SECOND WOMAN:

You ought to be ashamed of yourself, you should so,
to lie like this to a stranger.

—Look, friend,
this son of a bitch broke in here this morning
to pick us women's pockets.

MNESILOCHOS:

Base yelping brach,
On me discharge the venom of thy hate!

EURIPIDES:

Damsel, what hag is this accuseth thee?

MNESILOCHOS:

'Tis Prôteus' daughter, the Lady Theonoé.

SECOND WOMAN:

Now this is a little too much. I'll have you know
my name's Kritylla, just plain Kritylla,
and my old man's name was Antitheos, by God,
and we hail from Gargettos. And you're a bastard.

MNESILOCHOS:

Rail as thou wilt, I will not wed thy bro.,
Nor fail my Troyan Menelaos so.

EURIPIDES:

Soft, soft! What word is this assails mine ears?
Oh turn on me those orbs enlaked in tears!

MNESILOCHOS:

I blush to shew thee my reviled face,
But natheless—

EURIPIDES:

Angels and ministers of grace!
What eye is this I eye? 'Tis praeterhuman!
My brain swoons with surmise. Who art thou, woman?

MNESILOCHOS:

Nay, who art thou? My symptoms are the same.

EURIPIDES:

Art thou a Hellene, or indigenous dame?

MNESILOCHOS:

A Hellene. And thou, stranger, what thy race?

EURIPIDES:

Lady, on thee detect I Helen's face?

MNESILOCHOS:

And Menelaos' I on thee? I know,
Because thy vegetation tells me so.

EURIPIDES:

In sooth, thou contemplat'st that wretched wretch.

MNESILOCHOS:

To thee my wifely arms do I outstretch.
Oh hold me, hold me, hold me in thine own!
Come let me kiss thee, making murm'rous moan,
And let us then be going, going, gone!

SECOND WOMAN:

Any going going on around this place
is going to get a touch of this torch of mine.

EURIPIDES:

Yea, is't e'en so? Wouldst thou keep Tyndar's daughter

From the bed and board her legal husband brought her?
SECOND WOMAN:
I get it now. You're in this plot too,
you and that talk about Egypt. I might have known.
Well, he'll get what's coming to him, all the same.
Here's the Chief now.
                    [*Enter* MAGISTRATE *with an oafish* POLICEMAN
EURIPIDES (*apart, to* MNESILOCHOS):
                            That play of mine, it seems,
Failed to work out. Ah well, we tried!
I think I'd better be going.
MNESILOCHOS:
                            What about me?
EURIPIDES:
There's nothing whatever for you to worry about.
Not while I live
shall it be said that I abandoned you.
I've still a trick or two up this sleeve of mine.
MNESILOCHOS:
Yes. But this last trick buttered few parsnips.
                                        [*Exit* EURIPIDES

MAGISTRATE:
Is this the rapist that Kleisthenês reported?
SECOND WOMAN:
It is, your Worship.
MAGISTRATE:
                    H'm. Typical.
Notice he can't meet my eyes.
                            —Very good.
Officer, take this prisoner inside,
tie him to a plank, bring him out and prop him up.
Do you understand me?
POLICEMAN:
                    Yass, Marse Chief.
MAGISTRATE:
And guard him with your life, Officer.
If his accomplices attempt a rescue,
remember to use your whip.
POLICEMAN:
                        I use it, yass.

SECOND WOMAN:
Goodness knows he may have to! Just now
there was some sort of travelling salesman here
trying to spring him.

MNESILOCHOS:
Commissioner, by that eager
palm of yours, I implore you:
Grant me a favour, since sentence has been passed.

MAGISTRATE:
What favour, fellow?

MNESILOCHOS:
Before your associate
attaches me to the plank that you have mentioned,
have him strip me naked. If carrion crows must eat me,
it would be wrong to spoil their meal with the sight
of this saffron gown.

MAGISTRATE:
Denied. The Court has ruled
that you must suffer in your peculiar gear.

MNESILOCHOS:
Absurdly decked, must I absurdly die?

[*Exit* MAGISTRATE
Alas, I am a saffron mockery.
[*The* POLICEMAN *and the Guards take* MNESI-
LOCHOS *inside.*

HYPÓRCHEMA: DANCE SONG

KORYPHAIOS:
The dance, the women's dance, at the holy hour
When the Two Goddesses lead the solemn games,
   And Pausôn himself, starved, dry,
      Burns to multiply
The rigours of fasting for ever in their names.

         Whirl, whirl in a round
   Follow the beat
         of the clever feet,
      And whirl, hand
         circling hand

body bent to the sweet
                strict saraband:

CHORUS:
                Sing for the gods   [STROPHE Iα
                Olympian deathless Sing
Timeless hours in the lyric rage of the dance

                No woman's tongue   [STROPHE Iβ
                Contrive in this ritual
A word of hate for any hateful man

                All our art   [ANTISTROPHE I
                Draw the mystical round
Of the central Awe, the cyclic Mystery

                I dance in the name   [STROPHE II
                Of Apollo: O Music!
                I dance in the name
                Of Artemis: chaste Archer!
                        Defence from afar!
                I dance in the name
                Of Hêra: Bride Goddess!
                        Guardian of Marriage!
                        Join my dance.

                I dance in the name   [ANTISTROPHE II
                Of Hermês: O Shepherd!
                I dance in the name
                Of Pan and all Nymphs:
                        May they attend us!
                I dance the women's dance,
                The circle recircled,
                        In this holy season:
                        Join my dance.

KORYPHAIOS:
    Iô Bacchos
                Coronal of ivy
                        Wild Master
                Leap for us

Lead us
>Spin for us in the dance

CHORUS:

>Descend O child of Sémelê thou   [STROPHE III
>>Tumultuous Flame
>O son of Zeus come down upon us now
>>—*Evion evion evohé!*—
>>In song cascading
>From hills where the Maenads chant Dionysos' name:

>>>[ANTISTROPHE III
>>Kithairon shudders with music a shout
>>>Bursts from the stone
>The upland thickets howl in the nymphic rout
>>>—*Evion evion evohé!*—
>>>Of the cortège advancing
>As the smitten god strides on to join the dancing.

🎐 SCENE

>[*Reënter* POLICEMAN *and Guards carrying* MNESI-
>LOCHOS *bound to a large plank, which they de-*
>*posit at the foot of the altar*

POLICEMAN:
>Sure and it's all outdoors you got now
>to screech in.

MNESILOCHOS:
>>I implore you, Lieutenant—

POLICEMAN:
>>>No soap.

MNESILOCHOS:
>Prithee undo this knot.

POLICEMAN:
>>Knot? Yass.

MNESILOCHOS:
>Confound your incompetence, you're making it
>tighter!

POLICEMAN:
>>More tight, Boss?

MNESILOCHOS:

Ouch!

POLICEMAN:

Yass?

MNESILOCHOS:

You're killing me.

POLICEMAN:

Yerra, make up your mind!
—Now you wait here, Boss. I go in and get
soft seat to sit on. I come right back.   [*Exit*

MNESILOCHOS:

This is the persuasive art of Euripides,
and you can have it.

> [*He looks offstage, startled.*

—But what's this I see?
Almighty everlasting Zeus, it's Euripides
himself! He has come back! He would not leave me
desolate, forsaken, but returns disguised
as Perseus; and from the signs that he is making,
I must play Andrómeda. Well, I'm chained tight enough.
I will be Andrómeda, and thus I begin
my girlish lamentation:

> [*The following aria is accompanied by sporadic musical effects offstage.* MNESILOCHOS' *singing wavers unpredictably between treble and bass.*

Ye dolorous maids, ye virgins, coronal
Of my bright days enduskèd now in doom,
O playmates mine: Behold me now
Reject,
      abject,
           disject,
The object of a vile policeman's whim.
O Echo, Echo,
Dost hear me in thy cavernous concave?
Speak, Nymph: wilt thou show
Compassion, damn it all, and send me home
To my poor wife?

> (Yea, woman's life
> Is hard, but far harder
> The heart of my warder.)

Girlish coëvals, quondam confidantes mine,
Is it for this I have engulphed the wiles
Of antic harlots at their festival?
Is there to be no quiring hymeneal,
No sweet prothalamy, for wretched me?
Rigid, rapt
On this slivery joist,
No true-love knot adorning, but loveless
Links and buckles bite my nubile limbs,
Pure virgin meat, more meet for clasp
Less cruel!
              And Glauketês,
Remorseless fish,
Lurks, lurks i' the wave, a monster moist,
To maul my shrinking flesh.

I am the most unhappy man that ever lived.

O all ye Nymphs that pass by on the road,
Sing me no nuptial lay, but a threne, a threne,
Beating your bright breasts.
                          A maiden's curse
On the inhuman cad that ruined me,
Shaved me, plucked me, left me in saffron gown
To suffer at the pleasure of this select
Sorority!
              Yet who can bend the Fates?
No, rather the daystar sag from the firmament
And solar rage encrisp me to a turn!
Then, as I burn,
I'll wind my lamentable neck in death
And pass away on a melodious breath.
                    [*The voice of* EURIPIDES *is heard offstage.*

EURIPIDES:
Greetings, fair Princess; but a malediction
on the unnatural parent who staked you out
here on the rocks.

MNESILOCHOS:
                    Whose is the voice I hear?

EURIPIDES:
Echo I'm called, Echo, illusive nymph

yielding antiphonies to human speech.
This wild strand knows me well: a year ago
I performed here for Euripides.

                    —But you,
Lady Andrómeda, have you learned your lines?
Begin with a groan.

MNESILOCHOS:

                    You will groan after me?

EURIPIDES:

Groan for groan and grunt for grunt. I swear it.
        [*In the following passage* EURIPIDES' *voice, as off-*
        stage echo, should be different in timbre and
        much louder than the phrases echoed.

MNESILOCHOS:

O holy Night,
Along the bright
Starspangled aether how slow thy flight!
Thy car celest,
Proceeding west,
Caresseth high Olympos's breast.

EURIPIDES:

                    PUSSY'S BREAST!

MNESILOCHOS:

Is this the price
A virgin nice
Must pay for connubial surmise?

EURIPIDES:

                    HER MICE!

MNESILOCHOS:

O Fate inexorable!—

EURIPIDES:

                    BULL!

MNESILOCHOS:

For God's sake, stop your chattering!

EURIPIDES:

                    AT A RING?

MNESILOCHOS:

Damn you, can't you see I'm busy?

EURIPIDES:

                    IS HE?

MNESILOCHOS:
How can I render a Euripidean monody
if you keep on talking?

EURIPIDES:
KEEP ON TALKING!

MNESILOCHOS:
Damn you!

EURIPIDES:
AND YOU!

MNESILOCHOS:
Is there no hope?

EURIPIDES:
NOPE!

MNESILOCHOS:
I despair—

EURIPIDES:
I'D A SPARE—

MNESILOCHOS:
I stutter—

EURIPIDES:
ICED UDDER!

MNESILOCHOS:
Woe, woe!

EURIPIDES:
WHOA!

MNESILOCHOS:
I'm a wretch!

EURIPIDES:
I'M A-RETCH!
[*Reënter* POLICEMAN *with a footstool*

POLICEMAN:
Who you talk to?

EURIPIDES:
YOU TALK, TOO!

POLICEMAN:
You get funny, yass?

EURIPIDES:
FUNNY ASS!

MNESILOCHOS:
God no, Officer! It's this woman.

EURIPIDES:

HIS WOMAN!

POLICEMAN:
I no see woman.

EURIPIDES:

NOSY WOMAN!

POLICEMAN:
You son of bitch, I find you!

EURIPIDES:

BEHIND YOU!

POLICEMAN:
Where that woman?

MNESILOCHOS:

Seems to have gone now.

POLICEMAN:
Boss, that woman talk too much.
[EURIPIDES *suddenly appears suspended over their
heads by entirely visible wires. He is in the costume of Perseus—winged sandals and helmet—
and carries a shield emblazoned with the head
of the Cheshire Cat.*

EURIPIDES:
*What alien shore is this, ye gods, upon
The which my rapid sandal doth descend?
Cleaving the vast inane, I hasten on
To Argos with this Gorgon head in hand.*

POLICEMAN:
What you say, Chief? You got Marse Gorgos' haid?

EURIPIDES:
The Gorgon's head, vile varlet!

POLICEMAN:

Yass. That Gorgos.

EURIPIDES:
*But stay! Upon these cruel rocks a rich
And maiden form is drapèd in distress!
As men a dory to a mooring hitch,
So hitch'd is she by cables merciless.*

MNESILOCHOS:
*Stranger, in Pity's name I thee conjúre:
Dissolve my bondage.*

POLICEMAN:

Pretty funny, yass.
You damn fool, Boss: you talk too much too late.

EURIPIDES:
Virgin supine, I see and pity thee.

POLICEMAN:
Him a virgin? That old goat? Ha!

EURIPIDES:

Barb'rous dog,
'Tis Kêpheus' girl, Andrómed, that thou doggest.

POLICEMAN:
Girl, yass? She got big ramming machine.

EURIPIDES:
Give me thy white hand, lady.

POLICEMAN:

No!

EURIPIDES:

Officer,
as man to man: each one of us
has his own little weaknesses, don't you find?
Well, mine is a sudden and desperate passion for
this radiant maiden.

POLICEMAN:

You got funny taste, Chief.
I turn him over, yass? and you do your stuff.

EURIPIDES:
For me t' unbind her, churl, it were more meet,
And then to gambol on the nuptial sheet.

POLICEMAN:
You bet. You want to lay this old bastard,
you go right ahead. I no object.

EURIPIDES:

Nay, by Heav'n,
I'll loose those loops!

POLICEMAN:

Not while I got this whip.

EURIPIDES:
Aroint thee!

POLICEMAN:

Go to hell!

EURIPIDES:

Alas the day,

What argument will melt this brutish clay?
Yea, what avails the honey tongue of sense
To lick the sap of impercipience?
Some other circumventing means must I
Devise to combat the gendarmerie. [*Exit*

POLICEMAN:
That old fox think he make monkey out of me.

MNESILOCHOS:
Perseus, remember me,
A maid betrothèd to adversity!

POLICEMAN:
Silence in the court! You see this whip?
[MNESILOCHOS *subsides; the* POLICEMAN *sits down*
upon his stool and immediately falls asleep.

🕸 CHORIKON: CHORAL INTERLUDE

KORYPHAIOS:
I call upon Pallas. Hear me, Goddess!

CHORUS:
   Maiden peerless, Lover   [STROPHE I
    Of choric song, descend:
   Thou Keeper of the City's keys,
    Almighty Friend!

KORYPHAIOS:
I call upon Pallas, Destroyer of Tyranny.

CHORUS:
   Warrier Virgin, Patron   [ANTISTROPHE I
    Of Athens town, be near:
   To women suppliant incline
    Thy gracious ear.

         [STROPHE II
 And the two august Ladies whose ritual
  We sing today,
 Let them send down a benison to fall
  On us at play.
   Here no male insolence

        Dares violate
    The holy ground whose awful innocence
    We consecrate.

    Hear us, O Goddesses! If as of old   [ANTISTROPHE II
        You mark our prayer,
    Flame down in radiance twofold
        From the bright air.
            Come, O Persephonê,
            Demêter, come!
        The sacred dance with double instancy
        Summons you home.

🏵 ÉXODOS

        [Reënter EURIPIDES, dressed as in the Prologue,
        carrying a lyre. He is accompanied by a boy flute-
        player and a nearly naked dancing-girl.

EURIPIDES:
    Ladies, I have a proposal to make to you.

    If you are concerned, as I am,
    to make an end to this lamentable feud,
    I promise, for my part, never again to write
    or speak any ill of women.
KORYPHAIOS:
                            That is handsome.
    But why this change of heart?
EURIPIDES:
                            The gentleman
    attached to the plank there is my father-in-law.
    He is my motive. Release him, and you and I
    are friends for ever. Refuse, and I
    will publish every naughty secret you have
    when your husbands come back home.
KORYPHAIOS:
                            Fair enough,
    so far as we are concerned. But you'll have to persuade
    this constable.
EURIPIDES:
                That should be no problem.

Look, Fleurette: [*To the dancing-girl*
Do you remember what you're supposed to do?
Dance over in front of him, give him
a waggle or two, and dance back.
                              —You, Terêdôn,
let's have a Persian polka on your flute.
                    [*While the girl is dancing,* EURIPIDES *disguises*
                    himself as an old woman. Near the end of the
                    dance the POLICEMAN *wakes up.*

POLICEMAN:
Sweet moosics do I hear?
                              —What is this? A
floor show, yass?

EURIPIDES:
                    Sir, we beg your pardon.
This little lady has been engaged to dance
at a big convention down town, and we stopped here
for a kind of rehearsal.

POLICEMAN:
                    Is O.K. by me.
Maybe you let me rehearse her too?
How quick she wiggle, like a flea in the whiskers!

EURIPIDES:
Your dress, Fleurette, your dress! Slip it off,
do.
        There.
                    Now sit down on the gentleman's knee,
and I'll unstrap your sandals.

POLICEMAN:
                              Yass, sit down,
Baby, and I unstrap too.
                              —Oh the little tits,
all stiff, round, yass, like little parsnips!

EURIPIDES:
Pick up the tempo, Terêdôn.
                              —Fleurette,
don't tell me you're bashful with this gentleman!

POLICEMAN:
And a tight little ass, yass.
                              I feel
funny, like I want something.

EURIPIDES:

                        I'm sure you do, sir.
—That's all, Fleurette. Put your dress back on.
It's getting late.

POLICEMAN:

             Maybe she kiss me, lady?

EURIPIDES:

Kiss the gentleman, Fleurette.

POLICEMAN:

                   My God, a sweet kiss!
Oh little tongue, so good, so curly, like
Attika honey.
            —Maybe she sleep with me?

EURIPIDES:

Really, sir, there are certain things
that—

POLICEMAN:

          No, no, lady. I pay. I pay good!

EURIPIDES:

A drachma, say?

POLICEMAN:

              One drachma, yass.

EURIPIDES:

                     Let me see

your money.

POLICEMAN:

             Lady, I have no money.
I give you this belt.
    [*He unbuckles his belt and hands it to* EURIPIDES.
    Then, to the girl:
            —Now you come.
                    —Lady,

how you call her?

EURIPIDES:

          Her name is Artemisia.

POLICEMAN:

Hattie Mischa? I got it.
         —You come now, Hattie Mischa.
    [*Exit* POLICEMAN *with the girl.* EURIPIDES *strips off
his disguise.*

EURIPIDES:
A job well done, I swear by Hermês the Diddler!
—That's all, Terêdôn. You can go. And take this lyre.
—Now to the rescue.
                    —Father-in-law,
now that you're free, I advise you to make tracks
for your inconsolable wife and your little ones.

MNESILOCHOS:
You advise right.

EURIPIDES:
                    There's the last rope! Now let's get going
before the policeman comes back here.

MNESILOCHOS:
                                     You said it.
                                          [Exeunt

                    [Reënter POLICEMAN solus, dishevelled

POLICEMAN:
Lady, I thank you for little girl. She real nice,
she not so slow!
                    —Lady? Where old lady go?
I smell mouse.
                    —And old man? He go too?
I been buggered!
                    —Old lady? Old lady?
This not very nice of you.
                                —You, Hattie Mischa?
Yerra, where is old lady? Hattie Mischa?
She fix me up, all right.
            [Seeing his discarded belt on the ground, and
            kicking it
                                Yass,
and you, you son of bitch, you sure
belt me one in the bushes! You go to hell!
Ladies, where is old lady?

KORYPHAIOS:
                                You refer, sir,
to the respectable person with the harp?

POLICEMAN:
Yass'm, you bet.
                    [KORYPHAIOS points in wrong direction.

KORYPHAIOS:
                    She went that way,
and there was an elderly gentleman with her.

POLICEMAN:
He have saffron dress on?

KORYPHAIOS:
                              Now that you mention it,
I believe he did. If you hurry you may catch them.

POLICEMAN:
This way they go? This way?
                              —You, Hattie Mischa!

KORYPHAIOS:
No. Not that way. Over there.
                              —Really, sir,
you'll get nowhere running around in circles.

POLICEMAN:
Yass, I run in circles, but I go!
—Hey, Hattie Mischa!
                              [*Exit in the wrong direction*

KORYPHAIOS:
Go, and hell take you!

                              [*To the audience*
—Friends:
It is late, and our play is done. Let us all
go quietly home and pray the Goddesses
grant us their blessing at this Festival.

GENERAL NOTES

Σ = Scholiast

Page

261: *Persons Represented*: Mnesilochos is nowhere named in the play, and the textual evidence for his name is contradictory. Σ says, 'Mnesilochos prologuizes,' and identifies him as a κηδεστής—that is to say, a relative by marriage—of Euripides. I have followed a venerable but suspect tradition in making him the poet's father-in-law.

261: *'If winter comes', they say*: The Greek proverb is, 'When will the swallow come back?'

262: In the opening lines of the play A. is making fun of the metaphysical jargon of the Sophists, with whom he (more or less unfairly) associates Euripides.

262: *to become suddenly lame*: Then he would not have to walk at all.

266: *I libel them*: This was certainly Euripides' reputation, although such plays as *Alkêstis* and *The Trojan Women* should have been enough to offset the misogyny of the *Hippolytos, Medea,* and (presumably) the lost *Melanippê*. It should be said, however, that even Euripides' virtuous women have a Cordelia-like inhumanity.

266: *assemble with the Assembly*: No men were admitted, of course.

266: *you take the cake*: Already proverbial in A.'s time.

268: *in the style of Aischylos*: Mnesilochos cites the Lykûrgian Tetralogy of Aischylos (now lost), where, in the second play, King Lykûrgos is impudently questioning the god Dionysos, not knowing who he is. It is the effeminate manner and dress of Dionysos, like Agathôn's, that gives the travesty its point.

270: *Brevity . . . is the soul of wit*: The original cites two lines from the (lost) *Aiolos* of Euripides.

321

270: *'You love the sun . . .'*: Quoted from the *Alkêstis* of Euripides (691).

271: *Off with that cloak*: Σ says that this depilation scene is 'taken' from a comedy (variously called *Idaioi* and *Empipramenoi*) by Kratinos.

275: *it is your heart, and not your tongue*: This famous evasion, from the *Hippolytos* of Euripides, seems to have amused A. particularly. He cites it again, with crushing effect, near the end of *Frogs*. In the original, of course, it was the tongue, and not the heart, that swore.

275: The *Párodos,* or Entrance of the Chorus, brings us into the Temple where the Festival of the Thesmophoria is being celebrated. The liturgical passages that follow are of considerable interest because they parody or imitate ritual formulas and practices of which little is actually known. A formal invocation in prose is followed by a more extended one in verse, which I have cast in the form of a Litany; and this, in turn, passes into a Ritual Cursing of the kind that may still be found in the Anglican Service of Commination, prescribed for Ash Wednesday. These curses are summarized in a rather perfunctory concluding hymn, and the business of the meeting follows immediately.

276: *Givers of Law*: The dual number is used, for the Givers of Law are Demêter and her daughter Persephonê. The Festival is called *Thesmophoria* after them in this aspect (Θεσμοφόρω). It was a three-day feast, celebrated in November; and in this play we have arrived at the Second Day, *Nêsteia,* which is given over to fasting and secret business. The mysteries are inviolable, and consequently the invasion of them by a man is a scandal of horrifying proportions.

277: *consort with the Persians:* The warning against treason was a part of the regular ritual; the warning against Euripides is a part of the parody.

280: *the vegetable dealer's son*: A. is never tired of asserting that the mother of Euripides, Kleitô, sold greens for a living.

280: *'th' adult'rous guest'*: The allusion is to the *Sthenoboia,* a (lost) tragedy by Euripides, but it is so contorted that I have tried to render it by a paratragic line. The sense is that a guilty wife, thinking of her lover, drops a pitcher and breaks it.

280: *'morning greenness'*: Euripidean parody again, but of an unknown source. A brother notices with suspicion that his sister is inclined to be unwell at breakfast-time.

280: *'What's wedlock . . .'*: From the (lost) *Phoinix* of Euripides.

282: *brought up on wild vegetables*: See note on p. 280, *supra*.

285: *the proverb says*: It says 'Under every stone there's a scorpion.' A. substitutes 'orator' for 'scorpion': a frigid joke, though not so frigid as my rendering of it.

286: *chopped her husband up*: Σ refers to Klytaimestra, who murdered her husband Agamemnon.

288: *mad about women*: That is to say, he wants to resemble women; he is a pathic. —A. invents a verb, γυναικομανῶ; so in *The Birds*, ὀρνιθομανῶ: 'I'm bird crazy'.

290: *Whoozis*: Mnesilochos keeps repeating τὸν δεῖνα, just as we say 'Whaddyacallum', and the Spaniards 'Fulano'.

291: *that appendage*: Mnesilochos is wearing, and concealing with increasing difficulty, the prominent ritual *phallos*.

294: *has torn my precious babe*: The First Woman, providing against the austerities of the Day of Fasting, has wrapped up a wineskin in baby clothes and brought it to the Assembly. A. is fond of the idea that the women of Athens are too much given to drink.

296: *counting from last Dionysia*: That is to say, seven months.

297: *that Palamedês of his:* The *Palamedês* of Euripides was one of a trilogy performed in 415 B.C., the two other tragedies being *Alexandros* and *The Trojan Women*, with *Sisyphos* as satyr-play. Of these only *The Trojan Women* has survived. Palamedês himself, a Greek chieftain in the Trojan War, was murdered at Troy: 'and Euripides shows in [this play],' says Σ, 'how Palamedês' brother Oiax . . . wrote an account of the death on several oar blades and cast them into the sea', in order that one of them might carry the news to their father Nauplios.

299: *Parábasis*: At this point the action is suspended and the poet addresses the audience through the Chorus. As a dramatic form, a *parábasis* has a rather complicated structure; but it was subject to change (and even to omission), and in this play it is severely curtailed.

301: *the* Helen: The *Helen* of Euripides was produced in 412

B.C., the year before our comedy. In it the dramatist accepts the counter-myth, recorded by Herodotos and others, that Helen was not taken to Troy by Paris, but to Egypt, where she was impounded (as it were) by the kindly King Prôteus, and later retrieved by her husband Menelaos. (The Helen at Troy was only an *imago* of her, a phantom of delight.) Aristophanes' delightful recognition scene is a masterpiece of friendly parody.

302: *Protéas has been dead*: The sentry woman, Kritylla, has never heard of King Prôteus of Egypt, and confuses the name with that of one Protéas—an Athenian citizen, presumably, of whom we know nothing, nor is it necessary that we should.

303: *What realm is this*: Menelaos, returning from Troy with his wife—or the phantom of his wife, although he does not know this—, has been blown to the shore of Egypt, where he is startled to find a counter-wife, the real Helen, seated upon the royal tomb.

305: *a . . . POLICEMAN*: The ordinary Athenian policeman was a Skythian archer. A. makes this one speak a barbarous, though by no means consistent, dialect or perversion of Greek. The translation pushes this tó an extreme: I had in mind a Comedy Cop, minstrel-show blackface with bright red hair, a surrealist nightmare of jargon.

309: *I will be Andrómeda*: The *Andrómeda* of Euripides, now lost, was produced in 412 B.C. This time Aristophanes' parody seems more cruel: the heroine's pathetic monody, with the graceful echo device, is reduced to utter absurdity; and the interpolations of the Policeman, a caricature of the sea-monster Glauketês, are a devastating final touch.

316: ÉXODOS: The resolution of comedy is perfunctory enough: the sudden agreement between Euripides and the Chorus is improbable, to say the least, and one feels that A. is looking for the quickest and easiest way to make an end of the business. Plot, however, is of minoʌ̆ importance in most of A.'s compositions, the *Lysistrata* being a notable exception.

318: *this belt*: In the original he hands over his quiver, an essential part of his equipment; and this produces, a few lines later, an indelicate pun that can not be taken over directly into English. 'Belt' makes a less explosive pun possible.

❧ INDEX OF PROPER NAMES

ABBREVIATIONS:

AV:	*Birds*
LY:	*Lysistrata*
RA:	*Frogs*
TH:	*Ladies' Day*
Σ:	*Scholiast*

Dates, unless otherwise noted, are B.C.

ACHAIAN: Greek.

ACHARNAI: A town in Attika.

ACHERON: A river of Hadês.

ACHILLES, ACHILLEUS: Son of King Peleus of Phthia and the sea-goddess Thetis; mightiest of the Greek chieftains at Troy.

ADEIMANTOS: An Athenian admiral whose career culminated in surrendering the Fleet to Lysander at Aigospotamoi, less than a year after the unflattering mention of him in RA. His father's name was Leukolophidês, 'Old Whitey'.

ADONIS: A fertility god from Asia Minor whose cult became common in Greece. The *Adonia* was an annual celebration of his death and resurrection, participated in exclusively by women. On the day of the departure of Nikias's fleet on the ruinous Sicilian Expedition, the women of Athens were wailing the Adonis-dirge ('Αδωνιασμός), and this was taken to be an evil omen.

AGAMEMNON: King of Argos; commander of the Greek forces in the Trojan War.

AGATHON: Dramatist, dilettante in the arts and philosophy; satirized frequently by A. for his affected manner and supposed effeminacy; *fl.* 406. At some time before the production of RA he had left Athens for the refined pleasures of a life in Macedonia.

AGENOR: A king of Phoinikia; father of KADMOS, *q.v.*

AGLAUROS: One of the three daughters of Kekrôps, King of Athens, the two others being Pandrosos and Hersê. Σ says that

325

it was customary to swear 'by Aglauros!' or 'by Pandrosos!', but never 'by Hersê!'.

AGORA: The forum in Athens.

AIAKOS: A son of Zeus and Aigina; father of Telamon and Peleus, hence grandfather of Achillês. Renowned for his integrity, he became one of the Judges of Hadês after his death. In RA he is ludicrously diminished, appearing as a kind of porter in Pluto's palace.

AIAS: Ajax, one of the Greek heroes at Troy; in RA, 'Aiantos' is merely the genitive case of this name.

AIGAIAN: The sea between Greece and Asia Minor.

AIGYPTOS: A king of Egypt who married his 50 sons to the 50 daughters of his estranged brother Danaos, King of Argos. At Danaos's command, all but one of the brides murdered their grooms on the wedding night.

'AIOLOS': A lost play by Euripides.

AISCHINES: An impoverished braggart politician; his 'castles' (AV 822) are what we should call 'castles in Spain'.

AISCHYLOS: Tragic poet (525-456); the reference at LY 88 is to his *Seven Against Thebes*.

AISOPOS, AESOP: A semi-legendary writer of fables.

AITHER: The upper air, or ether; in RA, invoked as a pragmatic deity by Euripides.

AKROPOLIS: The Citadel of Athens, sacred to Athêna; at AV 827, the inner fortress of Cloudcuckooland.

ALKAIOS: Lyric poet (*fl. c.* 600).

'ALKESTIS': A play by Euripides, produced in 438.

ALKIBIADES: A military commander and politician of great brilliance and even greater unpredictability. Twice exiled from Athens, he had no compunction about going over to the enemy side; yet many thoughtful and patriotic Athenians still regarded him as the man of the hour. He was murdered in 404, the year after Aristophanes had cited him in RA.

ALKMENE: A mistress of Zeus; mother of Heraklês.

ALOPE: A mistress of Poseidon.

AMEIPSIAS: A comic poet, rival of Aristophanes.

AMMON: A famous temple and oracle of Zeus in Libya.

AMORGOS: An island in the Aigaian a little southeast of Naxos; famed for the quality of its flax, of which the 'very thinnest gowns' mentioned by Lysistrata were made.

AMPHION: Husband of Niobê; the quotation at AV 1247 is an absurdly jumbled parody of a passage in the [lost] *Niobê* of Euripides.

AMYKLAI: A town in Lakonia, centre of a cult of Phoibos Apollo.

ANAGYROS: A village in Attika; LY] also the name of a marsh which gave off a strong odor when too closely investigated.

'ANDROMEDA': A [lost] play by Euripides, produced in 412; TH] the heroine was a daughter of King Kepheus of Ethiopia, who, guided by an oracle, had her chained to the base of a seaside cliff and left to the mercy of a sea-monster, Glauketês; whence she was rescued by Perseus, who later married her.

APHRODITE: Goddess of love.

APOLLO: The sun-god.

ARCHEDEMOS: A demagogue and political trouble-maker; RA] although resident in Athens for at least seven years, he had never become a citizen.

ARCHENOMOS: Apparently a treasonable politician; but the reference in RA is so obscure that even Σ is silent.

ARES: God of war.

ARGO: Jason's ship on the voyage for the Golden Fleece.

ARGOS: The chief city of Argolis; one of the capitals of Agamemnon.

ARISTOGEITON: See HIPPIAS.

ARTEMIS: Goddess of the hunt and of virgins; sister of Apollo.

ARTEMISIA: A warrior queen of Halikarnassos who commanded a private fleet in Xerxes's expedition against Greece.

ARTEMISION: A promontory in Euboia; scene of a naval battle in which the Greeks successfully engaged the fleet of Xerxes.

ATHENA, ATHENE: Daughter of Zeus; goddess of wisdom; tutelary divinity of Athens.

ATHENS: Chief city of the district of Attika.

ATREUS: Son of Pelops; father of Agamemnon and Menelaos.

BABYLON: The Assyrian capital, on the Euphratês River.

BACCHANTES: The frenzied women attendant upon the rites of Dionysos.

BACCHOS: A name for Dionysos.

BAKIS: A celebrated and indefatigable Boiotian soothsayer.

BASILEIA: AV] 'Sovereignty', or 'Empery', personified as a housekeeper of Zeus and, later, as the bride of Pisthetairos.

BELLEROPHON: A prince of Korinth who murdered his brother and fled for refuge to the court of King Proitos of Tiryns. See STHENOBOIA.

BOIOTIA: A country lying north of Attika; LY] noted for the crudity of its inhabitants and the excellence of its edible eels.

BRAURON: LY] A town in Attika where every five years the festival of Artemis Brauronia was celebrated. The thematic legend tells of a village girl who was killed by a tame bear sacred to Artemis.

Her brother in turn killed the bear, thus committing a sacrilege that the quinquennial festival must expiate. On this occasion girls between the ages of five and ten, dressed in saffron gowns and walking in procession, represented little bears and were thus symbolically dedicated to Artemis. [Σ] But some say that Iphigeneia was sacrificed by her father Agamemnon at Brauron, instead of at Aulis; and it will be remembered that she was dressed in saffron robes for the occasion.

CHAIREPHON: AV] An Athenian friend of Sokratês, nicknamed 'Bat' because of his squeaky voice and sallow complexion.

CHAIRIS: A musician, 'somewhat frigid' according to Σ; here, a crow accompanying the Chorus on a flute.

CHAOS: A pre-Olympian deity; primal matter.

CHARON: The ferryman of the dead.

CHIANS: The island of Chios supported Athens early in the Peloponnesian War, and a clause for the Chians was accordingly added to prayers for the public good. After the Sicilian Expedition, Chios defected to Sparta.

DAREIOS: King of Persia (549-485); in Aischylos's *Persae* his ghost rises, to the consternation of the Chorus, and speaks.

DELOS: An island, one of the Cyclades; birthplace of Apollo and Artemis.

DELPHOI: A famous shrine and oracle of Apollo in Phôkis, on Mount Parnassos.

DEMETER: The earth-goddess.

DEMOSTRATOS: An Athenian orator and jingo politician.

DIAGORAS: A native of Mêlos, Professor of Philosophy in Athens; AV] accused and condemned *in absentia* for atheism.

DIEITREPHES: A self-made man, manufacturer of wicker baskets, who bought his way into the upper echelons of the Government.

DIKTYNNA: A Kretan epithet for Artemis Huntress.

DIOMEIOS: RA] An epithet of Heraklês as object of a quinquennial rustic celebration [Σ].

DIONYSOS: The wine-god; son of Zeus by Semelê; RA] as deity presiding over the Theatre, his priest is invoked.

DITYLAS: See NOTES on RA, p. 110.

DODONA: A notable oracle of Zeus.

ECHIDNA: A chthonic monster, half woman and half serpent; to the giant Typhon, whose reaction is unrecorded, she bore the following menagerie: the Hydra, the Sphinx, the Nemean Lion, the dogs Orthos and Kerberos, and the Chimaira.

ECHO: An attendant of Hêra who seems to have played Hedda Gabler to Zeus's Ejlert Løvborg. She betrayed Zeus's amorous secrets to his wife, and was punished by being deprived of the power of spontaneous speech. See NOTES to TH, p. 309.

EILEITHYIA: Goddess of childbirth; cf. the Roman Juno Lucina.

EMPUSA: A spectral monster said to haunt men in various shapes.

ENGLOTTOGASTERS: 'Belly-tongued'; at AV 1696, used to designate political informers and the officials who employ them.

EPOPS: The Hoopoe, *Upupa epops;* see NOTES on AV, p. 164.

EREBOS: A pre-Olympian deity; usually, son of Night and Chaos; the infernal depths.

EROS: Son of Aphroditê; god of love.

ERYXIS: RA] Unknown, except that Σ describes him as misshapen and morose. He seems to have had yellow hair—a sign of effeminacy—and it is certain that his father's name was Philoxenos.

EURIPIDES: Tragic poet (484-406).

EUROTAS: A river of Sparta; see LEDA.

EXEKESTIDES: A parvenu alien living in Athens.

FOXDOG: The nickname of one Philostratos, a brothel-keeper.

FURIES: The three goddesses of infernal vengeance.

GARGETTOS: A suburb north-east of Athens.

GENETYLLIS: A name applied to Aphroditê as goddess of procreation [Σ]; in the plural, more broadly, the minor deities attendant upon that goddess. In LY, the reference is to a women's festival of Aphroditê.

GLAUKETES: A sea-monster; see ANDROMEDA.

GLYKE: At RA 1344, a woman accused of stealing a sleeping woman's rooster.

GORGON: Any one of three sisters, daughters of Phorkys and Kêtô, who were golden-winged, brass-handed and serpent-haired. The only mortal among them was Medûsa, whose face had the power to turn beholders to stone. She was killed by Perseus, *q.v.*, who cut off her head and carried it with him as a useful weapon in combat.

GORGOS: In TH, apparently an *ad hoc* name. The Policeman has never heard of the Gorgon, *q.v.*, and comes up with a name that sounds something like.

GRACES: Aglaia, Thalia, and Euphrosynê, daughters of Zeus and Aphroditê; goddesses of delight.

HALIMOS: A town in Attika.

HEBROS: A river in Thrace.

HEKATE: A goddess of witchcraft; assimilated to several other deities, as Selênê in heaven, Artemis on earth, and Persephonê in Hadês; hence represented as *triformis* (with three bodies) or *triceps* (with three heads); and understandably, in TH, a favourite oath among women.

HELENA, HELEN: Daughter of Zeus by Lêda, Queen of Sparta (King Tyndareus being the nominal father); wife of MENELAOS, *q.v.*; seduced and abducted by Paris, a prince of Troy, she was made the pretext for the Trojan War. See NOTES to TH, p. 301.

HELIOS: Apollo as god of the sun.

HELL: Used in RA to translate 'Hadês', merely in the sense of 'the place of departed spirits'.

HELLAS: Greece.

HELLENE: Greek.

HERA, HERE: Sister and wife of Zeus.

HERAKLES: Son of Zeus and Alkmenê; most celebrated of the legendary Heroes; often represented as a glutton, a braggart, and an indefatigable gynecomane.

HERMES: The winged Messenger of the gods.

HESIOD: Didactic poet (died *c.* 750).

HESTIA: Goddess of the hearth; as 'Nestiarch' (AV 865), absurdly assimilated to the Bird Divinities.

HIPPIAS: A Tyrant of Athens, died 490. He reigned with his brother Hipparchos until the assassination of the latter, in 514, at the hands of the patriots Aristogeiton and Harmodios; driven into exile, he took refuge in Persia and was killed at Marathon, fighting against his own country.

HIPPOBINE: In RA, an invented (or so one hopes) name of scandalous import.

HIPPOKRATES: In TH, an unpopular Athenian notable, nephew of Periklês. His sons were vulgarly known as 'the swine of Hippokratês'.

HIPPONIKOS: AV] An illustrative name; see NOTES on p. 177.

HOMER: The epic poet.

HYMEN: God of marriage.

HYPERBOLOS: A demagogue of humble origin, d. 411; for his occupation in Hadês, see KLEON.

IACCHOS: A name of Dionysos, used mystically in his revels.

IBYKOS: Lyric poet (*fl. c.* 540).

IDA: RA] A Kretan mountain.

IOPHON: A dramatic poet, son of Sophoklês. He is generally awarded a certain amount of respect, but doubts as to his originality and artistry are recorded, notably by Σ.

IRIS: The rainbow goddess.

KADMOS: A Phoenician prince who migrated from his country to Boiotia, where he founded the city of Thebes.

KALLIAS: A wealthy and dissolute Athenian amateur of philosophy. In AV, verse 283, the name is illustrative; see pertinent note, p. 177.

KALLIGENEIA: TH] 'She who brings forth beauty': an epithet for both Demêter and Persephonê; later dissociated from the goddesses and made a spirit (δαίμων) attendant upon Demêter [Σ].

KARIA: A country in Asia Minor; RA] its characteristic music is also mentioned by Plato; AV] the Karians were said to prefer fighting on mountain tops as offering better opportunities for flight: hence [292-3] the pun on 'crests'.

KARYSTIANS: Inhabitants of Karystos, a town in southern Euboia. Though allies of Athens, they were regarded with distaste for their uninhibited behaviour and primitive morals.

KASTOR: A son of Zeus and Lêda; brother of Polydeukês, as well as of Helena and Klytaimestra.

KEPHEUS: A king of Ethiopia; father of ANDROMEDA, q.v.

KEPHISOPHON: The evidence, which stems largely from RA, suggests that he was a musician who assisted Euripides in the lyric portions of certain plays. There is a scandalous rumour that he was intimately entertained by Euripides's wife.

KIMON: An Athenian general, sent with an expeditionary force to the aid of Sparta; see PERIKLEIDES.

KINESIAS: AV] A dithyrambic poet of Thebes in Boiotia; he is outrageously represented in LY.

KLEIDEMIDES: Unknown except for the allusion in RA.

KLEIGENES: RA] A small man, 'indigent and uncouth' [Σ], adhering to the jingoist policies of KLEOPHON, q.v. He apparently had a lowly job in the Public Baths.

KLEISTHENES: A beardless, effeminate person [Σ], apparently a naval officer; in TH his function is that of a Women's Advocate (πρόξενος), and Rogers's note is worth repeating: 'So thoroughly is he identified with the womankind, that the Chorus express no indignation at his appearance among them'.

KLEITOPHON: An elegant young idler, disciple of the sophist Thrasymachos of Chalcedon.

KLEOKRITOS: AV] An effeminate fat man with large feet who looked like an ostrich [Σ].

KLEOMENES: LY] A king of Sparta. In 508, after a more or less abortive attempt to restore Isagoras to power, he seized the Athenian Akropolis. There, with Isagoras, he was besieged for two days; on the third, he and his men were allowed to depart for Sparta under a truce. (See Herodotos: V, 69-73.)

KLEON: A tanner who became an outstanding demagogue, one of

the most destructive jingoist elements in Athenian politics. He died in 422. RA] In Hadês, associated with HYPERBOLOS, *q.v.*, he is reduced to the status of legal mouthpiece for proletarian women.

KLEONYMOS: A corrupt politician and shameless informer, a cowardly soldier who became famous for having thrown away his shield in battle; see NOTES on AV, p. 231.

KLEOPHON: An Athenian jingoist of Thracian origin, one of the never-say-die super-patriots; see NOTES to RA, p. 114.

KLEPSYDRA: A sacred spring beneath the walls of the Akropolis, near Pan's Cave.

KOKYTOS: A river of Hadês.

KOLIAS: Epithet pertaining to Aphroditê; from a promontory of Attika where there was a temple of the goddess.

KOLONOS: A small town, suburb of Athens.

KORINTH: A city of Greece, situated on the isthmus connecting Attika with the Peloponnesos. Its women enjoyed a reputation for loose behaviour, if the comic poets are to be believed.

KORKYRA: The modern Corfù; in AV, the 'first-class goods' [1463] are whips, which were manufactured there.

KORYBANTES: Priests of the Phrygian goddess Kybelê.

KOTHOKIDES: TH] A town of uncertain location.

KRANAOS: One of the mythical founder-kings of Athens, succeeding Kekrops.

KRATINOS: A writer of comedy; in 423 his *Bottle* won first prize over Ameipsias's *Konnos* and Aristophanes's *Clouds*.

KRIOA: A deme of Attika.

KRONOS: Father of Zeus.

KYBELE: An Asiatic goddess worshipped as *Magna Mater,* the Mother of the gods; at AV v. 875 she is the Great Ostrich.

KYKNOS: 'The Swan.' Both Arês and Poseidon had sons so named. In RA, a character in a lost play by Aischylos.

KYPRIAN: An epithet for Aphroditê.

KYRENE: RA, TH] An accomplished and notorious prostitute.

LAISPODIAS: AV] An Athenian general with a limp [Σ], or possibly the reference is to sexual incapacity [Σ]. The Triballian has draped his cloak as though to conceal his left leg—inelegant and pusillanimous behaviour.

LAKONIA: A country of the Peloponnesos; chief city, Sparta.

LAMACHOS: An Athenian general who died on the Sicilian Expedition.

LAMPON: A noted soothsayer.

LAUREION: A town of Attika famous for its gold mines; AV] the

Owl of Athêna was stamped on coins: hence, at v. 301, we might say 'coals to Newcastle'.

LEDA: Wife of Tyndareus, King of Sparta. While bathing in the Eurotas she was approvingly observed by Zeus, who descended to her in the shape of a Swan. Of this union were born quadruplets: two daughters, Helena and Klytaimestra, and two sons, Kastor and Polydeukês.

LEIPSYDRION: After the assassination of Hipparchos, the patriots were obliged to flee from Athens. They fortified Leipsydrion, on the slopes of Mount Parnês; but after a gallant defence they were forced to surrender. LY] Since this event took place in 513, about a century before the action of the play, the personal reminiscence of the Chorus is patently absurd.

LEMNOS: An island in the Aigaian Sea, opposite the Troad. Hephaistos crashed there when he was hurled down from Olympos. LY] 'Lemnos-fire' seems to be dragged in for the sake of a poor pun: Λήμνιον: λῆμαι, 'Lemnian' and 'sore eyes'. Σ, however, says that the women of Lemnos were lewd; and that Hephaistos established a smithy there.

LEONIDAS: The celebrated king of Sparta who with three hundred men confronted the entire army of Xerxes at the pass of Thermopylai (480). The Spartans fought to the last, and only one of them returned home; 'and he', as Lemprière puts it, 'was treated with insult and reproaches, for flying ingloriously from a battle in which his brave companions, with their royal leader, had perished'.

LEOTROPHIDES: A dithyrambic poet, 'thin and corpselike in appearance' [Σ].

LEPREON: A town in Elis; AV] the name suggests leprosy.

LESBOS: RA] This island was noted for its tradition of poetry and for its perverse sexual customs; see NOTES on p. 141.

LETHE: The river of forgetfulness, in Hadês.

LETO: A daughter of Kronos; mother, by Zeus, of Apollo and Artemis.

LIBYA: A region of Africa.

LOKRIS: A district of Greece, extending from Thessaly to Boiotia.

LYKABETTOS: A mountain in Attika; RA] 'Lykabettos-language', therefore, would be high ranting.

LYKIS: RA] A third-rate comic poet [Σ].

LYKON: LY] His wife, according to Σ, was a certain Rhodia, 'much lampooned for her licentiousness'; but the Greek text—τὴν Λύκωνος—is ambiguous and could just as well refer to Lysistrata, since we do not know her husband's name.

LYKOURGOS: AV] 'Called Ibis, either because of his Egyptian extraction or because of his skinny legs. There is a redundancy of the ibis in Egypt'. [Σ].

LYSIKRATES: AV] A venal Athenian official.

MAENAD: One of the ecstatic women in the train of Dionysos; see BACCHANTES.

MANES: A slave name.

MANODOROS: A slave name.

MARATHON: A battle (490) in which the Athenians defeated an enormously superior Persian army.

MEGABAZOS: A Persian nobleman, general in the service of DAREIOS, *q.v.*

MEGANEITOS: RA] He was a follower of Aischylos and his nickname was 'Manês'—the slang term for an unlucky throw at dice. Nothing else is known of him.

MEGARA: LY] The 'Legs of Mégara' was a fortified corridor connecting that town with its seaport, Nisaia.

MEIDIAS: AV] A corrupt and perverse politician; 'Quail' seems to have been a cant term in boxing, as we might say 'Punchy', and it may well refer to Meidias's dazed and glazed expression.

MELANION: Nothing is known of this paragon beyond what the old men of the Chorus tell us in LY. Xenophon mentions him in his treatise on hunting, and there seems to have been a proverb: 'as pure as Melanion'.

MELANIPPE: Heroine of one of the lost tragedies of Euripides; noted, apparently, for sophisticated morals and guile.

MELANTHIOS: A tragic poet, effete and afflicted with leprosy [Σ] or some disease resembling it.

'MELEAGROS': A lost play by Euripides.

MELETOS: An incompetent poet of some repute in Athens who became one of the chief accusers of Sokratês.

MELIAN: An inhabitant of Mêlos, which in 415 was blockaded by the Athenians under Nikias and starved into submission. Its male citizens were put to death, its women and children enslaved.

MELPOMENE: Muse of Tragedy.

MEMNON: A son of Teithônos and Eôs, killed in combat by Achillês.

MENELAOS: King of Sparta; husband of HELENA, *q.v.;* see also NOTES on TH, p. 301.

METON: AV] A famous astronomer and architect. He opposed the Sicilian Expedition and feigned insanity in order to avoid serving on it.

MIKON: A celebrated painter.

MILESIAN: An inhabitant of Milêtos, in Karia. LY] The city had abandoned the Athenian cause shortly before *Lysistrata* was composed—hence the outburst on p. 12; but there is also an indelicate reference to a phallic apparatus reputedly manufactured there.

MNEMOSYNE: Goddess of memory; mother, by Zeus, of the Muses: that is to say, the memory of the past engenders the arts and sciences of the present.

MOLOSSOS: A region of Greece noted for its large and alarming dogs.

MORISMOS: A tragic poet, several times mentioned with distaste by A.; Σ reports that he was abnormally uninspired and a good eye-doctor.

MUSAIOS: A legendary poet, said to have founded the Eleusinian Mysteries.

MUSES: Nine goddesses presiding over the arts and sciences; daughters of Zeus and Mnemosynê.

MYRMEX: RA] 'The Ant': a politician, obviously sinister, who is mentioned only here.

MYRONIDES: An Athenian general, *fl.* 450.

NAUSIKAA: A princess of Phaiakia; daughter of Alkinoös, who befriended Odysseus.

NEMESIS: TH] Divine retribution, occasionally represented as a goddess.

NEREUS: A sea-god; father, by his sister Doris, of fifty sea-nymph daughters known as Nereïdês.

NIKIAS: The celebrated and disastrously unfortunate commander of the Athenian forces on the Sicilian Expedition.

NIKOMACHOS: RA] A politician of mean birth whose dilatory tactics contributed to the confusion in Athens after the fall of the Four Hundred.

NILUS: River in Egypt.

NIOBE: A daughter of Tantalos; wife of Amphion; mother of fourteen children killed, because of her pride in them, by Apollo and Artemis.

NYSA [-BORN]: According to some, Dionysos was born and brought up on Mount Nyseion, or Nysa, in Thrace.

ODYSSEUS: Wiliest of the Greek leaders at Troy, and hero of Homer's *Odyssey*; at AV 1560, the allusion is to his performing the sacrificial rites necessary for summoning up the dead in Hadês (*Od.* XI).

OIDIPUS, OEDIPUS: RA] Son of Laïos and Iokastê of Thebes; slayer of his father and husband of his mother; father (and brother) of Antigonê, Ismenê, Polyneikês, and Eteoklês.

OINEUS: RA] A king of Kalydon. On one occasion he forgot to sacrifice to Aphroditê, who immediately sent a ferocious boar to devastate his kingdom.

OLOPHYXOS: A town near Mount Athos; in AV, the name was chosen for the sake of a heavy pun.

OLYMPIA: LY] The Olympian Games.

OLYMPIANS: The gods, as living upon Mount Olympos.

OLYMPOS: A mountain in Thessaly; seat of the gods.

OPUNTIOS: AV] A one-eyed grafter; but the word is also the proper adjective from OPUS, q.v.

OPUS: A town in Lokris.

OREAD[E]S: Mountain nymphs attendant upon Artemis Huntress.

ORESTES: RA] Son of Agamemnon and Klytaimestra; AV] an Athenian footpad who has assumed the heroic name: see NOTES on p. 197.

ORPHEUS: A philosopher, poet, and musician, widely celebrated in the early legends.

PALAMEDES: One of the Greek commanders at Troy, ruined by the machinations of Odysseus; TH] subject of a lost tragedy by Euripides: see NOTES on p. 297.

PALLAS: An epithet for Athêna.

PAN: An Arkadian sylvan god, sometimes associated with the orgies of Dionysos; LY] the allusion in v. 998 is to the god's lascivious and mischievous tendencies.

PANATHENAIA: Festival of Athêna, at Athens.

PANDORA: AV] 'The Earth, since it gives us everything necessary to life' [Σ]; not to be confused here with the Greek equivalent of Eve.

PANDROSOS: See AGLAUROS.

PANTAKLES: RA] Σ says: 'P. is ridiculed here as being inept in military deportment. Eupolis [the poet] . . . refers to him as gauche.' There was a lyric poet by this name, and he may be meant.

PAPHIAN: An epithet for Aphroditê.

PARDOKAS: RA] See NOTES on p. 110.

PARIS: Prince of Troy, son of Priam; Aphroditê bribed him to award her the prize in the most notable of all beauty contests.

PARNASSOS: A mountain in Phôkis.

PARNES: A mountain in Attika; RA] for the allusion, see LYKA-BETTOS.

PATROKLOS: Achilles's beloved companion at Troy; RA] he appears in the lost Myrmidones, by Aischylos.

PAUSON: TH] A miserly painter; he 'burns to multiply the rigours of fasting', because fasting costs no money.

PEISANDROS: LY] A reckless and mercenary politician who at the moment A. wrote was bringing to success his plot to overthrow the Athenian democracy and establish in its place the hateful rule of the Four Hundred.

PEISIAS' SON: AV] Apparently a traitor; but the allusion is hopelessly topical.

PELARGIC WALL: AV] The Stork Wall, *Pelargikon,* of the Akropolis at Athens.

'PELEUS': A lost play by Euripides.

PELOPONNESOS: The great peninsula lying south-west of Attika; its most important city was SPARTA.

PELOPS: Son of Tantalos who gave his name to the Peloponnesos.

PENELOPE: Wife of Odysseus; TH] perennial model of constancy in marriage.

PERIKLEIDES: In 496, after an earthquake that devastated most of Sparta, the helots rebelled and were supported in their insurgency by troops from Messenia. Sparta sent Perikleidês as ambassador to Athens, urging assistance. Athens sent Kimôn with 4,000 hoplites to the aid of the distressed city.

PERSEPHONE, PERSEPHONEIA: Daughter of Demêter; Queen of Hadês; see NOTES to TH, p. 276.

PERSEUS: Son of Zeus and a mortal girl, Danaê, daughter of King Akrisios of Argos; *cf.* ANDROMEDA.

'PERSIANS': RA] A tragedy by Aischylos, produced in 472.

PHAIDRA: Wife of King Theseus of Athens. RA] In the *Hippolytos* of Euripides she kills herself after falsely accusing her stepson of ravishing her.

PHALERON: A port of Athens, notable for its sea food.

PHARNAKES: A Persian nobleman operating as an 'enemy agent' in Athens; AV] the Inspector [1028] is in his pay.

PHILEMON: AV] 'Lampooned as a foreigner, and a Phrygian one into the bargain' [Σ].

PHILOKLES: TH] An unsuccessful tragic poet, nephew of Aischylos; AV] he was nicknamed 'The Lark', and wrote a play called *Tereus, or, The Hoopoe,* much of it apparently plagiarized from Sophoklês.

PHILOKRATES: AV] The proprietor of a bird shop.

PHILOMEL: An Athenian princess ravished by the Thracian King Tereus and subsequently changed into a swallow (or, some say, a nightingale); hence, RA] a dismally twittering harbinger of outrage and disaster.

PHOIBOS: A name for Apollo as god of the sun.

PHOINIKIA: Phoenicia, a country in Asia Minor.

PHONÉYA: AV] An invented name. The Greek is *Phanês,* the root of which suggests the pseudo-patriot informers who are alleged to live in that country.

PHORMISIOS: RA] An adherent, although apparently a non-literary one, of the poet Aischylos; Σ says that he was heavy-set and bearded, and that he accepted bribes; another source reveals, more hopefully, that he died βινῶν ἅμα.

PHOSPHOROS: Artemis as moon-goddess.

PHRYNICHOS: RA] I: A comic poet mentioned depreciatively by Xanthias and Dionysos. II: A tragic poet, *fl.* 500, mentioned ambiguously by 'Aischylos'. III: A seditious politician, assassinated in 410: see NOTES on p. 114. The reference in TH is to the second of these.

PHRYNONDAS: TH] A swindler of such heroic capacity that he became proverbial; no details are known.

PHTHIA: A city in Thessaly; home of Achillês.

PINDAR: Lyric poet (518-438).

PISA: A city in Elis, famous for its horses.

PLATHANE: RA] A low name; see NOTES on p. 107.

PLUTOS: TH] Ordinarily the god of wealth (Πλοῦτος), but here assimilated to Plûtôn (Πλούτων)—that is to say, Pluto—as god of Hadês and husband of Persephonê. [Σ]

PLUTO: See PLUTOS.

PNYX: The meeting place of the Assembly at Athens.

PORPHYRION: One of the Titans in the conflict with Zeus; AV] the Purple Waterhen, *Porphyrio veterum.*

POSEIDON: God of the sea.

'POTTERVILLE': RA] Kerameikos, the Potters' Quarter in Athens.

PRIAM: King of Troy.

PRODIKOS: A prominent sophist, reputedly a teacher of Sokratês.

PROKNE: AV] The Nightingale; wife of TEREUS and sister of PHILOMEL.

PROMETHEUS: A son of the Titan Iapetos, and hence a semi-divine being; reputed to have created man and to have stolen fire from heaven for the comfort of his creation, for both of which acts he was persecuted by Zeus.

PROTEAS: TH] see NOTES on p. 302.

PROTEUS: TH] A legendary king of Egypt; see NOTES on p. 302.

PROXENIDES: AV] An irresponsible boaster; he comes from the wholly imaginary town of Kompasai, a word derived from the verb κομπάζω, 'brag'.

PRYTANEION: The town hall in Athens.

PYLOS: A town on the west coast of the Peloponnesos.

PYTHANGELOS: RA] An obscure tragic poet.

PYTHIAN: TH] An epithet of the gods as associated with the shrine of Apollo at Delphoi.

PYTHODELIAN: AV] The Swan, sacred to Apollo, takes Apollo's epithets: Pythian, as god of the Delphic Oracle, and Dêlian, as native of Dêlos.

SABAZIOS: A Phrygian god, assimilated to Dionysos.

SAKAS: AV] Popular name for a foreigner aspiring to Athenian citizenship.

'SALAMINIA': A state galley in the Athenian service; at AV 147, a kind of glorified police boat.

SALAMIS: A large island in the Saronic gulf, south of Attika.

SAMOS: An island off the coast of Asia Minor.

SARDANAPALOS: A lavish and splendidly dissolute king of Assyria.

SEBINOS: An invented name of indelicate derivation.

SEMELE: A mistress of Zeus; mother of Dionysos.

'SEVEN AGAINST THEBES': A tragedy by Aischylos, produced in 467.

SIDON: A city in Phoinikia; original home of KADMOS.

SIMOIS: A river of Troy.

SIMONIDES: An Ionian poet (556-468).

SKAMANDRIAN: Adj. from Skamandros, a river of Troy.

SKIRA: TH] The annual Parasol Festival of Demêter and Persephonê (or, as some say, of Athêna) near the beginning of July.

SKLEBYLAS: RA] See NOTES on p. 110.

SKYTHIANS: The Athenian police force was made up largely of Skythian archers, barbarians from the north.

SOKRATES: The celebrated philosopher (469-399).

SOLON: The lawgiver (639-558).

SOPHOKLES: Tragic poet (497-406).

SPARTA: Chief city of Lakonia.

SPERCHEIOS: A river in Thessaly.

SPHINX: RA] A she-monster who proposed a riddle to the citizens of Thebes and killed those unable to answer it.

SPINTHAROS: Lampooned for the same reason as PHILEMON, q.v.; otherwise unknown.

SPORGILOS: AV] A barber.

STENIA: A one-day festival preparatory to the THESMOPHORIA, q.v.

STHENOBOIA: A queen of Argos who falsely accused her husband's house guest, Bellerophon, of attempting her virtue. Later, in remorse, she killed herself. Heroine of a lost play by Euripides. Cf. PHAIDRA.

STYX: In Hadês, the river of the dead.

SUNION: An Attic promontory and town, site of a temple of Poseidon.

SYRAKOSIOS: A politician; author of a law forbidding the comic poets to introduce real persons into their plays.

TANTALOS: A king of Phrygia; son of Zeus; father of PELOPS and NIOBE, *qq.v.*

TARTAROS: The infernal and punitive depths.

TARTESSAN: RA] Eels from Tartesos; but the Greek word also means 'sea-serpent', and the threat is associated with ECHIDNA, *q.v.*

TAURIAN: LY] An epithet of the goddess Artemis, who was worshipped at Taurica Chersonesos, in the modern Crimea.

TAYGETOS: A mountain range in Lakonia, overhanging Sparta.

TEITHRASIAN: RA] Adj. from Teithrasos, an Attic deme noted for its impoverished and truculent inhabitants; applied, *in terrorem*, to the Gorgons.

TELEAS: AV] An unstable Athenian, adequately described by his own words quoted in vv. 169-70.

'TELEPHOS': An early (438) play by Euripides, now lost.

TEREUS: A king of Thrace, transformed, for his outrageous behaviour, into a Hoopoe; see NOTES on AV, p. 164.

TEUKROS: RA] A son of King Telamon of Salamis, consequently brother to AIAS; suitor of HELENA; therefore a member of the Greek expedition against Troy. Character in *The Salaminians,* a lost play by Aischylos.

THALES: Mathematician and philosopher (*fl.* 590).

THASIAN: LY] A fragrant and greatly prized wine from the island of Thasos.

THEBES: The chief city of Boiotia.

THEOGENES: AV] A boastful, showy man of largely imaginary wealth.

THEOGNIS: TH] A tragic poet, contemporary of A., whose work was so lifeless that he was nicknamed 'Snow' (Χιών); not to be confused with the famous gnomic poet who wrote some hundred years earlier.

THEONOE: An Egyptian princess, daughter of PROTEUS, *q.v.*

THERAMENES: RA] An elegant and resourceful boulevardier of the Sophist, or Euripidean, persuasion.

THERMOPYLAI: A narrow pass between Thessaly and Lokris where in 480 the Spartans met the invading Persian force; see LEONIDAS.

THESMOPHORIA: A festival of Demêter and Persephonê, celebrated in November; see NOTES to TH, p. 276.

THESEUS: RA] A notable Athenian hero, one of whose exploits was to invade Hadês and attempt to abduct Queen Persephonê. Thereafter the trans-Styx ferry fare was doubled, presumably to discourage similar adventurers.

THESPIS: The founder of Greek tragedy (*fl.* 534).

THRACE: Roughly. the territory north of the Black Sea.

ᴛɪᴍᴏɴ: A celebrated Athenian misanthrope.

ᴛɪᴛᴀɴs: Pre-Olympian divinities who revolted against Zeus and were defeated by him in a battle on the Phlegraian Plain; at ᴀᴠ 824-6, the great combat is reduced to a riot of braggarts.

ᴛʀɪʙᴀʟʟɪᴀɴs: A savage Thracian tribe.

ᴛʏɴᴅᴀʀᴇᴜs, ᴛʏɴᴅᴀʀ: A king of Sparta, nominally father of ʜᴇʟᴇɴᴀ; see ʟᴇᴅᴀ.

 xᴀɴᴛʜɪᴀs: A servile name.

xᴇɴᴏᴋʟᴇs: An obscure tragic poet.

ᴢᴀᴋʏɴᴛʜɪᴀɴs: Inhabitants of the island of Zakynthos (now Zante) off the west coast of the Peloponnesos.

ᴢᴇᴜs: Father of gods and men.